YOUR ALASKAN DAUGHTER

By

Harriet Walker

CONTENTS

For Harold

INTRODUCTION

The letters are old and faded. They are carbon copies of letters that I wrote more than fifty years ago. The copies have resided in folders squeezed into an old file cabinet, one of the first items loaded onto the truck whenever our family made a move. Some of the incidents included in those letters have become traditional stories told and retold in family circles through the years. But until now the letters themselves have remained untouched, unread.

Recently my granddaughter, Karen, became interested in this file of letters. She wanted to read about our life in the primitive village of Hope, Alaska, the winter that her father was born. It started as a way to fulfill a requirement for a Communications course she was taking. But as we worked through the letters in-route to fulfilling her assignment, we discovered so much more. As a senior in college, Karen is just a few years younger than I was when we made that move to Alaska. Her questions about that experience have caused me to reflect on aspects that I had not considered at that time.

I realize now, for example, that our leaving secure teaching jobs in Kansas and moving to the territory of Alaska, with all its unknowns, was hard for my recently widowed mother to accept. Even though, immediately after her wedding, she and my father had left their families scattered on various Kansas farmsteads and had gone to the mission field in Africa.

At the time we were planning our move to far-away Alaska, I reasoned that her own experience in Africa would surely make it easier for Mother to understand the spirit of adventure that challenged us. I think now that the awareness of the many hardships that accompany that very spirit of adventure may have made acceptance even harder for her. But the minute we decided to move to Alaska, we felt we had Mother's total support. Most of the letters I shared with Karen were written to my mother eagerly sharing experiences of pioneer life on the last American frontier.

When Karen asked if this decision to move to Alaska was a sudden one, a whim of the moment, I explained that from early on in my relationship with my husband, Harold, I had known of his interest in Alaska. He seemed drawn to that raw, unknown area of our country. It was an area that was waking up and stretching itself and already thinking of the possibility of becoming one of the United States. The fact that he already had two sisters and their families living there enhanced the attraction for him.

After he returned from WWII and before we were married, he spent a couple of summers in Alaska. Then, when we were married, and teaching in Mullinville, Kansas, summers loomed free and open. Alaska was enticing. So twice we flew to Alaska to spend our summers absorbing the frontier experience. During those summers, Harold worked longshoring, loading and unloading ships at the docks in Seward as well as logging with his brother-in-law, Ross.

More and more we moved in the direction of thinking of Alaska as a potential permanent location for us. We saved money for this eventuality. We bought equipment for the sawmill we hoped to establish in Alaska. Then in the spring of 1953, when I was pregnant with our first child, we cut our ties in the states and headed for the wild and wonderful territory of Alaska.

What follows is the story of that adventure told through letters; letters to people who needed to know the events of our daily lives. I've also included some of my e-mail correspondence with Karen because it helps to put the story into perspective and answer a few stray questions.

CHAPTER 1

June 1953: Over the Alcan

D ear Karen,
     I am excited about this project you are doing for your Communications course! So is Harold! He insisted that we run right out and get a scanner so that we can send the letters to you electronically attached to e-mails like this one. I didn't object because I've always wanted a scanner for some of my other projects as well.

I looked at the piles of letters. They are a little disheveled, but they are in chronological order. I'm going to divide the letters into groups. I'll scan them and then send them off to you with a little commentary. Feel free to use any of my comments as a text for your project. If you have any questions, e-mail them to me, and I'll try to answer them with the next batch I send.

I know from your last phone call that you are worried about the amount of work your grandfather and I will be putting into this project. Don't be! We do need to go through these letters to pick out the right ones to send so that the story can unfold itself properly. You wouldn't be able to do that if we just sent the whole box. Besides, this is an exciting adventure for Harold and me to revisit and reflect on a very important part of our lives. Those months in Alaska were formative for the way we have lived the rest of our life together. So, don't worry about our time and please accept our thanks for this fascinating challenge.

You will find the first group of letters attached to this email. - - These letters describe our trip to Alaska via the Alcan Highway. I am aware that through the years you have heard some aspects of that Alcan experience, but maybe reading the letters in sequence will give you a better picture. Because I wrote most faithfully to my mother, four of the letters are to her. One of these letters, however, is written to three of my college friends, affectionately called roomies, who shared various living arrangements with me during our college years. The four of us had a round robin letter system going all during the time I was in Alaska. As the packet of letters traveled around to each of us in turn, we would take out our old letter and put in a new one before sending it on.

The starting point of this saga was Mullinville, Kansas. We had come to love that little community where we had been teachers for three years. Leaving there was harder than we had guessed it would be. We were frequently required to justify our decision to move to Alaska in response to the incredulous questions of our many friends and relatives. But this process only made us more determined than ever to pursue our Alaskan destiny. The fact that Harold's mother would be making the trip with us seemed to satisfy the general concern about my being pregnant.

As you know, I had been to Alaska twice before. I already had a clear picture in my mind of what the village of Hope would be. Particularly easy to picture was the welcome that we would have from Harold's sister, Alma, and her family. They had been wonderful hosts to us on the previous visits.

Harold and I repeatedly traced the route on the map. I had a chant of sorts going through my head. We would go from Kansas through Colorado, Wyoming, Montana, and then through Alberta, Canada. But it wasn't until we got to Dawson Creek in British Columbia, that the Alcan Highway officially began. All those other miles were traveled only to reach the place where we could enter the celebrated Alcan Highway. Dawson Creek was the true start to our drive to our new home in Alaska.

Now that we had succumbed to the allure and promises of Al-

aska and its potential, we had come to think like Alaskans as far as considering the United States in the familiar Alaskan term of "Outside." We would be making our home in the U.S. Territory of Alaska, but our families would be living Outside.

An important part of the planned Alcan trip was Mom Walker. I wish that you could have known your great-grandmother Walker, Karen. Harold's mother was a woman possessed of a good sense of humor, adventure, and much wisdom in that she approved of me completely! What a fortunate daughter-in-law I was. She was willing to share the possible hazards of an overland trip to Alaska to have the summer there. She was especially looking forward to seeing the homes of her two Alaskan daughters, Elsie and Alma. Harold's younger sister, Elsie, had just recently made her home in Alaska and since she had been a college classmate, I was looking forward to visiting in her home as a sister-in-law and as an old friend. Elsie lived in Wasilla, Alaska. Alma, Harold's older sister, would be a neighbor of ours in Hope. So, we three very enthusiastic, very optimistic people headed for Alaska.

On the recommendation of my doctor who authorized the trip, we had bought a big used Buick for more comfortable riding. We had stripped down our possessions for this move but kept two recently purchased pieces of furniture, which were part of our dream life. One was a heavy-duty dressmaker-head Singer sewing machine in a lovely walnut desk cabinet, and the other was an up-to-date record player console. The irony of these two choices will become more apparent to you as you read the letters because we never actually had electricity in our home the whole time we lived in Alaska. These, along with many cherished books and miscellaneous items, were loaded into a trailer that followed us faithfully as we headed off to Alaska. Little did we know the adventures ahead.

However, I don't want to spoil it for you with explanations. I'll just let you read the letters.

Love,
Grandma

Slave Lake, Canada
June 2, 1953

Dear Mother,

You remember we said that we could make it from Mullinville, Kansas, to Alaska in seven or eight days--if nothing happened. Well, something happened!! Here we are, stuck in Slave Lake, Canada. Slave Lake! What a dreary and appropriate name.

I'll start at the beginning. We were making good time and enjoying our trip very much. We got out of Edmonton and hit bad, bad roads. We crawled along at a snail's pace when whop! We heard a loud sound. On went the brakes. Out jumped Harold muttering, "Bet it's a trailer tire." But he could see at a glance that it wasn't that. So, he began to fear it was one of our good front tires. But no! Now we wish it had been any tire or even all of them rather than what happened. You're doubtless thinking -- "get on with the story." But I assure you I won't be rushed. As I have mentioned before, I have lots of time. Besides, I am not enough of a mechanic to know just what did happen. Something called the torque tube broke under the car. The unfortunate event took place Sunday evening. It looks like we can't get all the replacement parts we need in Canada. We may have to send to the States for the particular torque tube that fits our car. In the meantime, we have had some parts sent out from Edmonton, and we are going to try improvising a solution to get us on our way--if possible.

If we get out of here in a day or so, we'll still make it to Alaska in fair time. With luck, we are only four days driving time from Elsie's place at Wasilla. On the other hand, if it looks like we may have to stay much longer,

OVER THE ALCAN

Mom Walker and I are going to build an adobe house as she did at the mission station in New Mexico. Just kidding, but this six-dollars a night dust-trap, which passes for a camp cabin, is sure the berries. I don't know why we couldn't have been stranded close by some of those lovely motels where we stayed back down the road. This town has a water shortage. You even have to ask for it to get it with meals.

If we are still here in six months or so when the baby decides to come, I'm going to name the baby for this lovely resort city. Just see how nicely it would work. Slavina Lakena if a girl and Slavo Lakeo if a boy. Slavina Walker! Sounds musical, doesn't it?

Because people needing major and minor repairs are just jamming the local twenty-four-hour garage, Mom Walker and I believe that this town pays the highway department to keep the roads in such horrid shape. Some truckers have been waiting around for days for parts. So, they must eat. They must sleep. See! The roads are responsible for a booming business.

LATER

Harold just got back in with the not-so-good news that we will have at least a four-day wait for parts. Whee! But he also did some scouting around and found us this nice, clean little motel about a half mile from town. We have clean floors, beds, etc., running water, a Coleman stove, a shower, a stool (the last place had a "stinking" chemical toilet) and closet and drawer space--one room is a bedroom. The other room serves as a living room /kitchen with a sofa that makes into a bed. And it all costs the same price we paid at the last place--$6.00. Even though we have to walk farther to get to town, the little Coleman stove enables us to prepare our meals, which also saves money.

So, we're very happily situated and are going to enjoy our little stay. Mom W. is a real jewel as far as accommodating cheerfully and helping make it all seem a lark. We have been playing three-handed Rook, and there is some swell fishing around here. Mom and Harold came in this afternoon with a nice catch of fish. Harold said that Mom had fun with the fishing. He laughed about how she would help the fish get reeled in by hurriedly walking backward while she turned the crank. Oh, and then, bless her heart, she prepared the fish for supper. Delicious!

Here is an interesting footnote to the fishing story.

When Harold went to check on the non-resident fishing licenses, his inquiries met expressions of incredulity--licenses to fish? The good news is that there is no licensing for anyone. The fish are just there for people to catch and use.

Harold found out that the ordered car parts aren't really expensive, and we'll be eating cheaply. We have a swell location. Lots of people would pay a pile of money for a week's fishing here in this part of Canada, and you might say we're just getting it thrown in for almost nothing. Anyway, it'll be a real vacation--lots of sleep, games of Rook, fish suppers, etc.

I wish that the list of the baby gifts I received at the shower in Mullinville hadn't been packed so deeply, because now would be a dandy time to get my thank you notes off. Besides, I'd like to tell you in detail what I got. But I'll be doing that yet one of these days.

Well, I'll close this rambling letter and get it off to you.

Love,
Harriet

Slave Lake, Canada
June 4, 1953

Dear Roomies,

I know that you won't be surprised to hear that we are stuck somewhere in the wilds of Canada. You'll think, "Isn't that just like them?" But you'll be surprised when you learn that I'm writing my installment for the round-robin even before I get the envelope. I think of the times in college when we longed for time on our hands. Believe me, girls, it's not all it's cracked up to be. I have all kinds of free time, and any handwork I brought along to occupy idle hands is buried deep under stuff in our trailer. Fortunately, Harold wisely kept the portable typewriter handy. It is staring at me conspiratorially. Charge this letter from your old college roommate to pure desperation.

Give Harold credit. He thought he had all the bases covered for our move to Alaska. He checked with my doctor about the feasibility of taking his pregnant wife up over the Alcan Highway. The doctor assured him that a nice long trip like that would be no problem if we drove in a heavy car. So we got hold of a 1948 Buick Roadmaster. To still Mother's concerns about the trip, we assured her that Harold's mom would be going along. Both Alma and Elsie have wanted their mother to come to Alaska to see them. So, this was a golden opportunity for her and a blessing for us.

Anyway, we loaded up the big doctor-recommended car and a practical-sized trailer. We packed pots, pans, bedding, towels, books, clothes, and dishes into the trailer and the back of the car. Harold arranged the things in the back seat so that one could sort of lie on top of much of the stuff and snooze. Now when I tell you what else we are taking to this little Alaskan village, which has no electricity, you are going to feel that you have further reason to doubt our sanity. I want you to remember, however, that this is a move for the long haul. We plan to be there a while, and we are optimistic that shortly there will be electricity available.

Therefore, we are taking the two nice things that we have bought since we were married. First was that Singer sewing machine in a lovely cabinet that you know I had been coveting for so long and a nice record player console, also in beautiful dark wood. You are not surprised about that choice, either, since you know how Harold enjoys hearing his wonderful collection of records - all of which add to the weight in the trailer.

So you are wondering why I am writing a letter from a town named Slave Lake instead of moving on up the highway to our destination. In three words, "we broke down." The neck of our torque tube, whatever that is, fractured.

You remember that Harold and a couple of his pre-college buddies made that trip to Alaska the summer after our junior year. Well, at that time the authorities had a list of spare parts required for each make of car before one would be allowed on the Alcan. Yesterday, ruefully Harold said that even if that list of spare parts were still required, he doubts that on the list would be "torque tube." However, they do still require that

you have a certain amount of money before leaving Edmonton for the Alcan Highway. Fortunately, Harold and I had saved long enough to have two or three hundred dollars more than what they required. Of course, the amount they require assumes that you have made it to Dawson Creek where the Alcan starts, and are not sitting three hundred miles short in Slave Lake with a busted torque tube.

So here we are in Canada, and it's a bit of a shock to realize that the parts for our Buick are not obtainable in Canada. The local repair people tried Edmonton and Vancouver without finding anyone who has the parts necessary. So, as I write this, they are in the process of trying to weld our poor crippled car's innards together and send us on our way.

When we do get on our way, we will head first to Elsie's place. You won't believe how different Elsie is from college days. I don't mean that she and Harold don't still have that brother and sister thing. They do. No, what I mean is that she has become quite domesticated. She married Dave Philo who has a dairy farm between Palmer and Wasilla, Alaska. He also has a milk route and hauls milk to a creamery, which, among other things, supplies ice cream for the military at Elmendorf Air Force Base near Anchorage. We plan to stop off at their place for a short visit and then head to Anchorage where we will stock up on a wonderful bunch of supplies and then, at last, get over to Hope.

The good news is that Alma has found a swell little house for us to rent while we are getting set for buying land and building. There are a chicken house and an extra log build-ing, which Harold's mom is fantasizing as being her "camp-site" and, of course, that other extra little building delicately referred to as an "outhouse." What delights Mom Walker the most, however, is the fact that there is a large garden site, which Alma says the owners already planted. We can move in and get busy gardening. And you know how my mother-in-law enjoys gardening. Harold's mom is also excited about the fact that the owners had a weekend cafe last summer and wanted it continued. I am still a foot-dragger at the thought.

The feature of the new arrangement that appeals to me most is that it is there and available. Because Hope is such a small village, I have had some concern that we might end up having to live with Alma's family for a while. The Millers are warm and welcoming, so that's not the problem. But try to imagine a story-and-a-half house with one large main room and two little upstairs bedrooms occupied by Ross and Alma's family. In addition to them, there are also two teenagers, Lewie and Erma Ann, plus little six-year-old Linda, and Vince, a young man who has been living with them looking for work. Our arrival would have added Harold and his pregnant wife, plus Alma and Harold's mother (one person). And we also need to count numerous pets-Billy the dog, goats whose names I don't know, semi-named rabbits and unnamed chickens. Well, the animals live outside, but you get the picture. Having our own little house to move right into is a delightful thought. Now if only our disabled Buick can get us there.

Your Ex-Roomie,
Harriet

Dawson Creek, Canada
June 6, 1953

Dear Mother,
I am writing this letter from Dawson Creek--just three hun-

dred miles up a hectic road from Slave Lake. We didn't get to leave Slave Lake until around noon yesterday, Saturday- six days of waiting!

We rather enjoyed our stay at Slave Lake after we moved to the better cabin. The proprietor of those cabins was a retired businessman who became attached to Harold. He took us on excursions, fishing, to town, etc. He even found work for Harold to do one day so that we could get out of paying that night's rent. Harold couldn't work for hire because Canadians protect their workers by not letting foreigners work. But the little boost of a night's lodging surely helped. By cooking, ourselves we also were able to save a lot on meals. Those savings are important because the government requires that we have a certain amount of cash on hand before we enter the Alcan proper. We are still on track for that requirement.

But wouldn't you know it! After five glorious sunshiny days at Slave Lake, it began to rain yesterday. This country around here is even newer and rougher than Alaska. I hadn't realized that. This part of Canada is just being opened up, it seems. The point is that it isn't waterproof yet. Everything is a big sea of mud. The few scattered towns have no sidewalks. The roads soon turned into treacherous mud-traps. Anyway, we slugged out of Slave Lake yesterday in the highest of hopes. We drove carefully down the road for twenty miles, constantly being splashed by cars coming at us and, unfortunately, by cars passing us, when what should happen but we heard an ominous noise down in the workings of the car. Poor Harold. I never saw anyone so crushed as he was.

Well, as luck would have it, we discovered we were only a half-mile from town. Harold hitched a ride into town. When he found a good garage, he had our car towed. All this time the rain continued to pour! After looking the car over, the mechanic diagnosed two things. First, the Slave Lake mechanics had failed to re-lubricate the differential gear correctly. We were very fortunate to have stopped the minute we heard the noise because a burned-out rear end would be extremely expensive--maybe a couple hundred. Second, they also discovered that the repair job was imperfect and there was no way to fix it. It seems that when the drive shaft in the torque tube gets heated too much, something gets to knocking and then seizes up -just like putting on the brakes. The only thing that we could do when that happened was to stop and let the car cool down before driving on. But we did keep driving on!

I won't go into the details about last night, but with the rain, the roads were deteriorating quickly, and Harold felt we must keep moving or by morning they might have become impassable. We kept moving, frequently stopping to let the driveline cool down. Harold took advantage of some of these stops to catch a few catnaps. I slept most of the time. It took us about twenty-four hours to travel the three hundred miles from Slave Lake to Dawson Creek. Now that we have arrived at Dawson Creek, we are ready to start on the Alcan Highway proper. Everyone knows that the worst roads are before you hit Dawson Creek. We have about eighteen hundred miles yet to go. Believe me! Flying to Alaska as we have done other summers, is the simple, inexpensive way to get there.

Dawson Creek is the last outpost of civilization before we get to Elsie's place. The rest will be just filling stations and the like. So, we'll stay here until we can get the car in shape--maybe a day or two. Luckily, we got a good deal here in the way of a cabin. For four dollars and fifty cents a night, we have a nice clean place with cooking facilities, a bed, and studio couch. Even though we have to share the bath, these accommodations are wonderful. We ate dinner, cleaned up, and Harold's spending this afternoon catching up on his sleep. He's sleeping and sleeping! How often he has reminded me of Daddy in one way. Through all this strain and worry there has never been a time when he was impatient or lost his temper. He still maintains the sweetest, calmest disposition. Hope the baby takes after him.

JUNE 8, 1953

Harold just got in with the good news. We'll be able to leave in the morning. Whoopee! He also met a couple that just came out from Anchorage and they say the roads are pretty good. Also, according to the map, we have around fifteen hundred miles instead of the eighteen hundred we thought to Elsie's place, and then it's about two hundred on over to Hope, Alaska.

Hope! What a beautiful word.

I've been feeling fine and in good spirits--

Well, must get this mailed. Will surely be glad to hear from you.

Love,
Harriet

Wasilla, Alaska
June 10, 1953

Dear Mother,

Harold's mom and I are here at Elsie's place. We would all be cozy and comfortable in Dave and Elsie's home except for one thing. Harold isn't here. We don't even know when he will get here. Let me tell you what happened.

We left Dawson Creek in such high hopes. Harold felt rested. We even sang a little as we started with me in the front seat and Mom W. in her corner of the back seat. I had been wrong in telling you that there was no more civilization between Dawson Creek and Elsie's place. There was Whitehorse, which felt big and civilized after the wilderness through which we'd traveled. We sailed euphorically into and then out of Whitehorse.

You may have already guessed what I am going to say next. About 200 miles down the road from Whitehorse we again heard that sound. Harold hurriedly got out, and once again his face wore that stricken look. I don't know much about cars,

19

but when I joined him, I could see that the bottom of the car had dropped out. It was not a good sign. Harold said with great discouragement that the faceplate had broken off the torque tube again.

Once again, we were in the middle of nowhere.

Although the minutes dragged as we were talking over possibilities of what to do, it wasn't as long as it seemed when finally, a single vehicle came down that very lonely road. This vehicle was a new GMC pickup driven by a clean-cut young Texan. He stopped and asked if he could help. As soon as Harold started asking him if he was headed to Anchorage, I had a sinking feeling about what was coming next. Sure enough, Harold asked this young man if he would take us - his pregnant wife and mother - to Elsie's home in Wasilla. I was sure that Mother Walker would immediately object. But she agreed with Harold that this was the prudent thing to do. The young man said that he would be glad to help in this way. Harold wrote out the directions. Mom and I joined our Texan in the cab, and the three of us drove off leaving Harold standing beside our broken car.

Our young chauffeur was the quiet sort, very quiet. I tried to initiate a cheerful conversation with him, but he merely answered with a politely drawled, "Yes, ma'am" or "No, ma'am." Conversation can soon lag with that kind of help.

I thought that this was going to be a long six hundred miles and truly I was not sure just what was the proper etiquette in such a situation. Hitchhiking is a skill I hadn't bothered to acquire. Mom Walker, on the other hand, seemed perfectly relaxed. She began to talk about plans for the cafe that she was eager to get up and running when we got to Hope. It was my turn for short answers because, as you know, I haven't even the faintest interest in a weekend cafe as she discussed food, our strong silent rescuer began to ask questions which Mom readily answered. She told him about the arrangement that Alma had made for us to rent that summer cottage in Hope. She explained that the owners live in Anchorage but were going Outside for the summer and had agreed to rent it to us for a few weeks. The summer before they had used the front room of that little house as a weekend cafe, which would hopefully attract customers from Anchorage. Alma had implied that they were interested in keeping this infant business going. You know all this, Mother, and you know how I feel about it. But when Mom W. explained it all and made it seem so simple and exciting to her, I felt selfish in my objection. Come what may, at least that weekend cafe business served a conversational purpose while getting some of the miles behind us as we went down the road.

Elsie was a bit surprised to see us arrive last night in the waning daylight. Our emergency driver graciously delivered us and our limited baggage to the door, accepted some cookies from Elsie, as well as effusive thanks from us. Then he drove off. This gallant young man had been hauling us for fifteen hours without any sleep.

And so now I am writing to you as Elsie, and her mother busy themselves around the kitchen and get caught up on all the news. I look out the window and wonder when, WHEN will I see Harold again? You know the focus of my prayers.

I know that it is unkind to send this letter off without a happy ending. But I have a chance to get it mailed in town and think I will go ahead and send it. I hope that in the next few days I can get another one off to you with that ending put to right.

Love,
Harriet

P.S. Have I forgotten your training so soon? No, I remind myself that we are warm and comfortable and, in a home, where people love us. I know that we are no longer a worry to Harold, and he can more speedily do what needs to be done to get back to us. I will include a prayer of gratitude with that which I mentioned earlier.

Hope, Alaska
June 19, 1953

Dear Mother,

Did you read that heading? Hope! We are here - all of us. Here is what happened to Harold after he packed us into that pickup and sent us on our way. I'm sure that he didn't give us all the details, but what I did get from him will give you a picture of what he experienced.

Sometime after we left, two happy Canadians in a large empty flatbed truck stopped to view his plight. They suggested that they tow him up the road about 80 miles to a small private shop. Harold said that this started O.K. However, they were soon traveling so fast that he could hardly see them ahead for the cloud of dust. On some of the sharp turns, he whipped around so far that it was like he was going to pass the truck. Harold said that he blew his horn and rode the brakes, but they just shifted down and plowed on. After what seemed an unending nightmare, they finally remembered that he was back there and realized that he wanted to stop. When they were all standing around out on the road, Harold became aware that a good deal of the happiness was alcohol-related. After an awkward exchange of parting remarks, the Canadian helpers fogged on down the road. Harold said that he was still shaking so much from the experience that he just crawled into the back seat of the car and slept until early morning.

Eventually, a heavy equipment operator who was on his way to a job in Alaska stopped, and they talked about his options. They decided that Harold would take the whole rear end out from under the car and get it to a machine shop at either the military base or the highway maintenance station a few miles back. The good Samaritan had with him a wonderful array of tools. He got out what he thought Harold would need and left the tools with only a casual request that Harold left them at a certain service station in Anchorage when he went through on the way to Hope.

As you know Harold has never had much interest in working on cars. Nevertheless, my non-mechanic husband now blocked up the car and removed the rear axle. With the skeleton of the rear end assembly over his shoulder he started down the road. Naturally, he assumed a hitchhiking position whenever he encountered a vehicle headed in his direction. The first possible ride was the truck that had towed him - now going the opposite way. Because they were now sober and still obliging, in a little over an hour, Harold and the car part were at the military camp. And, Mother, I think that you'll find this as hard to believe as I did. They told Harold, "Sorry, we aren't allowed to help civilians." They did help get Harold and his problem over to the highway maintenance station. And then, are you ready for this? After considerable deliberation, those highway department employees decided that if the military couldn't help him, they might have government trouble if they gave him aid. Their suggestion was to go a few miles down the road to a tavern whose owner had a welder.

Thus, on this thread of hope, Harold took his problem there only to have his hopes dashed yet again. It seems that the man had just come into a windfall from some copper stocks and since he and his friends were well into the second week of celebration, he had closed his business. But he pointed to a jury-rigged welding machine and invited Harold to help himself.

Harold had never used an electric welder, and it took him quite a while to get it to do anything for him. After about a two-hour siege of working with that thing and being afraid of electrocution the whole time, he finally got the faceplate tacked onto the rest of the torque tube. (I know ... I don't understand the terms either.) He tells about trying to "true it up by eyeballing it." Anyway, after a long time observing his struggles, the owner of the machine came down and said that Harold had been entertaining his friends and him long enough. He then "sewed it up" for Harold.

After several hours of waiting by the road, Harold and his iron luggage were freighted back to the jacked-up car by a fire fighting crew. When he finally put it all together again, our Buick was once more a mode of transportation. But what transportation! If it reached a speed of 20 mph, the car would begin to shudder violently. Then about every half hour or so Harold would have to stop and tighten some studs under the car. So, it took him more than thirty-six hours on the road to get to us. Even coming over here to Hope from Elsie's place we had to crawl at that under-20-mph pace. I held my breath the whole way.

As I write this, I can see the car out the window looking so whole and so innocent. I try not to think that it might be lurking there with a feeling of triumphant malevolence. I remind myself that in spite of all its contrary effort, we did indeed get here as did all those possessions that we had so cheerfully packed into the back of that car and into that overloaded trailer.

And yet, Mother, I need to tell you that we were the fortunate ones. Frequently on the way up on the Alcan, we would come across people who were leaving Alaska because things had gone wrong. At one place where we stopped to eat, we saw a woman trying to get the proprietor to give them food and some supplies in exchange for her wedding ring. Several of those fleeing the land of promise were families with small children. Like us, they had heard of all the possibilities for work and prospects for future success. Like us, they wanted to be a part of the development of this U. S. territory, which has such bright hopes of someday becoming an actual state in the U.S. Unlike us, however, they had no connection at this end. For example, we knew that we had a place to land when we got here even though getting here turned out to be more of a challenge than we had anticipated. And even if we had to spend our last twenty dollars in Anchorage for food, we did not panic because we had some money waiting with Alma and Ross and because we have excellent prospects for a secure financial future.

It almost seems strange to be here. I don't mean because of the difficult trip. I mean because this is a dream that we've worked toward for so long. Long before I knew that I was to wear the Walker name, I was aware through casual conversation how much Ross and Alma meant to Harold. Their taking him in to live with them in their little log home in Idaho gave to one very young Kansas dust bowl casualty an opportunity to regain his health. Even though they were trying to work out their dreams of making good by developing their quarter section of timberland in Idaho during the tight depression years, they had room in their little cabin and their hearts for this young brother. His respiratory problems disappeared in the Idaho mountain setting.

He lived with them those summers when Erma Ann and Lewie were little and then returned to Kansas after the first frost there. His sophomore year in high school, he stayed through the entire winter with the Millers. So, Ross was a sort of father figure to him. The bonds of affection there lie deep. I am sure you know all this. Harold has always felt an obligation to this family. So, we are thrilled to be here in an enterprise that will fulfill Ross' long-time dream of having a mill. If things work out right, we will also fulfill Harold's dream of law school and politics.

In another letter, I'll tell you more about the little cottage where we live. And, oh yes, Mother Walker sends her greetings. I have been so glad to have her along through all this. She has maintained a positive attitude, and most importantly, her sense of humor has rescued more than one bad moment.

Love,
Your Alaskan daughter, Harriet

CHAPTER 2

July 1953:Settling into Hope

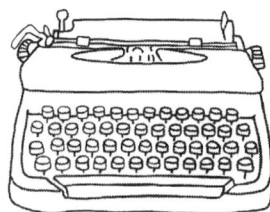

*D*ear Karen,
  I'm glad that you enjoyed reading the first group of let-ters. Let me answer your questions about them before I give you the second group. You asked about how I, a relatively new wife and soon-to-be mother, felt about moving so far from home.

I would have to answer that I was excited at the prospect and a little naive in my assumption that events would unfold as Harold and I had fantasized that they would. I was excited because I felt that I was following in the footsteps of my grandparents who were pioneers and early homesteaders in Kansas. And then, I remind you, that Mother herself had gone with my father to the mission field in Africa, a move which placed the words Freetown, Sierra Leone, West Africa, on my elaborate British-style birth certificate,

Thus, going so far from home just had the feeling of destiny ful-filled. I felt fortunate in that through the mail, I could continue to maintain the close relationship I had with my mother. During my first years away from home, letters to and from college were what had linked us. Telephone calls were for emergencies only. This con-nection through letters had continued into the earliest years of my marriage. So, I counted on a continuation of sharing our lives by mail.

Of course, I had been aware of the slow nature of the mail ser-

vice in and out of Hope. But during summer visits, that didn't carry the significance that it came to have when we moved there. Once we were living there, the inefficient system became a source of frustration to me. I soon learned, of course, to get with the rhythm of the postal system.

You see, Karen, each day mail coming into Anchorage would be brought by train to Moose Pass, which is approximately half way between Seward and Hope. There the mail would stay until Bill Bratton, the mailman, drove up from Seward on Friday. He would pick up the mail in Moose Pass and bring it on to us. Therefore, some of the mail could be nearly a week late when he retrieved it. Even so, believe me, Saturday morning was the great day of the week. Our letters would go out and that week's mail would come in.

Your other question was about the concern I might have felt about riding in the pickup truck to Wasilla with a man we didn't know. That certainly is a reasonable question. But, remember, we were stranded. If Mom Walker and I could be safely delivered to Elsie's house, it would leave Harold freer to do what he had to do with the recalcitrant car. "Hitchhiking" certainly seemed to be the lesser of two evils. Perhaps I should remind you that at the time these letters were written, hitchhiking was still a common and accepted practice for young men, as it had been all through World War II. Of course, true hitchhiking involved standing beside the road and signaling with a raised hand and thumb signal that one was seeking a ride. In this instance, Harold had an opportunity to talk with the young man and thus better assess the situation. I grant that not only did we not follow the pattern of thumbing for a ride, but also, we - a pregnant woman and her mother-in-law - did not fit the stereotype for hitchhikers. But when even Mom Walker agreed that this was a wise decision, I had to go along with it. The hard part, of course, was going off and leaving Harold without knowing when we would see him again.

Now Karen, let me tell you a little about the village of Hope that you will be reading about in this next group of letters. Until just before the time of these letters, the only access to this little village was by highway from Seward or by air from Anchorage. It was right on the ocean, but there were no docks, and even on high tide, only fishing boats could come in. Our first summers in Alaska we had flown into Anchorage from the States, chartered one of the many small planes available for just this sort of service and had flown into Hope. But by the time we made the move that you are reading about, the Anchorage highway was open enough so that Hope was accessible by car from either Anchorage or Seward. However, for most purposes, the port town of Seward continued to be the center of commerce, mail, medical help, and other such necessities.

The little cottage that we were renting was on the edge of town. It had been built by a couple who lived in Anchorage but enjoyed weekending in remote Hope. Harold and I had not yet met the Beutadahls when we moved up. They were planning to spend the summer of '53 Outside. Harold's sister, Alma, made all the arrangements for us to rent the Beutadahl's cottage. Right next to the cottage was the grade school with its apartment for the teacher up above the classroom. The school was a one-room affair that included students from grades one through eight. The high school students in Hope took their schooling by correspondence from the University of Nebraska that year.

The local church was Methodist. In the basement of the church was a very simple apartment where the circuit-riding pastor's family would stay while in Hope. He would have services throughout the week in other locations. Friday night was when he had the service for Hope. At the time that we were there, the pastor and his wife had a young son and a baby on the way.

The single source of supplies was the store run by Doc who carefully hid his tender heart behind a grumpy exterior. There was a town hall where every two weeks the community would gather for a potluck meal and a dance accompanied by your great-aunt Alma's accordion playing. The few residents in Hope who had generators saw to it that this hall was electrified for those occasions.

The residents in this village were, on the whole, very independent individuals. There were, for example, several men living there who were supporting families Outside. The lure of Alaska was often very strong for men but less frequently strong for women.

This, of course, is what divided the families. Residents tended to believe in the philosophy of living and let live, but would rally around to help in times of trouble. By the time we became members of this community, we had already developed respect for many of the individuals who peopled this little town.

Love,
Grandma

Hope, Alaska
July 3, 1953

Dear Mother,

Harold is not going to run in that annual Fourth of July race up Seward's Marathon Mountain this year. He's just not in shape like he should be to run such a race. He's very disappointed because, after those three Marathon third places, he still yearns for the big prize. But it was completely his decision, and I'm sure that it was a wise one.

For one thing, when we have been up here in previous summers, we didn't have a place to keep up and went to bed right after supper. This year there are so many things to do around the place, and the daylight tempts him to keep working. So, we just don't get to bed nearly that early. Weekends are no rest, of course, and his work has been only about half in the woods and the other half in the mill. Last year at this time, he was working exclusively logging in the woods, and that's the best training routine. I don't mean to imply that he's sick or anything, just that he's not in the condition to run such a strenuous race.

Therefore, this Fourth of July we'll spend right here in Hope sharing Mom's plans of luring some tourist money into our pockets. Hope is really going to celebrate the Fourth in a big way. They have a big picnic at noon and then a big folk-dance event in the evening. Most of the women have new dresses for the occasion. Guess it's second only to Christmas. Harold and I won't take in the festivities, of course, because of the cafe. Time enough for that another year.

We've decided to stay in Hope this winter. Harold really does want to make a try of a winter here working the mill. He would go to Palmer to teach in a minute if I were to ask it. But when I decided to come along with him up here, I did it so that he could really give this mill business a try at making us a living. I don't want to chicken out with only letting him half try it. But since we're short of cash, we're going to have to pull some of our plans in and settle for living on a smaller scale as far as buying land, building, etc., are concerned.

This is what we've decided to do. We'll build a little "shack" on some land less than a half-mile behind Millers. We'll build it on skids so that when we do find the land we want or decide what we want to do, we'll be able to dispose of the house as we see fit. We have the plans all made for the interior, and it'll be pretty swell, we think. Maybe I'll draw you a sketch in the next letter. There are several strong points in favor of our decision to stay in Hope for the winter:

(1) We'll be able to live cheaper here than we could in Palmer. We figure we can live for a hundred a month easily. We'll have wild game, berries, produce from the garden, free fuel, no rent, hardly any clothes to buy ... See?

(2) Harold can begin to do something concrete such as building the shack with virtually no cost because we have lots of lumber.

(3) We'll be able to make the trip "Outside" for a longer period. Teaching would limit us to only two weeks. If the baby were too small or I was too tired to come out as soon as Christmas, we'd lose our chance. This way, we'll just wait until Mama and Baby are ready and make the trip in grand style. Besides, it'll cost as much to make the trip whether for two weeks or for six. We figure it'll cost us a thousand dollars and we might as well spend some time in the States while we're at it. A two-week trip is not much for a thousand dollars, is it? Of course,

we're figuring on the people we visit just being so glad to have us come to visit them that they'll feed us and that'll help with our food bill. But we're under no illusions ... there are always incidental expenses. Baby "Slavina Lakena" will probably insist on our buying a few things too.

(4) We'll still get to have the doctor that I went to in Seward, and I like him so much.

(5) Harold will have more free time during the short winter days to help me and to enjoy our offspring.

Anyway, at present writing that's the way our plans are. So, we've decided about our winter.

You should see how the Millers have constructed a greenhouse that is a wonderful addition attached to the south gable end of their story and a half home. Alma gave me about a dozen blooming petunia plants, which she had raised there during the winter. The roof is made up of reinforced clear plastic. They have a wood stove out there for heating. This greenhouse allows them to start tomatoes in February, so they begin enjoying fresh tomatoes before summer. That greenhouse really expands the possibilities for fresh stuff up here, and I MUST have one someday. In the meantime, I accept these beautiful petunia plants with joy. I have them lined up along the front of our house. It is a little white house, and the effect of the colored petunias across the front is lovely, I think. Ah! I may make a gardener yet. But some incidents keep me humble. As you know, we arrived here with a massive garden all planted by the owners who were going Outside for the summer.

Mom W., of course, was delighted with the challenge of separating vegetables from the weeds which shared their garden space. And the part of the garden with flowers offered its own challenge. There were flowers planted that neither Mother Walker nor I had ever heard of and, of course, we weren't familiar with some of the native Alaskan plants. There was one lovely plant that I was nurturing and caring for very tenderly. One day Alma yanked it out ruthlessly. "That's a horrid weed," she told me. It seems that it spreads vociferously and local folk guard against it with hawk eyes.

Can you guess what the latest venture is? Canning! Harold says that to make it through the winter around here we must can up everything possible. So today Mom W. and I took all the spinach out of the garden and canned four pints. Then we cut a big pan full of rhubarb and made some rhubarb jam according to a recipe. The jam also contained orange peel and some pineapple. We were afraid it wouldn't be good, and when we got the ingredients measured out, we realized we were going to have a lot of jam. But it is delicious tasting, and so very, very pretty to look at. The color is amber, and the little chunks of rhubarb float all the way through it beautifully. Anyway, we're pleased with it, and I'm all on fire about canning and its possibilities. We have forty-four jelly glasses of jam, and we got them for a very small price, really, since we didn't have to buy the fruit. Later on, there'll be raspberries and strawberries to put up in jams and jellies.

There will also be peas and beans. Carrots, onions, cabbage, beets, turnips, and potatoes will go into the root cellar for winter eating. In late summer they'll hunt down a mountain goat, and Alma says that it is best to cook it right up and can it in the form of stew. Then soon there'll be a salmon run up these little creeks around here, and all the salmon we'll want will be there just for going down and picking them up out of the water. (Literally!) I'll put up a lot of them for soups, salads, sandwiches, and salmon loaf this winter.

Therefore, Mother, before I forget, I want to ask you about your big pressure canner. Whatever happened to it? I have only a little presto pan in which to can, and it does only three pints at a time. I can always use Alma's big canner, but this fall there will likely be many days when we'll both need to be canning at once. I was wondering if I could borrow yours if you still have it. If you have disposed of it, don't give the matter another thought, but if it is sitting some handy place unused, I'd surely appreciate it if it would find its way up here to Alaska. I'll be able to buy one myself in another year or so, but I'd be glad to put yours to some use in the meantime. I think air parcel post would be cost-prohibitive, but if it were shipped pretty soon by regular transport, it would get here in time for the salmon run and for putting up goat stew and the Fall meat that I have to can. Now, if it's too much bother, please, PLEASE forget it. If it can be done, swell.

Boy, you should see me! I am beginning to feel like I always supposed pregnant women felt - the over-worked idea of a watermelon swallowed whole. Every once in a while, I put my hand on my stomach and am amazed. It's surely in there. I can't push it in. It's tight as a drum. I hope my skin can multiply cells or what-ever it does fast enough to keep up with this growing organism inside me. I think I felt the first signs of life Saturday. It was just a faint thump. Felt it again today. Quite a thrill!

It's a quarter to ten in the evening, and it's a little dark to be typing inside the house. I don't think I'll go outside, however, because the mosquitoes are pretty bad. I know, I know, I could light that hurricane lamp, but then I couldn't impress you with writing about the strange daylight up here.

I hope you are feeling well and happy and that your plans for next year are shaping up nicely. I know, whatever happens, it'll work out for the best...because that's the way you are.

Love,
Your Alaskan daughter, Harriet

P.S. If you're going to spend your few summer vacation weeks with Evelyn and Bob in California, you really should plan on this summer. Next summer Harold, the baby, and I are counting on a Grandma visit. And we had in mind that you would supply the grandma.

Hope, Alaska

Friday, July 10, 1953

Dear Mother,

You mentioned baby sheets! I'll gladly accept your offer and hope that you meant you'd hem them too. You see I'm not likely to be able to do any sewing this winter. That lovely electric sewing machine that I had so long wanted just sits there accusingly. We use it as a sort of table and hope for better days down the road. This electrical beauty does make a nice sort of table, but it doesn't assist me in my desire to make baby clothes. I'll make up for this lack by turning out baby clothes mass production when we get outside to visit you. I will happily use your treadle machine and not say a word about how old-fashioned it is. You'll see.

Anyway, back to the sheets. We are going to use the baby bed that was Harold's, and which went to Alma's family when the first grandchild was on the way. Harold says that he can remember sleeping in it after he started to school, and Linda Lou has just graduated from it. I tell you this to impress on you the fact that it's pretty big. I haven't checked yet, but I wonder if the three crib sheets that were given me at the shower will fit. They are contour sheets and may be too small. I have one sheet that can be made over as you suggest. Don't worry about seams down the middle and the like. I'd rather have two imperfect sheets than one perfect one. The main idea, I believe, is to keep the baby clean and sweet smelling. If I don't get over to Alma's before I mail this letter, I'll send you the size of the baby mattress in the next letter.

You also mentioned making diapers. I've given up that idea. Nowadays most women so much prefer the new gauze diapers to the flannel ones that there must be something to it. They are lighter, less bulky, and dry faster, which will be a very important factor to me next winter. Besides, without a sewing machine that is functional, I'd have a heck of a time making diapers. I'm going to order the gowns and stuff that I need and maybe put a little embroidery on them to give them the homemade touch. I'll have plenty of time to do that after the summer and fall work is all done.

We have a sense of disappointment in our minister. With his particular personality, he isn't a good match for this kind of community. I've had enough experience at the other end of ministerial work, to hesitate before I criticize a minister, but after a few weeks of his ministry, I'm all ready to criticize. To Harold, the chief problem is that Rev. Elliot has a big voice and sings off key. Harold can't harmonize with the congregation nor can he drown out the notes that issue from the pulpit. I try to ignore it but I can't. And, of course, we sing and sing and sing. His sermons aren't so bad except that when he's through, you sometimes wonder where he was going.

Last summer the Elliots were Outside, and this church had a young couple serving as substitutes. They were so earnest and tried so hard. He sometimes stumbled in his delivery but he won the heart of his congregation with his sincerity, and he often had fifteen or more in his congregation. This year even Millers don't come very often. Grannie Clark comes. You'd like her, Mother. Also, young Mrs. Carter comes. She will be a neighbor if we get a home site on the bench. Aside from them, it is only Albert, who is mentally unbalanced, with the two and one-half Walkers that often complete the congregation. Of course, the Elliots often bring a couple out with them from Moose Pass so that there are a few more seats taken.

And that's just the trouble. The pastor and his wife don't seem to be the least bit concerned about the non-attendance. They almost never do any pastoral calling. I can't help thinking that there are people in this isolated setting who would appreciate a pastoral call. The Elliots do their duty by holding the services, and they don't seem to worry if no one is reached. Harold was talking with them about possible angles to improve the work here, but they are satisfied with it just as it is. Enough of this griping! Going to church isn't fun or spiritually enriching here.

Now I just happened to think of an instance that will serve

to illustrate my point, so I'm going on with my harangue. The winter that Ross hurt his foot, he was completely laid up for some time. The preacher did come to call. He expressed his sympathy and left. He didn't ask if he could help chop wood, or could get some neighbors to help with the hunting or anything. He just called. Now most ministers that we've had any contact with would have seen the Miller family's plight with winter coming on and the man of the house laid up-- but not this one. What happened to the pioneer pastors that I have read about? Where is the gathering of the community together in common cause? Fortunately, Ross had a small pension from the company for which he was working, and the family got along fairly well. The pension of about 110 dollars all went for groceries, you can bet.

I went birthday shopping for you today. The range of choice in Hope is very, very small. Shopping means Doc's store. Period. It is the only store in our village and purports to have anything anyone could possibly need. It is composed of several buildings, but the main building contains testimony to the evolution of lighting. Still mounted are kerosene lamp brackets, carbide gas lines, and two stages of electrical fixtures. At each stage of improvement, the old stay right there, and the replacement shares space with it in the ceiling and walls of Doc's store. Doc's name is Iver Neirhouse. I found that out by asking the Millers. I certainly had never heard him called anything but Doc. I believe that he did, at some time, have some pharmacy training, which earned him the title of Doc.

Doc has a huge dog named Prince who is treated to suit his name. He was the lead dog of Doc's old sled team. He is old, large, and part wolf. Often, when he is resting, he completely fills one of the narrow aisles in the store. He doesn't tolerate anyone getting too close to him, so if you wanted to go down the aisle that is his bedroom in any particular instance, you back up and go around another way. Of course, going down the aisle is just for looking and getting ideas of what is available.

Doc always picks up the item that is requested and puts it on the counter for tabulation. And his presence doesn't irritate Prince at all.

Doc's personality can sometimes make shopping much more of an adventure than you'd expect. Some days asking Doc for a particular item causes him to act like Prince when you're crowding his space. In those cases, it is better to just put the item on your list for another trip. For example, some weeks ago when Linda scraped her knees, Alma went to Doc's store to get some Vaseline for her daughter. Doc told her that was not what she needed and wouldn't sell it to her. He insisted that what she needed was a carbolated salve. It is evil-smelling stuff, but even in her irritation, Alma admitted that it had remarkable healing qualities.

Even though Doc can, on occasion, be grumpy and short with customers, I believe he has a proverbial heart of gold. During the winters, he sometimes gets so frustrated with his on-credit customers that he will just cut a family off from further credit. Yet when one of those families sends a list to the store with a little child, Doc just melts. Angry with himself, he fills the order and sends the child home with the requested items.

Doc is well up in years and moves stiffly around the store complaining about this or that ache. But at the dances after the potlucks when Alma plays the accordion music he loves -- a schottische or a polka --Doc is right out there participating in that dance with enthusiasm. I haven't seen it yet, but I understand he often goes ice-skating with the young people on sunny winter afternoons.

Another interesting tidbit about Doc is his collection of cars. Doc's favorite car was an old Model T Ford that he drove until he could no longer get tires for it. That car and a late 30's model Plymouth are both retired to their individual sheds. He was insulted by the amount he was offered for trade-in, so he just kept the cars and put them into retirement. His present car is a 1949 Ford that he doesn't drive, but has kept for community use. There hasn't been a whole lot of that because this car has less than nine hundred miles on it.

Even though the choice of shopping options in Hope is limited, the uniqueness of the one we have starts to make up for it. I found a gift for you at Doc's, and since it meets Doc's approval, he let me buy it. It'll be in the mail to you soon.

Hope the letter tomorrow from you tells me of your definite plans for next winter. Oh, I do see an advantage to weekly letters. I can count on hearing from you. How I look forward to those letters.

Love,
Your Alaskan Daughter, Harriet

Hope, Alaska
July 15, 1953

Dear Mother,

It is indeed a rare treat to be writing to you in the middle of the week and to know that the letter will be mailed right away. Our mail usually goes out when the new mail comes in at the end of the week. But I decided to take advantage of the trip that Harold's Mom is making to Elsie's place to get this letter mailed.

This stretch of hot, hot weather with several days well into the eighties has done the funniest thing. Instead of meaning a dry spell, it means a wet spell. We are literally being flooded. High in the mountains, last winter's snowpack is melting so fast that the streams are nearly all out of their banks. Harold and Ross spent Saturday afternoon using the bulldozer to fight a flood which threatened to do some damage to Miller's place and the mill site. Ironically, the bridge into town across Dry Creek was washed out, and only a few people from our side of the creek could get to town. They had to meet the truck at the creek to get the mail in and out.

They put a few timbers down across the creek, so a few brave souls ventured into town. But we Walkers didn't think there would be enough tourists to make it worthwhile to open the coffee shop. Hurrah! As far as I am concerned, there are no circumstances that would make it worthwhile to open that cafe. But I am trying hard to be a good daughter-in-law and assist Mom in her grand plan of making a fortune serving the few people that might just meander out from Anchorage on weekends. Harold just stands by and observes our "planning" with amusement.

Thus, there were three blessings last weekend. First, there was no cafe, Second, we took advantage of the heat wave to have a leisurely afternoon picnic in a lovely setting. Finally, there was a group of Methodist young people having a weekend retreat here in Hope. These kids held a nice church service Sunday morning. We attended that service and then had the Miller tribe over for chicken dinner.

The "Miller tribe" right now includes Vince. He is an attractive young fellow who has more or less attached himself to their family for a while. So, with church services and a family meal, Sunday really seemed like Sunday, if you know what I mean. Try as I do, I can't get adjusted to a week where the worship is on Friday night. Bible Study or prayer meetings on a weeknight are fine. But to have the worship service then just throws my week off. Of course, our "circuit -riding" pastor can't be at all his charges on Sunday morning, so I know I will have to adjust. I wonder what this says about my faith.

The garden is really full of good stuff to eat. We've been having fresh green things right along now. Strawberries should be ripe within a week. The only thing that we really miss and possibly suffer any for the lack of is good fresh red meat. Can't be had. Couldn't be kept if it could be had. But we fully intend to remedy that situation before another summer. Actually, there are several rather simple ways we could fix that up, and it would be worth it for the luxury of having meat when we want it.

When we get our car fixed, we're going to go to Anchorage or Seward more frequently and thus have fresh stuff more often. Harold says it won't cost more than four dollars or so for a trip and he thinks it's ridiculous for people to be without things for months at a time when they have a car, and the road is passable.

We'll plan a nice trip out of it each time ... maybe leave here soon afternoon, do our shopping, take in a movie, maybe eat out or picnic and get back in time for bed. That way we can have our fresh stuff and a little spree too.

I can't send you our house plans yet because they keep changing. But the plans are for a house about twenty-six feet by eighteen feet. It will have plenty of homemade, built in storage that should be adequate for us. We have picked out the site, and it won't be very hard to clear it and get the ground ready for a garden next spring. It'll seem funny to put work in on a place that belongs to us for a change. When I think of all the decorating that I've done in the various places that I've lived, I can't help thinking that I ought to be able to do this job to suit me.

You may be surprised to know that I have taken up knitting. The crocheting of doilies and placemats that I have done was enjoyable but not practical up here. It seems that there is nothing warmer than a pair of hand knit wool socks so, with Alma's coaching, I've begun a pair for Harold. Trying to handle all the four needles at times is a trial, but maybe I'll get onto it.

Friday will be a big workday again. I must clean up the house for the weekend tourist "non-rush." This weekend we are going to put out a kind of bench in the front of the cottage with fresh garden vegetables on it. We hope to attract the attention of tourists and to get them to stop and buy. I don't know how the folks who own the place made such fabulous sums of money last summer. Somewhere in my heart lurks the suspicion that they exaggerated the cafe trade because they wanted us to build it up. Maybe the figures they quoted were for the total summer's revenue, and we understood it as a week's return.

Love,
Your Alaskan Daughter, Harriet

Hope. Alaska
July 25th, 1953

Dear Mother,

Someone came up from Seward in the middle of the week and brought some mail. So, I got the package on Tuesday, the 21st, just a little over two weeks since you sent it. That's very good; too good to count on. I suppose one should plan on nearly twice that amount of time.

As your packages always are, this one was fun. I was, of course, most thrilled about the smock. I wore it the next day when we went to Seward to see the doctor. I have a string of pearls on a choker and earrings to match. They really looked nice with the neckline that way. I also wore the other outfit you sent to church last night. So, I'm very glad that it came when it did. And I'm very pleased with the nightgowns. I've really needed something like that. Your gift makes one less thing that I need to buy. The tea towel, apron, scarf, and baby rattle will all find good usage, I'm very sure. So again, I say, "THANKS."

When Alma took Mom W. to Wasilla to visit Elsie, we sent money for Alma to bring back some pint jars so that I could continue my canning. Therefore, since that time I've been putting up rhubarb. I hope that we get a lot of good out of it this winter. Mom also sent back some rare items, which can't be purchased out in this wilderness. She sent some tomatoes, some roasting ears of corn and some bananas. The bananas were so ripe by the time we got them that we have to use them in cooking. I've just taken a loaf of delicious looking banana bread out of the oven. It is delicious tasting too, I confess.

We just found out for sure that the place we're interested in isn't available right now. The ranger thought we might be able to get it within a year ... maybe ... but, of course, we' re needing something rather sooner than that. So, we're looking around for other home sites. We did find out an interesting fact, however, and that is that we can file on a home site and if we find one, we like better we can sell the improvements on that place to someone else and let that individual claim it while we move onto another home site. So, with that in mind, we may take a home site on the road close to where the mill is. It would have the advantage of being close to work and to the Millers and would also be a good property to sell when we get it fixed up. We should be able to get at least twice the price of our investment for any improvements we put on it. It isn't a site we'd care to keep forever, but it would be a nice solution for our present problem, we feel. We'll let you know as things work out along that line.

The doctor said that I was coming right along. He checked for a heartbeat and heard one. He predicts a girl! But he wouldn't promise. He needn't worry. It wouldn't go in an orphanage no matter what it is. I would just as soon have a boy as a girl. Actually, either one will be fine, so I can't lose.

Well, I have really turned out the work this week. Monday, I canned a pint of peas. Whee! Mom W. was here, and we picked peas and more peas. But all we had when they were shelled only filled one measly pint-sized jar. However, let's not undervalue that pint. It'll come in handy, I'm sure. I have also put up ten pints of raspberry jam and two pints of currant jelly. But the biggest project was chickens. We have more or less given up the idea of a deep freeze -- at least for a while. So we decided to can some chickens so that we can cut down on the cost of feed. We canned, in all, thirteen pints of chicken. That means a lot of head-chopping, dressing, and pressuring. I use my little pressure pan and borrow Alma's small cooker. I can do nine in a batch that way. But I think when I don't have any help like Mom W. gave me last week, that I'll do only my little pressure pan full. That would be four pints. I find that I get along so much better when I tackle these major projects in sections. I usually do only a small amount of jam at a time, for instance, but it is surely piling up.

I'm getting eager to see what a winter up here is really like. It's daylight so much of the time now that it seems hard to imagine Alaska any other way. I suppose I'll find out.

Harold has decided to have a basement under our house this winter and to have a heating stove down there. That way the floor of the house will be warm, and we won't have to keep the cooking stove so hot all the time. It does sound like a good idea, I think. It would be especially nice after the baby starts to crawl.

We think now that we will build the house eighteen feet by twenty-six feet. That would be plenty big with built-ins around and with the extra storage space in the basement. We're going to try to fix it up cute and modern so that it will sell better. Lots of people don't have ideas of their own and are willing to pay for ideas that others have worked out. Anyway, we hope that will still be true.

I neglected to mention that the docks have really been rushed in Seward this summer so anytime that we need cash that badly, Harold could put in a stretch of longshoring. So, we're not so hard up at all. He plans to try to get some long-shoring in when he is with me at the time the baby comes. The fact that he plans to go down with me and stay seems to be an intriguing novelty around here. It seems that the custom is for women from the remote areas to go into Seward safely ahead of time and to stay in some rented accommodation or with friends until time for the delivery. After the baby arrives, the new father is notified. Sometimes this notification is done by Mukluk Telegraph, which is a communication system unique to Alaska. It is a radio program that broadcasts personal items throughout the territory. After being notified, the father goes by road, boat, or plane into Seward to pick up his wife and baby. Harold has never considered anything else but that he will be with me through this little project of ours. I suppose it is self-indulgent of this new pioneer wife, but I can't tell you how grateful and relieved I am that he feels this way.

Guess this is all the rambling for this time. I do enjoy your letters so much.

Love,
Your Alaskan Daughter, Harriet

Hope, Alaska
July 25, 1953

Dear Roomies,

I flatter myself that you are curious about what has happened to your adventurous college friend, me. A fact borne out by the rate at which our letter packet has made the rounds. I got it with last Saturday's mail and will send it on with today's mail. As you recall, I wrote all of you from Slave Lake, Canada, many weeks and many adventures ago. You may be wondering where I am now. So, I mention the word "Hope." Hope is my frame of mind and Hope is where I sit writing a letter to all of you.

Let me tell you about life in this place called Hope.

Right now, we live in a little cottage on the edge of the village. The house is really quite cute - a little white gingerbread cottage. We are grateful that the Beutadahls, since they live in Anchorage, are willing to rent their summer home to us for a few weeks. The house has a main room with two smaller rooms behind. In one of those we have our bed, and the other could be used as a tiny nursery if we don't get our own little cabin built by the time the baby gets here.

The main room is in two parts - a living area and the kitchen. A long counter, open to either side, divides these two areas. This counter really is handy for use in preparing meals from the kitchen side. We have a wood stove for cooking, and I suspect that we will use it for heating when the weather cools. Harold keeps a pile of wood in the box by the side of the stove, and because of his careful coaching, I am actually learning which kind burns faster and how to use kindling to advantage. Also, I am learning to move things around on the stovetop to control temperature. Aren't you glad all my good brainpower is not going to waste? There are assorted cupboard spaces and a table that holds the water bucket. There is also a sink that taunts me because it doesn't deliver water into or out of the house. Still, Alma reminds me of how handy it is to catch wastewater, which can be drained into a bucket beneath. In a burst of optimism, this little house had been wired for electricity, and from the ceiling, some impotent light bulbs sneer down at me.

Lest you haven't grasped by now the concept of how modern our cottage is, I will point out that in regal splendor behind our new little home stands the outhouse. Now, I don't claim to be a judge of out-houses, but Harold assures me that this is one of the best built in town - a three-holer, no less. Should I be thrilled? I wonder ...

A little farther away is an old log cabin. It had long been unused, and the landlords have talked about fixing it up. But Mom Walker fell in love with it right away. She poured her boundless energy and enthusiasm into cleaning it up and making it pleasantly livable. So, when she's not visiting at Elsie's place, she stays out there in the old log cabin.

When Alma arranged for us to rent this place, there was a sort of caveat thrown in. The owners wanted us to keep the cafe open. Are your eyebrows lifting? You see, the non-kitchen half of that main room is not the cozy living space that, until this point, you may have imagined - an easy chair or two - possibly a sofa - some bookcases. No, it is equipped with two little cafe tables. Each of those tables has chairs around it. A summer or two ago construction on the road between Anchorage and Hope had finally been completed. The Beutadahls had the idea that they could open up a little cafe on weekends. This, they envisioned, would serve tourists who might wander in from Anchorage to look over the "quaint village" of Hope. They thought it might be strategic for their cafe in the long run if we kept it open this summer. I quailed at the thought of preparing food for someone who actually paid money for it. However, Harold's mother was delighted with the whole concept. She pictured weekend after weekend of happy tourists eating her sandwiches and pies.

Mom Walker is a bundle of energy, and she was a great help on our difficult trip up over the Alcan. However, I admit that we didn't see eye to eye on about the cafe enterprise. As the first weekend approached, Mom Walker's plans got specific. In high gear, she began making a variety of pies. Then she made dough for sandwich buns. That first weekend, three men stopped in. Their presence constituted the rush hour. Favorable comments on the pie paled before their appreciation of the sandwich buns. I walked around pouring coffee and listening to their happy comments. Great! The next weekend was much the same. Mom's buns made the sandwiches something special.

The little cafe sign didn't bring droves of people. The truth was quite the contrary. Yet it has to be admitted that we Walkers had great left-overs. Harold began to realize that this cafe plan might have unforeseen benefits. We sort of muddled along. One weekend the bridge to town was out, so we declared a holiday and went on a picnic. I felt guilty when we didn't open the cafe. However, I dreaded the results when we did. For Mom, the cafe was a lark, and she was very relaxed about it.

Then there came that fateful day when Mom again had a chance for a several-day visit with Elsie in Wasilla. I protested that this time she would be gone over the weekend. "Don't worry, Harriet. You can handle everything just fine."

I decided to make the buns first. I would do them a day ahead. The pies would thus be oven-fresh on cafe opening day. I mixed up the bread dough. I kneaded it and put it to rise. I hovered over that dough. Was it rising fast enough? I tasted a pinch from underneath the smooth ball of dough. Was it salty enough? Had I killed the yeast? I tasted another pinch of dough. I punched down the dough for the second rising. I thought that the dough lay there lifeless. It was my apprehension that began to rise. By now I was convinced that the bread would be a flop. What was I going to do?

Then I realized that I still had time to start over. My spirits lifted. But there was the matter of the dough on hand. Starting over would cost more, and the cafe enterprise was still not coming out even in the cash department. Of course, I wouldn't lie about it, but I preferred, strongly preferred, that nobody know about the fiasco. With buoyed spirits, I assured myself that I could do it right the second time. So how to get rid of the evidence? A sudden inspiration came- the outhouse. I took that batch out and dumped it down the largest of the vaunted three holes.

With great relief, I returned to the cottage to compose myself. Before I began the new batch of buns, I needed to visit the outhouse. I glanced down into the hole, which had recently received my dough. An ominous sight greeted me. The dough was alive. It was alive and growing. Horror filled me.

I retreated to the kitchen to grapple with this new threat. No insight arrived. Against my own will, I returned to the outhouse. The bread was still pulsing with life. Panic fueled my imagination. What if the dough continued to grow unceasingly? It would take over the outhouse and make its presence known as it crawled down the path toward our cottage. Perhaps it would slowly ooze along the village toward the schoolhouse. All those children and their parents would know about my disaster. I struggled with berserk fantasies as I fled the scene.

Time and again I went out to check on the new menace. I no longer hoped that I could conceal my sin from Harold. I just hoped he would come home in time to fight back the bread dough and comfort the mother of his future child.

Before he came home, however, the bread dough had finally stopped its menacing growth and slowly sank down into a sullen heap. I couldn't garner the courage to start another batch and just crawled into bed. However, when Harold saw me in such a state, he calmly walked to the front of the cottage and took down the cafe sign. He then came back to our bed-room and comforted me.

When she returned from Wasilla, Mom didn't seem the least perturbed about the closing of our big cafe enterprise. She was now excitedly making plans for roadside marketing of produce from her gardening efforts.

We are enjoying the long days here in Alaska. But it's not a time of leisure because there is a sense of rush throughout the village that as much as can be done must be done for winter cometh.

There are moments when I would like to go back in time before Alcan trips, college graduation, assorted progeny and just sit down on the bunk in our dorm room and have a good visit with all of you. This is one of those moments. But would I give up what has happened since? Except for berserk bread, I would have to say no.

Your ex-roommate,
Harriet

July 29, 1953
Hope, Alaska

Dear Evelyn,
Hey, how wonderful to receive a letter from you. I know that Mother keeps you up on the news of our great adventure. She also fills me in on how things are going on with you and Bob. Still, I am glad to get a letter directly from my one and only sister. So, you have earned one directly from me, your one and only sister. I'm going to have to hurry it a little since

there is so much to do to get ready for Harold's family reunion. But that's why I decided to sit down and get this letter written on Wednesday instead of my usual Friday writing time. You'll still have to wait until Saturday for it to get picked up by our prehistoric mail service.

It sounds like you will be going into this year of teaching with more confidence than you had last year ... and why not? You now know the set-up and are an experienced teacher with a good year behind you. So enjoy the year and get those Nebraska kids on track with their English. Remember to be prepared for all the little extras required of someone who also teaches music in a small school system. I remember the numbers that had to be prepared for PTA meetings, the Christmas program, the spring music contests, and the musical. I'm with you, Lil' Sis. You'll do great!

Life certainly has its strange turns. I think back to the Christmas vacation when you brought home from college the pair of awkwardly wrapped yellow angora socks that Harold sent with you as a Christmas gift for me. Opening that package brought the sudden realization that Harold David Walker actually thought of me as a person in my own rights - not just a mental sparring partner. Still, in the excitement of that realization and the hope that was born, I could never have guessed that so soon I would be pioneering in the wilds of Alaska. O.K. maybe I am overstating it a bit. "Pioneering" might not be completely accurate. But, believe me, in those letters to Mother, I left out some of the harder parts of the trip up over the Alcan. After all, she had made it clear that she thought Harold and I were very foolish to be going up there with a baby on the way. One day I reminded her of our pioneer ancestors who had made the long journey in covered wagons across the western plains, and she quickly reminded me of the graves that were scattered along the trails that the covered wagons took. Still, give her credit. Once we had actually decided to make a move, she has been nothing but supportive.

I am so glad that you and Bob are there close to Mother for

this one more year. Living in married student housing right there on the campus will make it easier for you to check in on her and do things with her. I find it hard to be so happy in my marriage and to think of her living alone in that little apartment and going to her daily work of managing the bookstore. I know that they say the first year of widowhood is the hardest. I suppose it is, but even with that time elapsed, it doesn't mean the complete end of grieving. I know that behind her brave front, Mother is very lonely at times.

But still, I am proud of her. Do you remember that when Daddy was recovering from his first heart attack, he pushed her into taking over their family business transactions? He even had to teach her how to write checks. Can you imagine? She had been an old-fashioned homemaker. She had never even written a check before. Yet, now she is managing the York College bookstore.

When I think of her bravely making her way to that bookstore each morning and doing what she has to do, I have a clear picture of a similar time in Africa. You were too young to remember when Dr. Conner's wife came down with diphtheria, the same disease that had taken the life of their little Max. Dr. Conner came to our home late at night and told Daddy and Mama that he would be taking his family and returning to America. It was decided that Mama would keep the little mission hospital going until a replacement doctor could be sent. Without the benefit of any medical training, she would have to rely on her sense of hygiene and her good judgment alone. Later that night, I lay in bed listening to something very unfamiliar. I could hear Mama crying and Daddy's low voice talking with her. But the next morning she put on her pith helmet, walked to the hospital and accepted the new assignment that God had given her.

As I think about that time and the one, she faces now, I feel very, very far away up here in Alaska. It is a great comfort to me that you and Bob are close to her for another year. Thank you, dear sister.

My last letter from Mother was a mildly scolding one. She was responding to the letter I wrote telling her all about the faults of the local minister ... his singing ... his seeming apathy. She reminded me of how judgmental I had been of some of the pre-theological students in college and how well their ministries have been turning out. Having lived in a parsonage, you and I know how unfair some criticism can be. And even more so, when Daddy was conference superintendent, you remember, he had many times when he had to intercede for a pastor. So, I try not to tell myself that this minister is different. Maybe if Mother could just be here, she would see what I see.

I really am trying to look at the whole picture. In the first place, the entire setup is hard. It is hard for me to have worship services on Friday nights. The week always seems a little out of kilter. But then I think how hard it is to be a circuit rider in this multi-church circuit. Rev. Eliot has a wife and son who travel with him most of the time. There is a little apartment in the church where they stay overnight after services and sometimes a night or so before the Friday event. I don't know their schedule, but it must be difficult. Maybe it doesn't leave enough time or energy for a minister to do all the contacting of people in his parish that I, Harriet Walker, think he should. When I think of the people in truly isolated places who manage to maintain a strong faith, I am a bit ashamed. Tuck my name onto the end of your prayer list, please.

I have met a most delightful woman, Grannie Clark. It didn't take long to realize why Alma is so fond of her. Her house is not very far from ours, and so I have frequently walked over there to spend some afternoon time visiting. She is a true old timer and has many wonderful stories to tell in her colorful style. She loves to relate those tales as her hands work away at knitting children's mittens. I had known about the mittens because Alma had told me that each year Grannie knits a new pair for every child in the village. One day I asked her if she would teach me how to knit mittens - might come in handy. "I can't teach you how to knit mittens," she declared in her abrupt manner. Then she said, "I guess I could show you how I do it." And so, I am beginning to learn the procedure. Fortunately, my work on the socks keeps me from being as awkward with those four needles as I was when I started learning to knit with Alma. But with Grannie Clark, as with Alma, there still is no pattern to follow. She says, "You do it this way." So, I try to do it ... "this way."

Grannie often looks askance at me when I stop knitting to take notes on some story, she has told me. I think she is secretly pleased. Perhaps, I will collect these old-timer stories of hers. Maybe I'll write a book someday featuring this wonderful old woman. Here is an example of the type of thing that she tells. She came from Texas to Alaska as a bride. And that trip was made in the winter - from Texas to Alaska in the WINTER. She and her husband traveled by dog sled with a group of men into the settlement. The first day of the long trip she was strapped into the dog sled. She said that she was too proud to tell her fellow travelers how cold and stiff she was. When they got the trapper's cabin where they were to spend the night, she couldn't move her legs at all. Her husband slung her over his shoulder like he would a quarter of moose and carried her into the cabin. The next day she told her companions that she would not ride on the dog sled again but that she would walk the trail with the others. She was wearing a long wool skirt that reached to her boots. Also, she had many layers of petticoats. As the day went on, the skirts collected snow and made her skirts heavier and heavier. Soon she was walking inside a frozen load that weighted her down. That evening she sat by the fire in the next trapper's cabin thawing out very slowly and very painfully. Then the following morning she shocked the group by declaring that she would wear some of her husband's clothes and walk the trail like a man. She paused for a minute in her knitting. "I did just that. I wore his clothes." She settled back with a satisfied look on her face.

She was also very proud of the fact that she had been one of the few women in that time to stay in Alaska with their men and not return to the I "lower forty-eight." "Texas was nice for growing up," Grannie Clark explained. But my home's Alaska." Even today, here in Hope, there are men for whom the allure of Alaska has such a pull that they remain even though they are supporting families Outside.

Visiting with Grannie Clarke, I am getting to feel like an Alaskan. I can even talk more like one, and I hope I am not as gullible as I once was. I remember right after Harold and I were engaged, we were sitting very close together on a sofa in the college reception room. Harold had his arm around me and was talking about his family in general and Alaska in particular. He told me that his brother-in-law, Ross, was a cat skinner. I can still remember that I jerked away and fought the revulsion that rose up in my stomach at the thought of this way of earning a living. Seeing my reaction, Harold laughingly told me that being a cat skinner meant being an operator of a large caterpillar tractor. He went on to describe how skilled Ross was and the admiration that this ability earned him. No, I am not as naive as I once was. I know that "cheechako" is an un-initiated newcomer. "Siwashing" is camping out with only the sky for a tent. A "dehorn" is a drunk. An "expectant mother" is your big sister. Oh well, you probably could have figured that last one out all by yourself.

Bob will soon be going back for his senior year at York, and you will be back teaching. It does indeed seem strange not to be involved once more with the beginning of a school year. This is the first autumn since I was in kindergarten that I haven't had that sense of new beginning that the first of the school year brings - as either a student or a teacher. I know that I will miss it. Give our love to that student husband of yours and any of our old college gang that is still around.

Your Big Sis,
Harriet

P.S. I neglected to tell you something about our little community church. Across the entire front of the church is a large picture window that shows a beautiful scene of God's world. No stained glass I have seen compares in beauty with the ever-changing scene revealed through the clear glass of this window. On Friday evenings of these long summer days, I have often been truly inspired as I gaze out into God's wonder that is Alaska. Why should I worry about worship with such a divine panorama?

CHAPTER 3

August 1953: Saw Mill

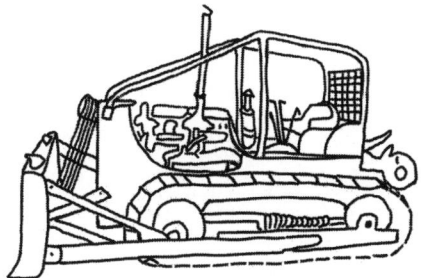

*D*ear Karen,

    Let me write out a little explanation of Harold's and my immediate families to help you place some of these letters. My sister, Evelyn, was teaching high school English and music in a small town near York, Nebraska, where she and her college student husband were living in married student housing. You probably picked most of that up from the letter to her in the last batch. I have a letter to my journalist brother, Clarke, in the next batch. He and his wife were living in Lincoln some fifty miles from York. So, both of my siblings were close to my mother, who was working at York College as director of the bookstore.

    The big event in this time frame was the Walker family reunion. You may think it odd that we had a family reunion for Harold's family in Alaska, which seems a long way to go for that sort of thing. However, bear in mind that Harold's two sisters, Alma and Elsie, and their families already lived in Alaska. Elsie, Harold's younger sister, lived in Wasilla, Alaska, as was mentioned in several letters. Alma, his older sister, was our neighbor in Hope. We had just moved to Hope, and Harold's mother was there visiting all of us. So to complete the family reunion, all we had to do was get Harold's younger brother, Cecil, and his older brother, Willard, to come up for a visit. Cecil and his wife, who were teachers in Esbon, Kansas, were not able to make the trip. But, Willard and his family, who were living in California, were able to come. So four of the five gathered with their mother for a reunion in high summer Alaska. It was a wonderful event.

In your last e-mail, you asked about how to control the temperature for cooking on the wood stove. There are several ways. Naturally, they are not as accurate as today's cooking ranges. The choice of wood helped regulate the temperature along with the rate at which one burned it. Harold would keep several kinds of firewood available for me. There would be the quick-burning kind and the slow-burning kind in neat piles by the cook stove. Actually, the main regulators were the draft and the damper. The draft opening was on the side of the stove. By opening and closing the draft, the amount of air supporting the fire could be controlled. The damper was located in the stovepipe and controlled the flow of air going up the chimney.

You will learn a lot more about the sawmill in the next set of letters. The sawmill was the primary reason we went to Alaska. It was the venture that was supposed to give us the economic independence for lives of public service in Alaska. Located on property owned by Ross and Alma, it was situated on level ground that gradually sloped into the bay but was high enough that extreme high tide would not reach it. Karen, you remember that Harold had a long association with his brother-in-law, Ross. Because of respiratory problems in Kansas, Harold had spent summers with Ross and Alma in their Idaho home from the time he was twelve until the beginning of WWII. During those years Harold witnessed the fact that Ross was familiar with all aspects of logging and running a sawmill.

After the war, Harold spent time working in the woods with Ross who was now living with his family in Alaska. These two often talked about having a mill. It was finally decided to start acquiring the equipment for both logging and milling operation. We did this as steadily as we could afford it. Harold and I continued to teach in Kansas, but we come up to help with the mill in Al-

aska during summer breaks. After two years of effort, the mill was in operation, and we had purchased a Caterpillar bulldozer and a truck. By the summer of 1953, we believed that the mill was well enough developed to sustain both the Miller and Walker families financially.

When Willard, Harold's older brother, came to Alaska for the family reunion that summer, he was full of ideas about improving the whole operation. Since Willard had experience in up-grading mills in California, Ross was intrigued with his ideas to the point that Willard was included as a future partner. Later letters will reveal how this played out.

The logs for our mill came from trees that we logged off U.S. Forest Service land. The local rangers were certain that the supply of merchantable trees was very small and that we'd soon exhaust it if we continued our operation. That might have been an issue if we'd just been selling the logs. However, We planned to turn the logs directly into lumber through our mill. We were the only sawmill in the area. On paper, it looked like there was a fortune to be made, didn't it?

I hope you enjoy this set of letters and I will look forward to your comments and questions.

Love,
Grandma

Hope, Alaska
August 7, 1953

Dear Clarke and Jean,

It was good to hear from you, Clarke. It was even OK to receive all those probing questions from you. You certainly have a journalist's skill for interrogation! Questions call for answers and answers require a letter, which your sly ploy now gets you!

Actually, I am happy to respond by letter. It's better than

having a brother waiting to interrogate me when I came home from a date, as you used to do. In fact, it will do me good to go back and rehash the steps that got us up here to Alaska. You're right that this would appear to be a detour from our plans for law school and politics. But that depends on how you define detour. We see it as a way to expedite that training and launch the political career.

The dream started a couple of years ago when we were up here in Alaska on the summer break from teaching in Mullinville. Ross and Harold were logging for the Bear Lake Mill down by Seward. Ross had long had a dream about owning a mill but had accepted the lack of any hope of it actually being realized. Harold, however, had begun to see a possibility for that very thing. Because of his strong relationship with Ross, I encouraged Harold when he suggested that we could help Ross realize his dream.

Ross was very reluctant to accept our financial help. He had always been fiercely independent and would never accept anything that meant borrowing money. When Harold eventually convinced him that the mill could be a good thing for both families, we developed a plan. Harold would use what savings we already had as a stake to get the mill started. We agreed to continue teaching for two more years in Kansas so that there was time to get the mill going well before it had to support two families.

During those first two years, Ross procured and set up the sawmill equipment using the funds we supplied. Harold and I also paid for the purchase of an old caterpillar dozer that Ross found near Hope. Back in Kansas, we purchased an army surplus six-by-six truck, which had been parked uselessly for some time. After its long wait in Kansas, that poor old army truck was destined to become both a logging truck and a lumber hauling truck in Alaska.

Last summer, Harold and a young fellow named George Windle drove that truck up to Alaska. George had been one of Harold's students at Mullinville. The trip was quite an adventure, as traveling to Alaska always is, but it was worth it. Many valuable things were hauled to Alaska on the back of that truck including a farm tractor, a refrigerator, and George's jeep. As you remember, I flew to Alaska after Evelyn's wedding to join Harold at the Alaska end of the trip. We were there together to see the sawmill cut its first slab off the very first log. It was an exciting moment.

Incidentally, George's jeep, after its long trip aboard the six-by-six truck, is still here in Alaska, as is George himself. He found this place to be a perfect fit. I think it may not be just Alaska that is holding George's interest though. It is generally agreed around Hope that he finds a local girl named Laura Stainbrook particularly interesting.

Harold is sure that the prospects for the sawmill to become a profitable enterprise are really good. We only pay the government $5.00 per thousand board feet in stumpage for the timber. After logging and milling, we get $90.00 per thousand board feet. That is for rough-cut, green lumber at the mill. We make even more when we haul the order to the customer.

I know this path through an Alaskan sawmill might seem like a detour. During the last couple of years, we have been putting aside money as a partnership stake in the mill. We really believe we have made a good investment on two counts. First, we plan to take advantage of readily available timber and make good money now while this territory is booming, and new building starts abound. This investment should soon earn back the capital with interest to enable us to go Outside, attend law school, and care for our growing family in a comfortable style.

The second reason this venture is a good investment of time and money has to do with the political opportunities in Alaska. There is, of course, strong talk about the positives and negatives of Alaska becoming a state. Whichever way it goes, there is a need for honorable politicians. Harold and I are quite excited about being a part of Alaska's political future. For that, we not only need Harold's law degree but we also need a stake in Alaska's future. The sawmill gives us that stake.

We agree that the venture is not without worries. Alma, for instance, worries some about a possible conflict between "the two men that I love-a husband and a brother." She is aware of the strong differences in their personalities. All this she has confided to me, and I have shared it with Harold. He tells me not to worry. In the first place, Harold really respects Ross and believes that he is a fair person whom we can trust. Harold is certain that no problem he can foresee will ever upset the apple cart. With my knowledge of my husband, I really believe him on that score.

Yes, it is true that we have moved to a primitive environment without the benefit of many modern conveniences that would make childbearing and family life easier. But, Clarke, I hope these answers to your questions can put some of your concerns to rest. Life in this community is really good. We have the essentials. The focus on daily activities necessary to make life possible has been good for me. I have been feeling well and enjoying the excitement of the many new elements of my life here. We are following a dream, an opportunity that few people have. Moving here and engaging in this adventure was an important turn in our life together and I am completely satisfied that we have done the right thing. Even if it doesn't turn out as we hope, the experience itself will be the treasure of a lifetime.

It's good to know that you continue to enjoy your newspaper work there in Lincoln. I am glad that Jean is making good use of her considerable talent as a commercial artist. Most of all, I am glad that you are there close to York so that you can have more frequent contact with Mother.

Love,
Harriet

P.S. If you have any questions about the above, I am sure I will hear from you. But I enjoy letters even if they are not interrogative ones. Remember that, please.

Hope, Alaska
August 7, 1953

Dear Mother,

Your last letter brought me a couple of very pleasant surprises. I can't tell you how thrilled I am at the thought of another addition to my maternity wardrobe. I shall be awaiting the package with eagerness. I have bought nothing since you did that sewing for me. Sometimes I regret that I didn't have more material on hand at the time. I am getting along nicely, however. I really don't like to spend money right now on something as temporary as waiting-clothes. I have the dressy smock you sent earlier, of course. I have the two everyday cotton wrap-around, which I practically live in. So the new smock will be a welcome gift.

We had decided that a baby basket was not essential, but when you mentioned it in your last letter, we reconsidered. It would surely be handy, especially for the trip Outside. Harold smiled at the idea of its being a birthday gift for him. I think he was very pleased. However, after checking the prices in the Sears and the Montgomery Ward catalogs, I've come to the conclusion that you had better make it a gift for both us. How about that? Baby baskets cost around $5.50 in either catalog. The pad would be another $2.50.

Today I'm resting, writing letters, and shopping. My, but it's hard work to shop by catalog. Locating products, comparing prices, filling out order forms, etc., is more complicated than it seems. We've been hoarding a little cash to buy some things for the baby, but Harold had to take it yesterday when he went to Anchorage. We still have a balance of $34.00 in the Mullinville bank, so we decided to order baby things with that. I got out the little book that the doctor told me to use and checked the "essential needs" list. My original list totaled way more than we could afford. Carefully, I have thought through what we could get along without. I finally got the list down to $32.00. This is what I'm ordering ... 3 kimonos, 1 plastic mattress cover, 1 rubber sheet, 4 cotton absorbent pads, 4 yards of outing flannel for receiving blankets, 4 doz. Diapers, 4 little nursing bottles for water and juice, diaper pail, thermometer, castile soap, baby oil, a package of cotton swabs ... and two nursing bras for me. Pretty good, eh? It'll be a nice comfortable feeling to have those essentials here in the house. Now if Harold can come back with some change in his pockets, we'll have enough to cover postage. Anyway, I'm proud of my shopping.

Maybe I should explain why I'm resting. The reunion is over, and the company is gone. Harold took all of them to Wasilla last night to spend the night at Elsie's place and then back to Anchorage this morning to catch the plane. He should be home any time now. Mom W. went too. She'll be back to spend about one more week here, then a week or so back at Elsie's, and then home to her mission work in New Mexico.

I know you can understand what a wonderful time this reunion was for Mom W. It was wonderful for all of us, of course, but the Walkers have been so scattered and now, to have most of them together, was pure joy for her. You remember that Willard is ten years older than Harold and Alma two years older than Willard. I know that those two made a pet of Harold when he was little. Alma wrote down the cute phrases that he said and her interest in music encouraged that gift in him, I believe. Willard would take Harold along with him on all sorts of excursions. Now that I know Willard better, I 'm amazed at his patience in having a little brother tag-along on the many exploits he had with his teenage friends. Those two older siblings have been very special to Harold all these years.

Elsie and Dave came over from Wasilla. So there were four of the siblings here. We were sorry that Cecil and Becky couldn't be here. Writing Cecil's name down reminds me of the story that Mother Walker laughingly told on herself at the reunion. She remembers the time that you and Daddy were at the church where Harold's dad was a pastor. You were going to give a missionary talk and suggested that Mom W. model an African costume. Do you remember that incident? Anyway, Mom W. says that she declined because she was expecting and felt "too pregnant." Without mentioning that you were pregnant as well, you went ahead and modeled the African outfit yourself. Mom W. laughs at the irony that her baby, Cecil, was born just three days before you had Evelyn.

The reunion was very successful. In fact, it was such a success that several people were very sad at the parting. This is the first time that Willard's teenage daughter, Jacque, has ever been able to play with young folks anywhere near her age. She has always lived a rather lonely life in a world peopled by adults. Thus, all five of Mom's grandchildren were together for a few days---six grandchildren, if you count Slavo or Slavina who still resides inside me.

Willard's little son, Willie, is a charmer. He loved the tiny sausages that we served him for one breakfast. I don't know if it was the taste or the name - Harold called them "little piggies" - but his appetite for them prompted us to go back to Doc's store and empty out his limited supply.

This was an important event for the adults as well. Alma and Willard hadn't seen each other for thirteen years. That time lapse seems hard to believe, but Alma moved to Idaho right after her wedding, and of course, Willard and Betty headed to California during the depression years. The Californians did visit the Idahoans once in '40, but otherwise, contact was limited to letters; so this was really a "reunion." A lot of catching up was accomplished, and I think it is safe to say, "a good time was had by all."

As you can imagine, because of planned family activities, the men didn't get much accomplished in the way of work, but no one is going to waste any regret over that. A major accomplishment of the stay, however, was that we got our car in running order. It will really be nice to have a car again. Willard is an excellent mechanic so we're hopeful that the car is really "fixed." If that's the case, then even the work loss will be largely offset by the benefit of having transportation again.

I'm not sure that having the men work the last few days would have brought us much monetary benefit anyway. Sales are really down. If the lumber doesn't start to move pretty soon, Harold and Ross are going to get some contracts for land clearing. That pays well, and they have the cat to use. That way they can garner enough money to get the two families through the winter before they continue working the mill and stockpiling the lumber. It'll sell. We're sure of that, but it may not be until next summer, now.

We still don't know where we are going to live this winter. We found one site, which we would love to have but I guess someone has already filed a claim on it. Maybe we'll be able to find the perfect spot yet. It won't take long to build the house when we find the place to put it.

I'll be very busy this next week canning. I notice that the raspberries, currants, and cranberries are going to be ready for jamming and jelling right away. I'll probably be putting up beets and peas before too long.

We have cauliflower and potatoes ready to eat any day now. Maybe I will rush the season a little and have some cauliflower for supper garnished with some very well ripened cheese that I bought from Doc. I looked at that cheese that had been hiding somewhere in the dim recesses of his multi-building store and wondered. But I understand that cheese improves with age. So tonight: cauliflower with cheese.

I put up lots of strawberry jam last week and some more rhubarb sauce. To date, I have made thirty-six pints of jam of assorted kinds. Needless to say, we don't have that much jam on hand considering the rate it gets eaten up around here. Alma says that a pint of strawberry jam is worth about a dollar and a half. I figure that the sugar and Certo that I have in each pint is barely over twenty cents worth. So see? I'm making money! Alma says that at the rate I am putting up foodstuff, I will soon have saved enough on grocery bills to make the rent payments. Thrilling thought!

I'm quite interested in your knitting project. Make the scarf and cap you are planning for me a nice bright red. I think that's the color that I'm going to use with my tan coat when I come Outside this winter. Should look pretty nice, I think.

Well, maybe someday I'll not wait until the last minute to write my letters. Erma Ann and another girl just came in to visit for a while, and it's too late to get into the post office today. I'll have to take the chance that this week's mail hasn't gone out yet in the morning when I go over to get last week's mail. The mail carrier usually waits around a while before starting back, and I'll hope that I am that lucky.

AUGUST 8, 1953

Harold got home after ten last night. It seems that the flight that Willard's family planned to take out of Anchorage was canceled and they will have to wait overnight for the next flight. I do hate that because they had to borrow to make the trip and extra expenses can take the edge off a good time. There is nothing that we can do about it though, so I'll just try not to worry.

I guess mom is going to come back over here to stay and visit Alma from headquarters here at our place. She likes the independence of staying in the log cabin that she cleaned up. Besides, she says that she thinks that she makes her two daughters nervous. I rather imagine she does. She's a lot like you in wanting to plan the day to get things done. That always works out fine with me because I like to plan the day too. I can't help thinking that the way to get things accomplished is just that simple. Anyway, neither Alma nor Elsie seems to do any planning. In fact, Alma is always kidding me when things don't go according to schedule, so I try to make no appearance of planning things around her. Sometimes at her house, when the men come in for dinner at noon, it isn't ready to eat until one thirty. I'd be very worried about that in her place, but it doesn't seem to bother her or the men a bit. Anyway, it bothers Mom, so she's coming back over here to spend the working part of her day with me, and she'll spend the playing part of the day with the Millers for the short time she has left here in Alaska.

It seems that our beautiful weather is going to last. We have been having quite a string of golden days. Today will be another one. It really has been a lovely summer. I hope all the good weather isn't used up so that there'll be plenty next summer -- for your visit.

How strange it seems to be writing this in such a hurry to get it into the mail so that I can read the one written previously by you. Seems like that's doing it backward. Doesn't it?

Love,
Your Alaskan Daughter, Harriet

Hope, Alaska
August 14, 1953

Dear Mother,
So, I know that you are dying to hear more about the U.S. territory of Alaska. Right? I was asking one of my new friends, Marge Carter, what she thinks of the winters here. She laughed. Then she said, "We rush around for months getting ready for the winter ... all summer and into the fall. Then all of a sudden, we are looking at seed catalogs and glorying in the lengthening days as we accept the arrival of spring. We are hardly aware of winter at all." Hmm. We'll see!

A couple of weeks ago the fellows came back with a bear. This particular bear had been high in the mountains eating berries and was the most delicious meat I think I have ever tasted. It was tender and rich. About three families were in on the division of that meat, and it was gone in short order. But it was really good while it lasted.

Mother, picture me as a merchant of chickens. People around here are pleased to pay for dressed chickens, so I am learning to do it. I mean all of it. So picture your prissy daughter with her hands inside of a chicken. I'm even learning how to scald them properly so that I don't have to use a pair of pliers to get the feathers out. The result of this effort is that I sell the nicely dressed chicken for a good price. We actually figure the cost of the chickens by live weight, but mostly, people buy them dressed. That's a strange term when you realize that they are really "undressed."

We are selling off the roosters and keeping the young pullets. Harold often mentions how much he is looking forward to having fresh eggs. He doesn't like the eggs that are shipped in. He insists that fried "boat" eggs just flatten out all over the plate. He is counting on some fried eggs that stand up and "look you in the eye." We may be selling some eggs too. It would be fun to be like the Kansas farm wives who raised chickens to have a personal spending fund from the egg money.

While I am talking about raising chickens, I should tell you about Peggy Nutter, a sort of legend who used to live near where we do now. She also raised chickens, and her chicken house is not too far away. Anyway, the ground here carries some gold, and the town area was never placer mined. Hence, the chickens were free to pick up nuggets along with the gravel that they need for their digestive systems. When she dressed chickens, Peggy N. would open up the craw and look for gold nuggets. She did the same with the contents of the gizzard. Harold has, on occasion, imitated her when he was around while I was dressing out chickens. He has found no gold, and I am certainly not staking any future wealth on that unpleasant task.

Lest you think that our diet will be strictly chicken and eggs now that the bear meat is all gone, let me assure you otherwise. The fellows came in the other day with a mountain goat. Alma had been telling me how wonderful goat stew was for a winter meal. She suggested that I make up a rich stew using the goat meat and the end of the garden vegetables. Then I could can it up into meal portions. This project appealed to me, and I am truly glad that it did. Mother, that stew is delicious. It had lots of meat, carrots, onions, some cabbage, string beans, and even a few precious peas. I am hoping that relating all this will impress you. Of course, finding a vessel big enough to contain the amount of stew that I intended to make was a challenge. I hope you won't be shocked when I tell you what worked perfectly well for this purpose. The un-used bright and shiny "awaiting" diaper pail was the cook pot. And delightfully promising jars of goat stew are the result.

So you see, Mother, we are making a fine living off the land here in the wilds. The garden has served us really well. We are getting a variety of good quality meats. At various times in late summer, depending on their species, the salmon come up the creek to spawn. One can go down to the creek and literally choose a good-looking salmon, reach down and snag it. This summer we have really been enjoying the salmon. Baked salmon is superb. Then, of course, there is the hope for a moose. That would result in a big batch of meat. Ross and Harold have already been talking about how they will work out a system for freezing that meat.

It looks like our mill business might get another partner. When Willard and his family were here a few weeks ago for the family reunion, Willard just fell in love with this country and the enterprise that has lured us up here. He seemed keen on joining in the corporation that we are setting up. If he could come up here for some extended weeks in the summer, he could be a real asset. He is just plain gifted with mechanical ability. We call our operation the M & W Mill for Miller and Walker. Get it? I know, it's bursting with originality. But, the men involved wouldn't consider any of my creative suggestions. So if Willard joined, I am wondering if it would still be the same W or if it would be the M&WW mill. Time enough to worry about that if it happens.

I guess that we are just about a year or so behind in the lumber game. Last year the market wanted un-finished lumber, but now no one wants to bother with it. So we have a huge pile of lumber sawed which isn't selling very well. But, of course, while it sits, it cures and will be able to command a choice price should the market ever want it.

However, we have decided that we are going to have to keep in step with the times. We know that several lumberyards would take our lumber if only it were finished lumber; that is if it has been planed to a smoother finish on more precise dimensions. So it has become clear that we will have to buy a planer. The problem is that we can't buy a planer until we sell some lumber and we can't sell lumber until we buy a planer. That's a heck of a mess, isn't it? Ross and Harold have been shopping around for planers. There is one between here and Anchorage that has been deserted. It is lying back from the road and is almost invisible because it is completely covered with grass and weeds. We've been trying to locate its owner to see if we can have it " cheap." Some folks have advised us to just take it since it has been neglected so long but, of course, we can't do that because then we'd be liable before the law and might lose everything. If we could get that planer at a reasonable price, we'd really be set.

The other deal that we've been considering is a terrific planer that belongs to a company that went bankrupt. Purchased new, a planer like that will cost nine thousand dollars. The company went bankrupt because they didn't have insurance to cover a legal settlement in favor of a man who was injured while working for them. Here is another planer that is just sitting idle, but for legal reasons can't be sold. We couldn't dig up enough to buy it anyway. But there is a possibility that we could rent it for a while with the option to buy. That way we could make it pay for itself. Anyway, we're looking into those two possibilities. If something should happen right away, we'd really be set yet this fall. That's because it wouldn't take long to run the lumber we have cut through the planer, and we could really get some more down and ready in short order.

If fall comes in too soon before we can sell our lumber, we'll just have to make it through the winter as best we can. Reaping the big harvest will just have to wait for next summer. Ross and Harold can be stockpiling logs like mad all winter. They can saw and plane it all as soon as the weather turns. That way, next summer will be the time of money making. If it should come to that, we'll charge our food over at Doc's store. Then, should we not have the money to pay for it, Harold and Ross can hew railroad ties for Doc who has a contract with the railroad to sell them. He got the contract so that some of his bachelor friends could pay their bills that way. But working for Doc might be a good deal for Harold and Ross because we can always be sure of food that way. Yet, it would be a detour from their working toward our goals. However, besides food, we'll have hardly any other expense. We can leave the house unfinished on the inside and finish it as we have time and money. Blue Cross will take care of most of the baby cost and with the doctor's fee comes three months of postnatal care for mother and baby. Should have things in excellent shape by that time, eh?

You remember Vince, the young man who is staying with the Millers? Well, he is still around. Bless his heart. He likes the country, I guess. He has made no indication of ever planning to leave. Harold thinks that Ross will have to ask him to leave before winter sets in because another mouth to feed is a sizeable consideration. He helps around and has really made a wonderful summer for the two Miller teenagers by taking them lots of places in his car. But he is not earning his keep. He may be planning to leave at the end of the summer. I have not heard. He is such a pleasant fellow and fits in nicely, so I hope that there is no rift in the relations as winter approaches. We'll see.

Well, I better finish this off for now. I'll get it on its way tomorrow when I go to pick up another letter from you ... I hope ...! hope!

Love,
Your Alaskan Daughter, Harriet

Hope, Alaska
August 21, 1953

Dear Evelyn,

It was so nice to have you write back in response to my last letter that I've decided just to keep this thing going and send another one right back to you. As you remember, when I wrote the last letter I was just getting ready for the big gathering of Harold's family here in Hope. Well, it really went well. Harold's family has really been scattered with two sisters in Alaska, a brother in California, a brother in Kansas, and until a couple of months ago, we were in Kansas. Suddenly, this summer, Alaska became the center of gravity for the Walker family. When Mom W. came up here with us, it left only Harold's two brothers in the States. Harold's older brother, Willard, and his family made the trip up even though Cecil and Becky were not able to come.

Sometimes I think of the "old days" when families weren't so scattered as they are now. Then I realize that I have to tread softly when I broach that subject because, in the case of our family, I am the maverick. I am the one who took off with Mother's future grandchild to the wilds of Alaska. In Harold's case, our heading to Alaska meant one more of the Walker siblings living in the same general area.

It had been a long time since Alma and Willard had been together. They did a lot of catch-up visiting, and even more reminiscing. Willard had so much enjoyment out of the trip and being here with us in Alaska. It really wouldn't surprise me too much if he would return before too long. The cousins had wonderful fun together. City-bred Jacque took no time at all to fall into the pattern of life here. It was intriguing to see how much she enjoyed Erma Ann and Lewie. At first, she was annoyed by Lewie's teasing, but it wasn't long until she was just lapping it up. Needless to say, he also enjoyed it very much. I suppose the lack of playmates is one of the reasons that Jacque has concentrated so hard on her acrobatic dancing.

She put on a show for the community here at the potluck Saturday night. I tell you, she is unquestionably the best performer of this sort that I've ever seen. I am amazed at the money that they pour into her training. Her costume alone cost over a hundred dollars. On the other hand, she is beginning to take in a nice amount of money for her shows. I know that helps some. She has been on several of the big name television and radio shows. She's no little person in her field, and yet I am sure this little California lass would have loved to spend the rest of the summer as a little tomboy in Alaska.

The two younger children, Linda and Willie, were truly a pair. Linda cried for some time after they left. She and Willie have had a perfectly wonderful time together. Like Jacque, neither one of them has had much chance to play with kids their own age. Teen-agers Erma Ann and Lewie have grown up having each other. Little Linda has only Billy, the dog, who was so jealous of Willie that he would growl whenever he came very close. Although Willie is about five months younger than Linda, they were just exactly the same size. Both talked with the same big voice. You could hardly tell which one was talking if you weren't looking at them. They were certainly cute together, and there were very few quarrels for such independent preschoolers. They would play together from morning to night, getting dirty as hoodlums, but enjoying themselves immensely.

One element of life up here really amused our sophisticated Californians. That was the radio programs. Nowhere else that we have lived have we found such amazing informality. These programs are broadcast from records sent to the Alaskan radio stations. So, the programs often give slight hints that they are out of date. Last week, for example, nearly every program had something in it about the Fourth of July. But who minds that? Because of the long daylight hours for working, we haven't taken advantage of the regular evening programs. Winter and the long dark nights will change all of that in a few months. When the Alaskan cold comes, you can imagine a pleasant domestic picture of your sister and brother-in-law sitting here in our little white cottage as the wild winter storms roar outside, cozily listening to "Gunsmoke," "The Six Shooter," or "Lux Radio Theater." Add to that picture my sitting in the big rocking chair knitting, yes Evelyn, knitting, and maybe you can stick in the view of us munching on deep smoked Alaskan salmon. How does that strike you?

Oh, you should hear the commercials! There is nothing like the commercials on Alaskan radio. Just got through listening to one that was a doozy. It started out with some stirring music, then the words "In seeking a route between the two great oceans, Captain Cook sailed into Cook Inlet and on into Turnagain Arm where he ran into the land. So he had to 'turn-a-gain.' Hence the name." (Music and a drum roll) Then the deep-voiced announcement, "Ladies and Gentlemen, the president." (More stirring music, another drum roll, the sound of a gavel rapping three times.) "Ladies and Gentlemen, the president of People's T.V. Center, would like to give away TV sets, but the vice president won't let him. Therefore, they have done the next best thing ... " etc. Through June, about every program was broken into with the thrilling announcement of how one auto sales company was getting along with its self assigned quota of a hundred new cars sold in June. The crazy part was that listening, I was secretly pleased as the announcement changed from "Thirty-three more cars to go" to "Thirty more cars to go." Why one should care, I don't know. But by the end of the month, I almost felt I must go right in there and help the poor guys out. They were so near and all. I never did know just how that race against time turned out. We let our battery run down without having a replacement on hand, so I had to wait a week or so and missed out on the end of that life or death struggle.

One program is really vital to life here in Alaska. It's called the Mukluk Telegraph. It broadcasts personal information all over the area as a way of getting messages to those who live in remote places -- like us. Through this service, weddings have been arranged, deaths announced, rescues made and often just little routine unimportant happenings recorded.

Let me get back to my description of the Walker family reunion. We spent a day up on Palmer Creek fishing and the whole group of fourteen people caught about 115 little trout. That was just enough to feed us when you remember that most people can eat five to eight of them in a meal. But everyone caught fish. I can't imagine why the fish were cooperating so well that day.

The next day we went gold panning. We also managed to have a few bits of gold dust to show for that day's work too. Not worth a dollar, I suppose, but something to show. We finished that day with a picnic cooked outdoors, enjoyed by all.

The last morning, just before leaving, several members of the group went salmon fishing. They caught ten salmon. Alma and I were just floored. That's a lot of meat with salmon being such great big fish - unlike those little guys caught up Palmer Creek. I was truly sorry to see the reunion break up. Harold, Mom W., and Willard's four traveled with Elsie back to her place in Wasilla to stay overnight before catching a plane the next day. Behind them, in the void created by their absence, they left two sisters-in-law, three dejected cousins, one delighted dog, and ten salmon. I took home one "dog" salmon and canned it. So now I have five pints of salmon as a start on my winter's supply. Alma baked some for supper, canned quite a bit and fixed the rest up for dog food.,

One of the most interesting aspects of the reunion is that Willard has taken an interest in the mill venture. Harold thinks that he is interested enough to come in as a partner. That would really be exciting! Willard is an extraordinary mechanic, and so much development of this enterprise depends on sound judgment and good decisions in the mechanical arena. Harold is sure that Willard would be a valuable asset to our work here. So cross your fingers, dear sister. We really need this business to work out for us. With our lumber selling so slowly right now, we have to take hope in the future and our ability to develop the mill long term.

Well enough of that ... Please greet your husband for us. I'm sure he is excited to get back to school to finish his senior year. That will be coming up very soon. Also, please give Mother a hug for me when you see her next. It's wonderful to keep in contact by mail, but now, especially with Mom W. gone home and life settling into the last dash to get ready for winter, I really miss her and you.

Your big sister,
Harriet

Hope, Alaska
August 28, 1953

Dear Mother,
Although it is still warm and summer-like here in Alaska, there are hints that Fall and its cold, cold successor are well on their way. The days have noticeably shortened. There is an occasional chill in the air. However, the most salient sign of the impending change is the flurry of activity as the community prepares to put the school back into session. I must admit to more than a little twist of nostalgia as school years prepare to start all over the world without my taking part in it.

Nevertheless, I find myself watching the local school with interest. The schoolmistress lives in an apartment over the classroom. She teaches all the levels through the eighth grade. Village high school students will be taking their schooling by correspondence. You won't believe where they get their curriculum. I've come all the way to Alaska, to this remote village in the hinterlands, only to have the local high school course of instruction come from Nebraska, where you live. It's a small world. Actually, the University of Nebraska has an excellent program for this. The Territory of Alaska contracts with the University of Nebraska to provide correspondence courses for students living in outlying areas.

The Miller kids, Erma Ann and Lewie, will be juniors in high school this year and take advantage of that U. of Nebraska correspondence program. Their freshman year they attended the high school in Seward where Ross was working for a logging/sawmill operation across the head of the bay from Seward. They lived in a house furnished by the company. Last year, they took their sophomore class work by correspondence and seemed to thrive on the independent study. So they anticipate no problems with this year's schooling plan.

This year, the five high school aged young people in this community are all taking correspondence courses. There are a freshman, two sophomores, and the Millers who are in their junior year.

I think that it is interesting that Erma Ann and Lewie are in the same grade although there is about the same age difference between them as between Clarke and me. The year that Erma should have been starting to school, they lived on the property near here known as the King Ranch. It was more than a mile from the school. The teacher was eager to have a boy in school because all the eight or ten students scattered throughout the eight grades were girls. He was sure that Lewie would be able to handle the work. Because Alma would be walking Erma to school each day, having them both in the first grade solved a logistics problem for her. So she started them both the same year. Each day she would walk them to school and walk to get them after school. Occasionally, I understand, she would just spend the day at school visiting.

Little Linda joined the family much later. She'll be a first grader this year. And Alma will be once again walking a child to and from school. They'll leave home each morning and return each evening across the salt grass covered mud flat that edges Turnagain Arm. From the Miller place to the school is a distance of about three-quarters of a mile.

Now, Mother, let me turn to the primary subject for this letter. Some questions in your last letter suggest that more news about our development of the mill business is in order. I also suspect that you have had a conversation with Clarke since I wrote in response to his queries about the course our lives have taken into this mill venture. I know we talked this through carefully before we left for Alaska. But when faced with the actual tasks of making such a venture work, it bears more discussion, especially when lumber sales are falling well below our expectations, as I reported a couple of weeks ago.

Harold says that we are making improvements to the mill every day. When it's running smoothly, the mill can easily produce more than a thousand board feet per hour. This means that the mill actually holds the promise we had originally imagined. Our thinking got a big boost when Willard visited us. Ross really respects Willard's abilities. With the possibility that

Willard might become a partner, we are hopeful that the mill might get on track to reach its full potential. Harold and I think that Willard sees the same vision for the mill's future that we do and believe that Ross might be willing to listen to Willard in a way he seems unable to accept from Harold.

The honest truth, Mother, is that Harold and Ross don't have the same aspirations for the future of the mill. Harold and I have talked about this a lot. As we think back over the last couple of years, the signs were there that Ross' vision differed significantly from ours. We are still very much hoping that Ross will come to see the same high potential for the mill that Harold sees. Let me try to explain this better.

We see the mill growing rapidly in the next few years to a large operation that produces significant amounts of lumber and employs many people in a growing community benefiting from the brisk commerce. This is crucial to our plans, not only to provide funding for Harold's schooling but also to provide evidence of Harold's worth to Alaska's political future. Ross, on the other hand, sees the mill as a small, two-man operation where he can serve his friends and neighbors by custom cutting lumber for their homes while eking out a living.

A perfect example of this happened recently when Harold returned from Anchorage where he was trying to drum up some business. Harold was all excited about three propositions he had for Ross. First, was an opportunity to furnish flatcar stakes for the Alaska Railroad. Ross rejected this because he said the territorial government ran the railroad and their payment would run sixty to ninety days after delivery. Ross was completely unwilling to take out the loan it would require to ramp up operations to make this deal work.

Another deal was for a huge order of one-inch boards cut in random widths but all eight feet long. This would furnish the material to build a fence around a large racetrack. Ross rejected this offer because cutting only one-inch boards would waste too much of what should be cut into choice dimensional lumber. This means the two- and four-inch material that is used to create the skeletal structure of buildings.

The last opportunity was from a retail outlet in Anchorage that said they would take all the rough-cut lumber that could be produced in any variety of sizes. What could be the objection to that deal? Well, Ross rejected this one because he felt there would be too much pressure to produce. He was worried that the retail business would soon try to dictate the species, length, and dimensions of the material they would accept.

Ross prefers to spend an hour helping a local customer make out an order for the lumber to be used in some new building while the mill sits idle. Then he takes lots of time setting the saw to get the most out of each cut while filling the order. Harold says that Ross is very good at doing this and derives a great deal of satisfaction from direct participation in customers' lives. However, it is hard for Harold to have the mill operate so slowly when he knows that rapidly sawing lumber and shipping it off to the voracious markets in Anchorage and Seward would be the quickest way to build the business. Hiring more workers would help to increase the mill's output and provide new jobs to help Hope grow. But since Ross refuses to borrow, there is no money to pay them. It may be that Ross wants to do the work as much as possible with his own hands.

With all of this, I suppose you may be worrying that there is potential for big problems between Harold and Ross. I know Alma worries about this some. But things will turn out OK. There has never been any open quarreling between Harold and Ross. Harold makes sure it stays that way. He is completely willing to do as Ross wants. He keeps hoping that Ross will eventually come to see his vision through gentle persuasion. We are quite hopeful that Willard will be a strong ally in bringing about this transition. Ross' respect for Willard could be just what we need to help him see what a bright future the mill could have.

I know, Mother, that you sometimes worry about our Alaskan adventure, and I really don't want to heighten your concern. However, it was clear from the questions in your last letter that it was better to lay out the truth for you rather than trying to gloss over the troubles. But I do want to put things in perspective as well. Remember that Ross and Harold are both very good and congenial people. Even if their visions for the mill's future differ, we are all confident that they will find an acceptable resolution. Our decision to embark on this venture was thoroughly considered and carefully prepared. Our primary rationale remains the political opportunity available in Alaska. Our hopes for our future are focused on being able to represent our community in the development of good government on the Alaskan frontier. Even Ross's vision for the future of the mill will probably serve that purpose if we can find a way to afford the schooling Harold needs to fulfill our larger purpose.

Harriet Walker

Even if someday we would need to walk away from the business for some unforeseeable reason, we are taking great joy in the process. The excitement of planning and preparing for the winter; being welcomed into the family-like community of Hope, and living out a frontier life in the modern day is precious to us. But I don't think it will ever get to the point that we will just leave it. Almost every day Harold tells about some improvement they have made to the mill. We are content to let this exciting prospect develop in its own time so that Ross will be comfortable with the changes. Even now, Harold is sitting across the room working on a letter for Willard. He wants to keep Willard filled in on all the mill developments. I'll type it up as soon as he is finished and we'll get it off with tomorrow's mail. In fact, he is telling me that he is nearly finished, so I suppose I should tie this letter off as well.

Just to let you know again, I am feeling well. We are going into the doctor in Seward next Monday for a checkup. We'll know for sure that the baby and I are as well as I feel. Life here in our little Hope cottage is lovely. There are lots of things to do every day with knitting, canning, cooking, and planning. I surely am looking forward to getting your next letter tomorrow.

Love,
Your Alaskan daughter, Harriet

CHAPTER 4

September 1953:
Preparing for Winter

*D*ear Karen,
    "How do you use a diaper pail?" Oh, Karen, I sometimes forget what a gap there is between my generation of parents and those in your generation. Our diaper pail was a white enamel pail with a handle and a lid. It was for soaking used diapers before they were washed. Now you know why I was worried that everyone would be horrified to know that I used a diaper pail to make goat stew. But the diaper pail was brand new when I used it for that purpose. And I assure you it never did serve as a cooking pot once we started to use it for its intended purpose.

    Your question about scalding chickens is also easily answered. After the chicken is killed, the feathers have to be removed. Dipping that chicken into scalding hot water makes it easy to pluck those feathers cleanly. However, once the chicken is featherless, it still has a sparse covering of fine hairs. Rotating the chicken over an open flame singes those off. Then the bird is carefully scrubbed and entrails removed. This whole process is called "dressing the chicken." It is ironic, as I noted in the letter because it leaves the poor bird in rather an extreme state of undress.

Karen, you asked about the sawmill operation. Your grandfather has given me some assistance in formulating an answer. Ross and Harold had laid the plant out with the expectation of using several men in the operation. However, we did not have enough cash on hand to hire extra help, and Ross was totally against incurring any debt. That meant that the mill had to be run with just Ross and Harold. Since Ross was in charge of the main saw, called the "head rig," Harold was left to fill in the rest of the work positions. Linda found it hilarious that her Uncle Harold was actually running up and down the length of the mill to keep up with his parts of the operation. He had many duties that had to be performed quickly if the mill was to be kept in steady operation. First, he had to select logs from the millpond and winch them up the slip to be ready for sawing. When working with the really big logs, he helped Ross roll them onto the carriage. He also had to be available at any time to help turn large logs on the mill carriage after the main slabs were sawed from each side. Harold also carried away the waste slabs and trimmings and loaded them onto the waste truck. Some of the slabs had enough usable surface that they could be trimmed into one-inch lumber. Harold would perform this operation while Ross was sharpening the main saw and the mill's power plant was available to run the trimmer. He also had to cut off the ends of newly milled lumber to standard lengths. And finally, he would sort and pile the lumber into stacks of the same dimension and length. Can't you see your grandfather dancing around that elevated mill platform?

When you read this next group of letters, I suspect you will realize that during September our efforts were bent in the direction of getting ready for winter. The long, luxurious days of summer were shortening, and work had to be squeezed into fewer hours. By then, Harold and I realized that we were running behind on this preparation process. Several little incidents had set our well-laid plans askew. More and more we had to rush to take care of the garden produce and to get the canning done. Winter was steadily approaching.

Still, I think back on that time as being one of anticipation. Harold may have been more aware of the urgency of our preparation, but I was infused with confidence. I had a sense of serenity and contentment in this beautiful country and in this new life with surprises around every corner.

Love,
Grandma

~)·(~

Hope, Alaska
September 5, 1953

Dear Mother,

Ross and Harold will take a load of lumber into Anchorage Monday, so again it was a treat to read your letter to me before I write to you. And, goodness knows, waiting to mail the letter in Anchorage when they go in on Monday will get it to you as fast as the regular way, if not faster.

Today proved to be quite a good day for mail. There was the letter and packet of pictures from you, a letter from Mom Walker, two or three magazines, a letter and box of baby shirts from Betty Walker and to top it all off, our order from Sears and Roebuck came. It was really like Christmas opening that box and seeing all the pretty and practical things that came for the baby. Harold was glad to see the order come, too, because it contained the pair of boots he needed for working at the mill. He's had to wear his logging boots and the calks on the bottom chew up the mill's walkway. We still have an order of baby things coming from Montgomery Ward, but the really essential things, diapers, wrappers, and receiving blanket material came today.

The Methodist church in this area has a camp for young people here this weekend, and I asked if I could be of any help. Lo and behold, they came in this morning with a huge kettle and an even huger bunch of carrots for me to cook for lunch. I fixed them. I'm still wondering if the kids liked them, "carrots and kids being what they are" if you know what I mean.

I was very pleased with your offer of the warm chenille robe. If you are sure that Evelyn doesn't need it, I'll accept it gladly. Things aren't quite so money tight up here as it looked like it was going to be. We've had a little of our lumber move recently. However, everything, like the gift of the robe, is still deeply appreciated!

I went to the doctor last Monday, as I told you I would. Our trip was very pleasant and uneventful. Just Harold and I went, and we left early enough in the morning so that we got some shopping done. It was the first chance to shop I've had since I was with you in Dodge City last spring. I bought enough yarn to finish out the socks that I was knitting and to do another pair. We also bought some more canning jars. I've got to keep going on putting up food for the winter. Mostly we shopped in the Army Surplus store. We were able to pick up some real bargains in the way of winter work clothes for Harold. When he starts working outside in the extreme cold, he must have the right clothes. Some of the things we got were second hand but looked very durable. The savings on the total group of purchases really gave our budget a shot in the arm.

You know the doctor, and I have been at variance about the expected date of Slavina's arrival. He said the fourteenth of November, and I always thought the ninth. I got to thinking that the five days difference might be from his misunderstanding me when I told him the date to figure from. Sure enough, he had thought I said the initial date February seventh when I'd really said February second. So now we're back on the same track. Now, what if Slavina does arrive on the fourteenth? Wouldn't that be funny?

We also bought a large supply of hamburger while we were in Seward, so we had the Miller tribe over for supper. I couldn't seem to get any heat out of the fire when I was preparing supper, and it wasn't ready when they got here. But they are patient so it all turned out OK, I guess.

Wednesday I had such a big wash that my heart failed me when I thought of doing it on the scrub board. I can't seem to get very close to that board anymore, you know. Something --someone-- has come between us. Anyway, I went over to Alma's and did the washing. She has a gas-powered machine that she sets up in her main room. A long exhaust hose takes the gasoline fumes out of the house. So although we have all that engine noise, we have little of the smell.

Alma had the boiler of water already going on the stove - bless her. So after Lewie got the machine started for us, I knew the luxury of washing all those work pants and other clothes with ease. Then Harold and I stayed over there for a rabbit supper. I always forget how good fried rabbit is. The Miller rabbits are definitely part of the atmosphere here because, although they have their own pen and hutches, they share much of the running-around space with the chickens and Billy, the dog.

Thursday, I made catsup. Yes, that's right...catsup. I made it out of high bush cranberries, which grow wild. First, you boil four pounds of cranberries with one pound of finely diced onions until both are soft and can be run through a sieve. Then you add sugar, allspice, cinnamon, cloves, salt, and pepper and boil until the right consistency. Pour into jars and seal. Although just a little darker red, it looks amazingly like regular catsup. Harold sampled it for supper and was ecstatic about it. He has commissioned me to make another batch, as I shall, as soon as I get the berries. It should taste very good on moose this fall.

I hope we score on that moose because Harold, over his early summer sick spell, has been eating well and putting on weight. He looks wonderful. He should be looking wonderful considering the amount of food that he now stows away. I look at him with apprehension when he is about halfway through the meal. That apprehension mounts and mounts as he continues to eat. But so far he hasn't over-eaten, so maybe I had better stop worrying.

Yesterday I canned some peas and did a lot of letter writing. Three nice long letters. One was to Mom Walker. Now that Mom W. has gone back to the mission, I will be writing her regularly, of course. I suppose I will be telling her many of the same things that I tell you. So I won't be searching for something to write about. And another good thing is that now I can look forward to getting letters from her, too.

Last night our church service was combined with the first session of the weekend camp. It was quite nice to have the church packed and to be in on a camp session again. I came home afterward, but Harold couldn't resist playing with the kids, so he stayed for the recreation hour. He enjoyed it very much.

Today, along with cooking carrots and opening our haul of mail, I'm writing the epistle you are now reading. I'm also looking forward to tomorrow being Sunday. There will be a worship service tomorrow to close out the camp. I always prefer to worship on Sunday. However, the best thing about Sunday is that Harold is home all day.

School starts Monday. Linda has a new pair of wool pants that Alma made out of an old skirt. Linda is getting so tall now though that it is almost impossible to get a pair out of regular skirts. That's bad news because it surely was a good economical way to use up old skirts.

Moose season starts Tuesday. The men will be out hunting until they are successful or the season ends. I do so hope that they have luck because a moose could make a much easier winter for us. We haven't been here long enough to establish residency, so Harold isn't eligible to hunt this year. But he can go along and help pack out, and that will earn us a share of the take. Erma Ann and Alma are both eligible. So, there will be plenty of legal meat if they can get it. They are also hoping for a goat or two. Meat is serious business here. Hunting for these fellows isn't the big spree that the hunting trips our Mullinville friends used to take when they spent so much money, had so much fun, and didn't give a hoot about shooting deer. Here in Alaska, hunting is an important part of preparing the winter food supply.

I cut my hair again this week. It's really short this time. But that isn't as remarkable as the fact that Harold finally got his cut. Alma cut it. Now I can see that I am going to have to learn how to barber because Alma doesn't like to do Harold's. She tells me that it is a much tougher job than cutting Ross's bristly bush. So I'll learn. I suppose this winter of seclusion will be as good a time as any to learn.

I'm glad that Evelyn has a nice set-up for this year. I look forward to seeing their home in the college's married student housing when we come out this winter. Even if they are Quonset huts, I know they can be fixed up quite nicely. Teaching can surely be an easier matter when the living environment is good. Having that nice and efficient apartment made my teaching in Mullinville much easier than what I did in Benedict, even though I did love that first year of teaching.

Yes, we're still planning to get Outside this winter. We're basing our hope on the money that should be returned to us from the Kansas School Retirement System. We'd sure like to make it by Christmas, but that's awfully soon after Slavina or Slavo gets here. It might not be wise. We'll see.

Love,
Your Alaskan daughter, Harriet

Hope, Alaska
September 12, 1953

Dear Mother and Mom Walker,
As usual, I have let time run out on me. I'm up early on Saturday morning, hurrying to get my correspondence complete before the mail carrier leaves. Rather than writing two short letters, I'm going to write you both a longer one. Toward this purpose, I am deeply indebted to whoever invented carbon paper. I've been spoiled by the trips that we've been taking out of Hope that have allowed me to wait until after I read your letters before writing to you. This time it is back to the se-

quence of my letter to you before I have read your letters to me.

Monday night Ross and Harold got in around ten o'clock. I had somehow managed to keep Harold's supper warm and not too dried out. He brought me two treats back from Anchorage. The first was a big roll of oilcloth printed in a cheerful design on a green background, and the other was a sack of fresh plums. I was delighted with both.

He also had some good news. We have found yet another opportunity to sell our lumber to the willing Anchorage market, and Ross seems to be more comfortable with this one. A secondhand dealer in Anchorage, Speedy Porter, through whom they do much business, is interested in acting as an agent to handle their lumber. The one hitch is that he can't undertake it until we can guarantee to have a minimum amount ready each week. Harold thinks that they can reach his standards fairly easily with some of the improvements that they have been talking over with Willard. When we get set up like that, Speedy will come and get all that we can

turn out and sell it for us. He'll buy it at our present price and make his profit above that, you see. So as far as we were concerned, it would be almost the same as selling to private individuals ... except steadier and handier. The mill won't be able to handle the rate this fall because of the need for improvements and because bad weather is closing in too fast. But it's a great opportunity for next spring.

Speedy Porter also traded Ross and Harold a good welder, which they've needed, for some lumber. He may want enough more lumber to almost pay for a pair of cat tracks which we must have before any excavation can be done for our house. The cat tracks we have now are worn so badly that they are a problem. Although they still work in the woods, we really need better cat tracks for excavating in rocky ground. Trading lumber for supplies really helps us to stretch our cash.

The same fellow that they delivered to Monday made another order of about the same amount. He said that it was excellent lumber and he couldn't afford to miss the chance to build a garage when he could get lumber at that price. So things are looking much better for lumber sales.

The fall weather has come in too soon though this year and has sort of fouled up a couple of things. In the first place, Tuesday was the rainy opening of moose season. Alma went along with Ross and Harold that day so that if they got a moose, it could be on her license. They didn't have any luck. The next day and the day after that they went out. Both days it rained fearfully, too. So in the three days of rain, they got nothing but some very thorough soakings. Honestly, you could wring water out of their underclothes when they got in. The experience took so much out of them that yesterday and today, both rainy days, they stayed inside to work in the shop. There are fourteen days of moose hunting left and a long time yet for goats, so they are still hopeful of bagging some winter meat.

Homer and Augustine Boe, who are good friends of Alma's living in Seward, got a moose the first day. Harold says that they won't get much for themselves by the time they divide with all their friends. Millers have always given them some meat, so Boes returned the favor with a big roast of moose. The point of all this is that we were over there for supper Thursday night and had a moose meal. It was so very, very delicious. I took a bottle of my catsup over. As usual, all the Millers were skeptical about it. Lewie especially loves to tease me, I think. However, I noticed that it wasn't left sitting idle on the table.

I almost forgot to tell you about my spree with the oilcloth. I cut scallops into it and lined the shelves above the sink. They had been lined with oilpaper, and soap and other things were always sticking. I never felt that I could get them clean. Now they are so bright and clean. I also lined the orange crates that I have by the stove and the bench under them. I still have enough left over to cover the kitchen table and the one in the living room. That way I could get rid of the plastic covers, which have bothered me so much because I can never get them completely clean. I had quite a day decorating up the place, and it surely is an improvement. Well, I think it is an improvement.

I have almost finished knitting another sock for Harold. That's number one in the second pair. He is pleased as punch with the first pair, and I find that I rather like knitting. It's nice to have something to pick up and take with me when we go over to the Millers for the evening.

Our evening at the Miller's the night of the moose meal also started an odd sequence of events that evolve into a rather funny story. On the day of that event, Harold had one cookie left from his lunch, which he brought and left on a saucer for Linda to eat after supper. One wouldn't think that such a simple, kind act could cause such uproar. However, to make it understandable, I will need to give you some more background.

The first graders are let out of school at 11:30 for lunch. However, Linda can't eat in the classroom until the rest of the students are released at 12:00. Her friends all go home to eat lunch and are back wanting to play before she even gets a chance to start the meal Alma has packed for her. The result is that she has been mostly skipping her lunch. Then she is starved by the time school is out, so she finishes her lunch after school. Then she is too full for supper, only to be hungry again by bedtime. So Alma wondered if Linda couldn't just come over to my house to eat her lunch when her playmates went home. That's why she now eats lunch with me. As you remember, we are next door to the school, so this works out well.

Anyway, when Alma brought the boxed lunch to me yesterday morning, she told me not to give Linda any cookies or candy that day because she had stuck in a nickel to get an ice cream cone at Doc's. Well, Linda came gaily in and asked me for a cookie. I was shocked. I told her what her mother had said. She thought that surely I was mistaken because she said her mother had told her to ask for a cookie. We had quite a squabble.

Yesterday was one of the days when Harold came home for lunch. I told him what had happened. I was quite unhappy about the whole deal because I had cookies and would gladly have given her one or more. But her mother had expressly asked me not to. When he got back to work, Harold told Ross the whole story. Ross asked, "Did she get her cookie?" Harold said, "You don't know my wife." Ross replied, "I know Linda."

The truth was that Alma actually had told Linda that she could ask me for a cookie because some heartless individual had eaten the one Harold laid away for her the night before. Then she completely forgot what she had told Linda and instructed me not to give her any. What a predicament. Harold personally delivered a cookie to Linda this morning.

Tonight is potluck supper for the community again. I think I'll take chicken fixed some way. I'll either fix it with noodles or with dressing. I don't take fried chicken as a rule because one little chicken doesn't go far in that mob and more than one chicken would really be more than our share. We are just two individuals and with chickens worth a dollar a pound live weight, more than one chicken would be an excessive contribution.

At the last potluck, a couple of soldiers from Elmendorf base in Anchorage were there. The two have sort of adopted Hope as their community. One of them, Willie, has his eye on Erma Ann, we believe, but so far it hasn't done him any good. Anyway, at the last potluck, these two brought half a ham, beautifully baked. You can bet they - and the ham - were really appreciated. Food like that is a rare treat. I wonder if they will be there tonight and what they will bring.

Because of the delay in getting our papers cleared on the Bear Creek place and the need for a better set of tracks for the cat before we can start to build, it is beginning to look like we'll spend considerably more time in this house than we had originally planned. That's all right, really, because it's warm and cozy. We would be quite comfortable here as long as we need to stay. It surely is a nice feeling to know that we have it. This plan will also allow Harold to do a much better job on the house because the pressure will be off.

Likely we'll be here now until after the baby is born, so I'm already designing in my head a set of shelves to be built in the living room for baby equipment. Harold just smiles knowingly. He's been married to me long enough to know I'll contrive a need for shelves at the slightest opportunity. But who said that a baby was a "slight" opportunity?

Sometimes when I get to thinking that things are moving too slowly, I have to stop and consider that we haven't even been here quite three months yet. When I remember that, it seems we've accomplished miracles. If we were to get the house ready to live in by the end of winter or early spring, we'd be doing pretty well. Full-time work at the mill still has to go on.

We don't know yet what our rent in this cottage will be. We'll settle that this weekend. Mrs. Beutedahl said something last week about Harold trading work for the house. They're considering a rather extensive overhaul to the old log cabin next door. Harold and I talked it over. Labor really is quite valuable for us right now. It would be hard to measure it fairly and still achieve a good deal for both parties.

Furthermore, we want Harold to spend his spare time working on our new house. So he told them the fairest thing would be to charge us rent. If they had work they wanted him to do, then they could pay him wages. So now we'll see what happens. I think if Mrs. Beutedahl sets the rent, it'll be very reasonable, but if Mr. Beutedahl does, it likely will be sky high.

Well, it's after nine, and I'd better walk down after the mail and slip these two letters into the pouch. I do hope that I haven't waited too long.

Love,
Harriet

Hope, Alaska
September 21, 1953

Dear Mother,

This is getting to be quite a habit ... waiting until after the mail comes to answer your letter. They still get there just about as fast. Don't they? Ross is taking a load of lumber to Anchorage tomorrow, so I'll have him take this letter in. Since next week is our trip to Seward to see the doctor, I'll be able to wait for mail before writing them as well. Surely makes it nice and makes the distance between us seem so much smaller.

The mill business really is making nice strides. We have the money now to buy the bulldozer tracks that are so desperately needed. The ironic thing is that they are having trouble finding a pair that will fit. We're especially eager to find them because there is an opportunity for about a thousand dollars' worth of bulldozer work here in town. However, the set of tracks on the Cat right now, although they work in the woods, would not stand up to construction and excavation work. Of course, what I'm really interested in is that as soon as they get the Cat fixed up and out of the woods, they can start the excavation for our house.

But the delay has served one good purpose! We got the home site we really wanted after all, and I'm just thrilled to pieces over it! When we thought we'd have to settle for the Bear Creek site, we planned to build and then to sell our improvements the first chance we got at a prettier site. Now we can do everything on a more permanent basis because our new site certainly is gorgeous. It is located at the end of a short road out of Hope on a bench overlooking Turnagain Arm. It has a priceless view. We're going to plan just how we want the place to look when finished and work toward that goal in stages. For example, the building that we put up first likely won't be on the site of our final home. We will plan later to convert it to a shop or guesthouse. We'll make it our home for now until we are ready to build the bigger structure. We can also plan our outbuildings with the final effect in mind. Now, I am not at all frustrated by the delay because it has allowed moving in a permanent direction.

The fact that we got the wonderful home site is just one piece of good news, however. The second is that Ross got his moose! He shot it a long way from the road. He then dressed it out and propped the chest cavity open for cooling. He packed out the heart and liver for immediate eating. He brought part of the liver over for us to have. Fresh meat is wonderful!

In several ways, packing out the meat is a major part of the hunting job. Ross never lets any of it go to waste. Last year he let a neighbor have a quarter of moose for helping to pack it out. This year there are plenty of "family" men to get it out. Early in the morning the next day Ross, Lewie, Vince, and Harold headed out to bring back the kill. Jim Carter, who will be our neighbor when we get our house built on the hill, also went along. He wants to use the hide and antlers for his taxidermy work.

I might mention that what complicated matters were the lack of a trail of any kind to where the moose was. The way was straight through the brush back into the rugged mountains. They all loaded into the old truck and drove upstream through the shallows of the river until they came to a hole so wide and deep that it was impassable. They then unloaded a rowboat, which they had brought along. They continued upstream, paddling the boat across the deep places and dragging it through the shallow ones. Do you have a mental picture of five very wet Alaskans? The stream kept getting shallower, of course, as they went further up. However, they were able to get the boat within three-quarters of a mile of the moose, which left only a short hike.

Jim Carter took careful measurements of the features of the moose head before removing the skin and horns. Jim was the one who packed the rack and the hideout. The men say that they made a big load. The part that was most important to the rest of us, the carcass, was cut up into four major chunks. Each of the remaining men packed out one of these "quarters."

After they got these loads down to the stream, they built up a mat of brush in the bottom of the boat to protect the meat in case they took on water. That proved to be fortunate because, once in fast-moving water, the boat hung up sideways on a rock. Quick movement from Ross managed to get it freed before it was swamped. The boat did take on some water, but the meat was safe. Nevertheless, the men had to stop, empty the boat, and repack the load before they could go on down. After that, things went smoothly all the way down to the truck where they loaded up and came home in triumph. The whole operation took them the full day, but they brought home 690 pounds of wonderful meat!

I am eager to know what our share will be. I'm guessing over a hundred pounds. In any case, getting this moose means that I'll be cooking delicious steaks, roasts, and stews for a while now and canning meat like mad. We figure that moose in itself is worth over five hundred dollars. Think how it'll cut down the grocery bill to say nothing of the joys of having fresh meat. Ross, as you know, cut up a lot of ice last winter and stored it in a sawdust pit. He has plenty there for us to use too. We plan to freeze a lot of the meat by packing it in ice and salt. That way the fresh meat will last a much longer. We're all quite jubilant about it.

Nearly every weekend there are soldiers here from Anchorage on short leaves. Vince and Erma spend their time with them. They sometimes have hikes, softball games, and various other amusements. It seems to me to be a good thing for Erma Ann because Lewie is the only male besides Vince anywhere near her age. It gives her a little more normal social life. These soldiers are such kids, you know.

But all this bores Lewie stiff. So, guess who comes rushing gladly to his rescue? Uncle Harold. I believe that Harold truly misses his contact with the high school boys that he taught. Lewie makes a very pleasant substitute. They really do hit it off nicely. Harold thinks Ross doesn't give Lewie enough credit for doing adult things. So Lewie has gotten to do more lately. Anyway, Harold and Lewie took a little excursion into the mountains when Ross was moose hunting and came back with a nice supply of wild low-bush cranberries. I made them into cranberry relish, some of which I intend to bring along for the Christmas dinner. Put it on the menu!

Yes, right now we plan to make it to York for Christmas. I may be a bit feeble so soon after the baby is born, but we think I could rest up there nicely, too. We don't have to rush around like mad; we could just visit quietly. Couldn't we? Then maybe we'll be able to do some rushing by the time I leave. Shopping in a real store comes to mind.

We may possibly come Outside by ship and bring the car along. Harold is tortured by the thought of not having a car. I think maybe we could get along nicely without one. But it's true that with the baby and all, a car would surely be handy. Our latest idea is to fly to Oakland, California, and to rent a car from Harold's brother, Willard, for the trip. It would take us a little longer to get to Nebraska that way but might be worth it. We'll see!

I think I told you that the fellows traded lumber for an electric-welder. Anyway, what I didn't know at the time was that this welder not only generates its own electricity but can be used to run other appliances. Harold says that maybe I use it to do some sewing in the spring. I suppose I would just move my sewing machine into the shop and go to work. We are hesitant about getting an electric plant ourselves because it is beginning to look like we might get electricity into Hope next summer. Wouldn't that be wonderful? Electricity run by a utility company is always more satisfactory than trying to keep up your own power plant. Diesel plants, which are cheap to run, are very expensive to buy. The little gasoline plants, which can be bought at a reasonable price, would cost a great deal to run, especially if you try to run them all day. A lot of the old timers around here with their own plants have been opposed to the idea of utility company power. We think they are gradually softening up. Harold has been plugging for it right along, and a couple of incidents make us think that utility company power could be a reality. So we'll see how that turns out.

In the meantime, let's go back to the thought of plugging my sewing machine into the welder. We have an idea for a project. Our future across-the-road neighbors, the Carters, have an idea for setting up a hobby and craft shop here in Hope to meet tourist demand. Well, potential tourist demand. Doc sells only picture postcards, and you know how people are. They like to have something to buy. This shop might also serve as an outlet for Jim's taxidermy work. Carters propose that they would sell anything made by Hopeites for a ten percent margin. So, we'd like to create something to sell to help them get their shop started and maybe make a little money for us. Alma is considering making stationery. She sketches some very nice letterheads with moose, bear, or other typical animals. She also is thinking of making winter bouquets from the beautiful straw flowers that grow so abundantly for her. I am thinking of using my potentially electrified sewing machine to make stuffed toys. What do you think of that?

Boy, I hate to think of your fighting that cold you mentioned in the last letter. I trust that by now you have the problem licked. Do take care of yourself. I'm not the least worried about you shirking any duties. I also know that sometimes you do things when you could ask others to help.

When I think of the mad rush that is your life at the college, and then I think of the easy leisurely pace that I lead, I wonder. Honestly, I go to bed early, sleep until six thirty or seven. If I'm tired in the morning, I lie down. I take a nice long nap in the afternoon. I don't think I've ever felt any better than I do right now. The weather has been lovely and fall-like these last weeks. I've taken some nice, long walks. Autumn here is lovely. Now that I have seen the beginnings of this season, I begin to wonder if Alaskans are hiding the best when they rave so about their summers.

Last night I was outside around 9:00 and it was almost as bright as day ... the moon was so clear and large. Ross says that sometimes when the snow is on the ground, and the moon is bright, it's like day outside with moonlight. Should prove interesting.

One morning last week Harold got up early with a bright idea. Would I like to go for a drive with him before breakfast? We drove along the road looking for spruce chickens, which he can legally hunt. We hadn't driven much over a mile through breathtaking scenery when we saw a couple of those little birds by the side of the road. Harold shot one, and we returned home. Harold dressed it out while I got breakfast. Presto! We had the makings of a spruce chicken meal for supper. Spruce chickens are smaller than a pheasant but considerably larger than a quail. Stuffed with some apple, bread and sage dressing and baked with potatoes, carrots, and onions, this bird made us a wonderful meal...just the right size and everything.

One of the things that Ross has Lewie and Vince doing is making a nice path between town and the Millers. They have done a really superb job of making a finished trail across the flat. They have put gravel on the path and built little bridges over the low places. Makes it nice because Alma and Linda come across the flat each morning to school. Linda could easily handle it on her own as evidenced by the fact that she comes home by herself. I think Alma still takes her because she just plain enjoys the walk.

I might elaborate a little on Vince. Millers first knew him as one of the soldiers who came over from Anchorage on the weekends. Recently, as a civilian, he wrote that he was coming up to Alaska. Millers invited him to stay with them until he found employment. He arrived two days before we did and has stayed with them ever since. He hasn't looked for work at all. We thought that he might leave when summer ended, but he seems to have no intention of ever leaving. He's a very likable kid and fits in nicely with the family, but he is another mouth for the mill to support and an adult mouth at that.

For a short time Vince worked with the men in the milling work, but because he was not fast enough in his assigned tasks, he held up Harold in his. Ross finally sensed that this wasn't working too well, so he put Vince to working with Lewie on little projects that needed to be done around the place. That proved to be an inspiration. Things got done, and the mill-work went ahead just as fast or faster than before. Harold was much happier too.

Vince and Lewie have built a shed for the goat's hay. They have built that path, gardened, picked berries for Alma, put up fencing, and various other jobs. I don't know what will happen when the kids' high school correspondence course gets here, and Lewie goes back to school. I don't think that it will work to have Vince go back to work at the mill.

Since the Millers got the moose and the lumber is moving now, I don't suppose they will ask Vince to leave. But really, I can't understand him. He is young, strong... just twenty-three, I believe, and yet willing to live there not making a cent for months on end. Of course, Harold says he has a good deal because he is getting room and board. For a while, that was more than we were making. But Harold has so many things he wants to do that he is frustrated trying to get them all into one little lifetime. He has ambitions and dreams. I can't understand a person like Vince even as likable as he is.

The other day when I was walking across the flat from Alma's place, I got a whiff of something that reminded me of my childhood. Momentarily I was back in the old markets in Freetown, Africa. It took a minute for me to figure out what it was. It was dead fish. You know that salmon come upstream to spawn and then die. Well, this time of the year there are lots of dead ones lying around. Needless to say, they stink. The amazing thing is that you can't smell them very far off - just when you cross the streams. That wouldn't be true in a warmer climate.

Well, I'm doing a horrible job of my typing. Hope you can find your way around this letter. And look how long this letter is already. Why weren't college assignments as easy to write as this five-page epistle to you is?

Love,
Your Alaskan daughter, Harriet

Hope, Alaska
September 22, 1953

Dear Roomies,
Seems like I have fallen into a regrettable habit of waiting until about noon on Friday to write my letters. Recently, I rarely seem to have time to get any more written than to the two mothers. This once-a-week mail business really breeds procrastination. It's also true that I held the round-robin packet an extra week, but it was because I was enjoying rereading each of your letters, not because I was procrastinating. However, if you will please check the date on this letter, you will notice that this is Tuesday. Remarkable! Commendable! Of course, you won't get it a minute earlier than if I were to have written it at the very last second before the mail pouch was closed this weekend.

According to my calculations - and who should doubt them - the baby should be showing its pink face to the light of day (or night) in about six weeks. In some ways, that will seem like a terribly long time because I am all ready for it now. I have even packed the clothes that the baby will wear home from the hospital. In other ways, I know the time will just whiz by. It's true that we now realize that we won't be ready to move into our own house before the baby comes. Reason? We may be ready, but the house isn't. So, we'll abide a wee bit longer in the small rented cottage where we are warm and comfortable.

Nevertheless, my thoughts move on to the little house that we are building. Harold and I are so eager to get a place of our own. I think I'll spend the entire first-week driving nails all over the walls. What fun to pound nails into unfinished walls with abandon! I am so sick of taking care of other people's property.

No, that's not true. We are very fortunate to have such a really nice place to rent until our own is finished. I've been collecting orange crates like mad. That way we can fashion temporary storage and put our stuff away as soon as we move in. Your old roommate is now completely addicted to a domestic organization.

I can't remember what I told you last, but I'm pretty sure that I haven't written to you since hunting season began. We were really pretty lucky. I'll amend that. We were very lucky. We scored one hundred percent. We got bear, mountain goat, and moose. Of course, Harold isn't considered a resident yet, so he had to confine his efforts to helping Ross pack out the meat. The moose alone yielded more than six hundred pounds of meat.

Packing that meat out was quite a process for the five men who undertook this project. Included in this venture was driving the truck up through a streambed and then using a boat to get near the site of the killing. I guess, in some ways, shooting the moose is the easy part. These guys also followed the tradition of a celebratory meal at the kill site. They had taken in with them a large cast iron skillet as well as salt and pepper. They used this to cook huge, thick steaks over an open campfire. Yum!

Harold spent hours and hours cleaning his share and cutting it up. He was so sanitary that I was really impressed. I guess the reason that so many people don't care for "wild" meat stems from lack of careful processing. That certainly won't be a problem for this little family.

I'm sure I have told you how far away Seward is. It's close enough to run in once in a while to have a baby, but at seventy-five winter miles, it is too far to make use of the cold storage lockers in there. But let me tell you the ingenious deep freeze that is preserving our meat so wonderfully right here in Hope.

During the winter months last year, Ross cut chunks of ice and stored them in sawdust. Those chunks of ice are the main ingredients in the deep freeze system that has been constructed for this year's moose. For the Millers' freezer, Ross started by building a very large wooden box, which I think is about five feet by five feet and not quite as tall as I am. A second wooden box was made to fit inside with over six inches space between that big box and the smaller one. The space between the two boxes was filled with sawdust for insulation to keep the cold in. But even the smaller box is large enough that a 55-gallon steel barrel is placed in it with several inches spare between the round sides of the barrel and the square inside the box in which it is placed. Are you following all this?

The inside box is lined with tarpaper and tarred so that it is impervious to water. A mixture of salt and ice is packed around the barrel immediately turning the inside of the top-less barrel white with frost. A snug cover fits into the top of the barrel, and an insulated cover matching the boxes' external double walls seals the top.

I understand that as spring approaches when warmth begins to creep in, the water can be drained off and replaced with a fresh batch of that mixture of ice and salt. If there is still meat left by April, say, this process of replacing the salt and ice mixture has to be repeated more than once a week.

I described the Miller deep freeze because it is more dramatic and impressive. Using the same technique, Harold has prepared a smaller one for us. Does this remind you of anything about summers in the Midwest? It makes me think of ice cream freezers. Anyway, that takes care of the moose, and now you know how to freeze moose meat without the benefit of electricity.

Although you probably won't really notice it, I just had an interruption in typing up this letter. Harold came in a few minutes ago quivering with excitement. When he was getting our water supply for the day, he noticed that the beach was covered with wild geese. He was hurrying to change his clothes and take his gun along as he walked across the mud flat from our place to his job at the mill. "Just in case," he said. He was so excited that he could hardly get changed into his rubber boots and the "tin pants," which is what they call heavy waterproof trousers. He's now headed off to the mill with an anticipatory look on his face and that gun in hand.

Harold really is thriving. He hasn't put on so terribly much weight, I find that baffling considering the amount of food he consumes. He is truly excited by what we are doing. Every once in a while, however, I think he does get a bit nostalgic about coaching. I think this because he talks about his boys and mentions how he would like to be working with them. We get the Mullinville newspaper and read every word of it. Sometimes I get transported back to Kansas in my mind's eye. I can easily imagine myself shouting until I am hoarse at one of Harold's football games, attending the church women's meetings or some exciting social function. I suppose, if I were actually back there, I would be grading papers or doing some other task I had let pile up.

Still, our life in Alaska is exciting too. It is really Fall here now. The leaves are wearing their autumn colors. The landscape is gorgeous. Snow is creeping down the mountains. The richness of evergreen green stands in contrast to the golden hues of other trees sprinkled between and highlighted by the brilliant red of the berry foliage. In the mornings it is quite cool, well, maybe cold. It warms up through the days and cools off again at night. The sun is shining right now, and I shall soon abandon my duties and take a nice long walk.

There is one thing about this weather, however. I can't get my heart set straight on seasons. I know that it is only late in September, but it feels like deep fall already. October, I'm sure, will tug my heart toward Thanksgiving gatherings. The way Alma, my sister-in-law, describes November sounds like well past time for Christmas. I'm already starting to have thoughts about Christmas cards, wrapping presents, and candy making. Maybe it's better to think of them now. I'll probably be too busy to give them a second thought when the true season does arrive on the heels of the young Walker.

Well, greet your families for us one and all. I'm hopeful that by Thanksgiving you'll be hearing of expansion to our little clan.

Your friend to the North,
Harriet

Hope, Alaska
September 25, 1953

Dear Mother,

Well, we were up on our home site looking it over today and the more we look, the happier we are. We can hardly wait to get started. As I mentioned, our chosen site on Porcupine Creek is on a bluff overlooking Turnagain Arm. That is a long extension of Cook Inlet and has extremely high and low tides. At high tide, we can look from our place about six miles across a body of water that fills the valley between the mountains like a sea. But six hours later, the water has all disappeared except in the lowest channel, which is too far toward the other side for us to see. This great movement of water in and out is like a living presence and brings quite a variety of vistas. We plan to build our house so that two large picture windows meet in the corner of the room that overlooks all this grandeur.

We've been digging potatoes. I helped Harold one evening by washing them and laying them out to dry. It's really quite a job, but we're making progress. We already have way more dug than we'll ever be able to eat through winter and we aren't half finished. We really have a nice crop considering that nothing was done besides planting them.

The days are getting cooler all the time now. There's snow on several of the mountains. Some mornings it reaches way down toward the valleys, but soon melts at the lower elevations. But the funny thing is that it still doesn't seem as cold here at the end of September as Alaska seemed that first summer I was here.

Speaking of the lowering temperature reminds me of the fact that, traditionally, one concern around here has been the digging of graves in the winter. The mixed clay and rock freeze up like cement. One old bachelor dug his grave in the summer every year so that if he died in the winter, no one would have to dig a grave for him. Then every year someone would die during the winter and permission was asked to use the old timer's grave. He always consented but speculated that between then and the ground thawing, he would personally need one. And eventually, that was the case. But, as it turned out, there were many willing hands and backs to chisel out the grave for this generous old fellow.

Well, the moose amounted to about six hundred and ninety pounds of meat. We've frozen most of ours. With this cooling weather, our ice and salt freezer is quite efficient. Also, I've canned about twenty-two pints of meat. Picture that this winter. Moose and noodles, moose stew, moose gravy on some of those many potatoes. Delightful thoughts!

I think that Vince is going to take me into Seward tomorrow. I need another check-up and Alma wants to have a general check-up too. Harold and Ross really need to take the best advantage of every working day left before winter, so having Vince as our chauffeur appears to be the best arrangement.

It's getting late in the evening, and I seem to have a little trouble collecting my thoughts. I surely am getting spoiled with the wonderful leisurely hours that I've been living. Alma smiles at me and says, "Just wait! When that baby gets here ... "

Harold was so crazy about the first two pairs of socks which I knit for him that I've decided to knit as many more as I can right away. In fact, I have just completed a pair, which I'll give to him Wednesday as a birthday gift. I am glad that Alma taught me how to knit these socks. Turning the heel is something that I am sure I could never have figured out from printed instructions.

Because some animal got one of our chickens last night, Harold located some old traps today and has them set. We've been selling chickens right along. Gives us some ready cash and cuts down on the feed bill.

I'm going to be writing Elsie soon to ask if she and Dave can come over for Thanksgiving. It would be fun to have someone else admire that new little Walker. And, of course, there's no question that this one will be admirable.

I love hearing news about your situation. I haven't completely decided whether it is better for you to have Evelyn and Bob so close or whether it is better for them to have you so close. I count on your keeping them up with the news.

Love,
Your Alaskan daughter, Harriet

CHAPTER 5

October 1953: Winter approaches

*D*ear Karen,

You have asked about our process of washing clothes. Lighter items could be handled nicely on the scrub board, and I counted on this as a solution for the baby clothes. For laundering heavier things like Harold's work clothing, I was willing to go over to Alma's house and use her gas-powered machine. This differed very little from the electric machines used at the time except that it was powered by a little gasoline engine with an exhaust tube running across the floor and out the door.

At Alma's house, the process would begin long before I arrived. Lewie would have filled large boiler tubs with water, and they would be heating on the wood stove. Hot water and soap would be put into the washing machine tub. Since that water would be used over and over, careful sorting of the clothes was important. Into the first washing would go the white clothes. Then that same water was used for successively darker clothes until the very last load of by-now very murky water accepted the heavily soiled dark work clothes.

Clothes from the wash water would be run through the wringer into the first tub of rinse water. The wringer would then pivot around so that the clothes could be moved through that wringer into the second rinse water and finally through the wringer into the clothes basket. This basket, with its heavy load of wet clothes, would go home with us and, as I remember it, that winter we hung all our clothes to dry on lines strung across the main room of our little cottage.

Washing the clothes on the scrub board was another challenge altogether. The idea was to move the clothes up and down across the ridges of the scrub board. This was an effective but labor-intensive way to get clothes clean. The rinsing twice was also part of this process. I admit to you, Karen, that Harold's strong arms were much more familiar with that piece of equipment than mine was. When I would protest feebly that he had been working in the woods all day, he would remind me that our partnership was not based on traditional conceptions of men's work and women's work. Even when I used the scrub board myself, Harold would often wring out the clothes.

Now, I'll try to describe oilcloth to you. I don't know when that stopped being used. It had a sturdy fabric backing and a very smooth, very easy to clean surface. This surface was similar to the good plastic cloths available today but was superior to anything in the way of plastic that we had at that time. It was bought by the yard and, as I noted in the last batch of letters, could be trimmed into scallops without the need of hemming. It was available in a myriad of colors and patterns. It had long been used as covering for kitchen tables. I remember well the oilcloth in my grandparents' kitchen. It is true that in time, oilcloth had a tendency to split and peel, but the roll Harold brought home was a source of many delights to the young Alaskan housewife who wanted to make her home more attractive.

You asked if those socks that I knit in Alaska were exactly the kind of socks with the turned heels that I taught you to knit last winter. Yes, they were.

I think that four-needle style of sock knitting is almost a lost art, so I am glad to pass it on to you. I know you enjoy the socks that you made to wear around the dorm room. But the knitting that I did in Alaska was for warmth against the very real danger of arctic temperatures. Thus knitting took on urgency as the days shortened rapidly and the sense of coming winter pervaded the village.

I knew from Alma that one couldn't buy socks or mittens that were as warm as those that we knitted. This was especially true when we used two strands of yarn. Neither Sears and Roebuck nor Montgomery Ward's catalogs had them. So, while Harold was busy with all sorts of preparations for the winter, I considered knitting as my way of preparing for the family's protection against the elements. I knit socks, mittens, and stocking caps.

I wasn't the only one knitting with gusto. Grannie Clark was busy knitting the mittens that were her annual Christmas gift to every child or teenager in town. She also had time to knit a soaker for our baby. Once, when I visited her, she was working on it. She had to explain to me what it was because things had changed in baby care since she was a young mother. The soaker was a heavily knit pair of panties that would go over the diaper and absorb excess liquid. I exclaimed over the cleverness of the idea but secretly was glad that I had on hand plastic pants which I was sure would be more effective.

The coming of our baby was not only a much-anticipated family event, but it had become a community event. Whenever I was at Doc's store, or the post office, or the church, I was well aware of the general interest in our impending event by this village where no baby had been born for years. Not only was there all the usual bustle of getting ready for winter but also this year there would be a new baby in the community.

Getting ready for winter dominated the fall season. There was a growing sense of urgency as supplies were laid in and firewood stockpiled, and produce from the garden was canned. There was also the anticipation that once winter settled in, those who were prepared would have weeks and weeks of leisure for hobbies or long-delayed reading. We were not among those who were really prepared for winter. So in addition to long days in the mill working,

Harold had to rush to get us ready. This batch of letters contains the evidence of how we were losing the race to get completely ready for winter. This was a fate that in an earlier pioneer era might have been fatal. For us, it was just uncomfortable, inconvenient, and more expensive.

We had been so excited about the location that was now ours for a building but disappointed that circumstances had prevented our finishing a new little cabin as we had planned. But winter was coming - ready or not. Tandem with that disappointment, however, was the awareness of how fortunate we were that in the coming months we could be tucked into that little cottage in the middle of Hope.

Love,
Grandma

Hope, Alaska
October 2, 1953

Dear Mother,

We finally have our potatoes dug. Harold really was rushed, poor lad. He rarely had an hour from the time he got home from work until it was too dark to dig. I don't think that Ross understood the situation - he has two boys to dig his potatoes - or he wouldn't have worked quite so late. That last night after we had had one small freeze and before a big one was expected Harold "borrowed" Vince and Lewie to help him get the last of the potatoes out. We have way more than we'll need and their crop wasn't so abundant. So the potatoes that we would have lost without their help may well be on the Miller table before the year is out anyway. We have been putting a little lamp in the log cabin with the potatoes, carrots, and beets each night to keep their little bodies warm.

The mornings are quite chilly, but by mid-morning the sun has warmed things up considerably. In fact, these last days have been gloriously beautiful and very pleasant. I keep thinking of some lovely Kansas Novembers. That's really what the weather is like.

Here is a good joke on me. I had been thinking for weeks that Harold's birthday was on Wednesday. In fact, just now I checked the carbon copy of my last letter to you, and even there I mentioned that I was giving him his birthday socks on Wednesday. Well, the first of October was Thursday, not Wednesday. I am chagrined that an intelligent, college educated person like me with a great big calendar hanging on the wall can't do a simple thing like keeping the days straight. Why didn't Harold notice? He might pay attention to the first day of moose season three years down the road but birthdays, even his own, just don't register. So he was no help in saving my pride. Now let me tell you the story as it played out and then you will understand why I'm feeling so embarrassed.

Tuesday night I talked to Harold about his birthday, and we decided not to try to have a big dinner with guests. You'll note that I'm really taking things easy now. Just after he had gone to bed Tuesday night, I laid out a pair of knitted socks which he didn't know were finished and I set a birthday card on top of them. I hoped that he would see these the first thing in the morning when he got up to build a fire. He did and was very, very pleased. Our private little birthday supper that evening also was going very well until he casually mentioned a conversation that he'd had with his sister just before coming home from work. Evidently, Alma walked out to where the men were working and said, "Harold, why don't you and Harriet come over tomorrow night for the birthday supper."

"Birthday supper?" exclaimed Harold innocently.

"Whose birthday?"

"Yours, you dope," retorted Alma in sister-like fashion.

"Why, today is my birthday. Isn't it?" responded Harold.

"You were born on October first if I know anything about it," she assured him.

As Harold finished this story, I checked the calendar and felt more foolish than I've felt for some time. We went to dinner at the Miller's the next evening anyway. Ross accused Harold of doing it on purpose to rate two big meals. But since Harold pays no attention to birthdays, I know the fault really rests with me. Anyway, the supper on the right date was very nice, and we all had a good time at the real celebration of that elusive birthday.

I'm not sure I mentioned it to you, but the Millers purchased a generator some time ago. Ross still doesn't have the house wired for electricity. I just can't imagine having a light plant that long and not having it installed. But I'm more of the impatient type - I may learn. Anyway, I suppose after having been without electric lights for years and years, a week or two doesn't make much difference.

Last week we got a new battery for our little radio. We have been without a radio for some time now and are really enjoying the simple luxury that one can provide. We have a very clear reception thanks to the fact that Harold strung the antenna from our house to an outbuilding. When he was in the process of putting up that lengthy antenna, he told me that our miner friends, Little Jim and Big Jim, had an antenna strung clear across the canyon near where they are gold mining. Their reception was phenomenal. With no electrical interference, we have the cleanest sound you can imagine. We now know what time of day it is. We can keep up on current music, get the news, and listen to radio drama in the evening. It really is a pleasure to us. You'd be surprised how domesticated we look in the evenings... Harold reading... Harriet knitting... and some sweet music coming from the radio.

Harold took that radio to work two days this week to listen to the World Series ball games. The guys were working in the shop, so it was possible to listen to the broadcasts. Today they were running the mill, so I have been listening to the games. The series begins in the morning at 8:00 and that will give you a little idea of how far west we are.

One of the best things about having the radio back is that

we are now able to rejoin all our fellow villagers listening to the daily broadcasts of the Mukluk Telegraph. This one-way message program is a wonderful service for those of us who live in remote places out of contact by telephone. Early evenings this "telegraph" is broadcast over the area. It is composed of little personal messages to individuals, and the length of the broadcast depends upon the number of messages to be sent out. The announcer reads the messages in a calm, almost bored tone of voice. I haven't heard it often enough yet to cease being amused at some items and touched by others. Let me give you some examples. There might be a message for Patrick Martin asking him to feed John's dogs tonight and tomorrow since John is stuck in Anchorage because he has to see the doctor again tomorrow.

Another example might be that the Walter Wrights want their friends in Kenai to know that their car was wrecked near Mile 58 this afternoon. They are wondering if their neighbors, the Petersons, would go over to their house and keep the fires going so that their supplies won't freeze. Sometimes the messages might be as simple as telling someone the date and time of a relative's flight into Anchorage.

Most of the messages are straightforward and uninteresting. They are just getting information across. This information is indeed gotten across to every ear across the vast array of listeners. Then again, some messages could be extremely important and carry a great deal of emotional impact like:

"Alex has bought the ring. He wonders if Marlene wants him to buy her a wedding dress or if she has something that she can use. He suggests September 14 as the date to meet him in Seward."

Or perhaps something poignant like: "Andy, I am sorry. Please come back. Jenny."

A really wrenching one we heard recently was: "The nurses at Trinity Hospital wondered if Mr. Berry Schell of Homer would please stop in sometime soon to pick up the bodies of his wife and infant daughter."

How can one describe such communication? Is it stark, revealing, poignant, or just plain crude? All over Alaska, in the little villages with once-a-week mail service and no telephones, in the trappers' cabins, in the isolated Eskimo settlements, and on fishing boats at sea, radios are tuned in to that program listening for the sound of that matter-of-fact voice who might be bringing a message of ultimate importance. This is part of the tapestry of life in remote Alaska.

According to my information, the Mukluk Telegraph got its name from Eskimo fur boots. I believe that mukluk means "large seal" in Eskimo and the boots or moccasins got their name in turn from that. I have heard that it also is a slang phrase meaning "word of mouth." But I prefer the idea of a message being brought personally by someone in a pair of those beautiful fur boots. Don't you?

I think we are getting close to being ready for winter in the clothing department. I was surprised at how much it costs to get a working man ready for winter. He has put better than $35 into just work shoes alone. They are essential and expensive. Then there are the $12 suits of winter underwear. Waterproof and wool lined trousers are also very expensive. But Harold is very conservative in his needs, and I think we saved maybe 50 dollars or even more by doing the shopping that we did at the army surplus store in Seward that I told you about. We also believe that once he gets these things, they'll last a long time, so we are getting ready for future winters in addition to this one. It's just that we have to pay for it now. I have ordered very little in the way of warm clothing for myself because I don't know what size I'll be and because I'll spend most of my time indoors where it's cozy and warm. Harold's Mom had given me two suits of long underwear which I can use when I need them, and I fail to see that I'll need much else. If I find the need for other things later, we'll get them. But there's no use going hog wild and ordering a lot of things that are both expensive and useless. Some of the housewives around here really dress warmly even in the house, and some wear essentially the same things that housewives wear anywhere. I'll need to see which kind of housewife I am, but I suspect I'll be the latter.

It's getting late, so I better quit. I'll try to add some more tomorrow before I send this if I get a chance.

OCTOBER 3, 1953

It's snowing a little bit this morning -- our first snow. I don't think it'll be enough to leave even any traces on the ground, but there are some snowflakes, nevertheless.

Last week Harold had a pretty bad cold. I wanted him to give up and go to bed. He seemed to get rather panicky at the thought, not joking like he sometimes does when I try to make him really sick so he can get well. Anyway, he slugged through it and is nearly over it now. Last night, I was saying something about how living like we are really made married couples very dependent on each other. I suggested that it might be a cure for some of the ills of modern marriage. He grinned and said that it had really come to him forcibly when he was fighting the cold. He said that he got frantic when he thought of being sick because of all the things that we need him to do. Last night he brought in an extra supply of wood which we'll probably lay back for an emergency. But he does do so many things around the place for me. He gets in a big supply of water and fills the teakettle and dishwashing pans before he leaves in the morning. He also fills up my wood box and empties the previous day's wastewater. Now that we close the heavy door as well as the screen on the chicken house, he does all their tending. Really, lots of those things I could do perfectly well, I'm sure, but he just rushes around and has them done in no time flat, and it would take me much longer.

I don't feel that he is quite so dependent on me, but he comes home at night very tired physically and does enjoy sitting down to eat a good hearty meal. He really does need me to do things for him like that. When we lived in Mullinville last year, he did most of the things I did. We just took turns doing them. This year a thing like keeping Harold's clothes mended is a constant job. Harold's work is really hard on clothes. As the weather has grown colder, his newly knitted socks have been a real joy to him. So, I'm not useless. After the baby comes, he'll need my work at childcare as much as I need his strong right arm. See what I mean? In modern life, women have appliances and club work. Here, the home is the center, complete center, of existence. I hope I learn some valuable lessons from this experience.

I looked across the table at H.D. this morning and laughed out loud. He surely is getting to look like a rough working man. He is bearded. His hands are so rough that he has trouble handling small things like a pen. He has on heavy work clothes. His pants are held up by heavy-duty suspenders. It's hard to believe that a year ago he was wearing suits, ties, and even a hat, no less.

My next knitting project is a pair of mittens for myself. When I dress up for my walks, the only part of me that gets the least bit cold is my hands. Making those mittens the way that Grannie Clark showed me shouldn't take too long. After that, I'll go back to my sock knitting. Well, I guess I've decided to make a stocking cap for Harold. I had planned to make one for him for Christmas, but he needs one now. Maybe I'll knit him a spare stocking cap for Christmas. His caps have been too short. Alma says that stocking caps up here need to be long enough to be pulled up over the ears double. I'm going to see that he has one like that.

I'm feeling fine and waiting eagerly for the next five weeks to be over. Oh, Augustine Boe was up here from Seward this week. She has been such a good friend of Alma's. Fortunately for us, that friendship spills over to Alma's little brother and his wife. She said she already has the bed set up in the basement for us. So at least we have a place to stay when we go to have the baby. Several homes in Seward regularly accommodate women who come in from "the wilds" to await the birth of their babies. But they charge money, of course.

I am also sending a letter to Evelyn thanking her for the gift. Thank you again for your share in the wonderful present.

Love,
Your Alaskan daughter, Harriet

꩜

Hope, Alaska
October 2, 1953

Dear Evelyn,

We are having real fall weather now. It's very CHILLY when we wake up in the morning. I just lie in bed like a woman of leisure while Harold gets the fire going and then returns to bed for a cat nap or two before we have to get up to begin the day's work. Then, as the morning progresses, the weather warms up considerably. We have had beautiful, sunshiny days.

By the most wonderful quirk of fate, we were able to lay claim to a beautiful little home site on a bench of land just above Hope. While processing this new claim will delay starting the building, it's worth waiting for what will become a permanent location for our home in Alaska. Before we got the chance at this place, we were afraid we'd have to settle for an intermediate solution, which meant building, selling, and then buying what we wanted.

I am feeling just wonderful. Alaska is surely the place to get ready for a baby. I have no trouble finding time for naps, walks, and all the other necessary things. It's really a lot of fun. You'll find it all out for yourself someday. Being so big is only a slight inconvenience, especially when your full-length mirror is turned to the wall as mine is. Truly, so far, I've just felt wonderful. I can feel the baby kick and jump about. Mine even turns somersaults, but what else can be expected when you think about who the masculine parent is. Already the little character displays a temper. He/she gets positively furious when I work over the wood stove too long. I mentioned it to its father but got little sympathy from him. He suspects me of egging the squirt on and insists that I begin firm discipline right now. So, I'm not going to get out of cooking duties that way. This baby also shows perverseness of nature, which I hope it won't continue through the rest of its life. It seems to think that the time for me to go to bed in the hope of immediate sleep is the time for it to begin its exercises. Thump! Thump! Bump! Bump! Roll over! Begin again! Well, in spite of all these inconveniences, I am really attached to it, as you know.

Thinking about being pregnant reminds me of a story that happened just the other day. We have an old fellow in our town who is known as Crazy Albert. Albert spends his time wandering up and down the roads and town streets. One never knows when he'll appear. He walks very silently and seems to be everywhere. He talks to himself when he walks and moans to himself in church. He is living in an ideal community for people like him because this town is good at minding its own business and letting people be just what they want to be. I've never seen him ridiculed. Not only is he tolerated, but he is treated like a person whenever he shows up. And he shows up everywhere.

What all this is leading up to is an amusing incident where we inadvertently contributed to Albert's malady. Harold and I were driving back from visiting some friends when I remembered that I hadn't had my walk for the day. So, I asked Harold to let me out about a mile from home, and I'd walk that distance. Harold drove on in our big, but very unreliable Buick and I came trudging my pudgy way home. But just wait. Who should be coming up the road but Albert? First, he saw Harold ride by in royal splendor; then shortly afterward came Harriet afoot as a poor pregnant woman. Albert stopped after he met me, turned around in the road and watched me, scratching his head. Harold, meantime, had realized what was happening, parked the car and crept around the corner to see the whole incident. So, I had only a little way to walk before I saw the parked car and Harold doubled up with laughter. Poor Albert! I'm sure he never will understand those Walkers. He joins others in this, of course.

Goodness gracious, here I am long into this epistle, and I haven't even mentioned the event which prompted this letter in the first place. I was really pleased when I opened the box from Mother to find the three darling little playsuits. In fact, it came as a bit of a start. I've been collecting things for immediate needs like kimonos and diapers. I'd almost forgotten that Baby would need other kinds of clothes soon. I think Harold was very relieved to see something that raised the subject of maturation in the near term. Thanks very much for the gift and also for the red jacket. It fits and will see good service.

I'm sincerely looking forward to seeing you at Christmas time. We'll sit down and have a good long visit. I hope your teaching is going well, Evelyn. And tell Bob that I hope his senior year at York is also going well.

Your big sis (in more ways than one),
Harriet

Hope, Alaska
October 9, 1953

Dear Mother,

Monday I was in Anchorage. It was the first time I had been out of Hope for any purpose other than to see the doctor in Seward since I got here. Harold was going into town to place a bid on some equipment that the fellows wanted desperately, and since the truck wasn't needed for any purpose, he drove it in place of our car. He asked me to go along because he thought I'd enjoy the outing. I did. Even though many of the buildings in Anchorage are still unfinished and some are only covered with tarpaper, it still had a city-bustle feel. It felt strange to be in a city again, and I must confess I almost felt like a country hick.

While in Anchorage we invested in a big Aladdin lamp. It burns coal oil, which we Alaskans refer to as Pearl Oil. The two five-gallon cans of oil we bought should last a while. The lamp really gives lots of light and is much safer than the Coleman gas lanterns. I am enjoying it so much, especially since the lamp itself is pretty. It is pink and stands up on its base like an electric lamp complete with shade. We need light earlier and earlier in the day as the darkness of winter grows.

We have the beginning of our new house made on our home site. Well actually, we have a little bit of a hole dug. We've revamped our plans again. Now we plan to have the root cellar under the house. That was our first priority since we have to provide storage for our winter's food supply. The house itself will be very small, but cozy. I can hardly wait to get it finished or should I say started.

I have my mittens finished and are they slick! They are really warm. I've advanced to the two-thread stage. I used two yarns, one two-ply and one four-ply, and the result is extra-extra warm. Now I am working on that stocking cap. Harold is afraid that I don't want to go back to socks but, on the contrary, I'll be glad to do it. Making a stocking hat is too monotonous. You just knit ribbing for inches and inches. The socks and mittens present a variety of challenges but not his old stocking cap. We got a big order in from Sears and Roebuck last Saturday. I was in ecstasy over all the different skeins of yarn. You know I've always been crazy about pretty yarns. And now it's even nicer since I can really utilize them, not just possess them.

I was quite pleased about Evelyn's suggestion about pillow-cases to be used as sheets for the little mattress in the baby basket. I measured, and it should work nicely. This next week I'm going to put into the basket all the things that I want to take to Seward for the baby's trip home. I'll also put in some yarn for me to work on in the hospital. I hope I feel up to knitting. There is also the possibility that I'll have to wait for the baby to arrive so I'll be able to put the time to good use knitting. By having everything in the baby basket, I'll be all ready to go. If we have to make a hurry-up trip, we'll just grab the basket and be off.

Oh! I should tell you that the fellows were high bidders on the cat that they wanted to get for salvage parts. That means that the mill bank account is nil again, but the new equipment should prove to be a really good deal. Ross and Harold had inspected the wrecked D-7 Caterpillar Dozer that was for sale as government surplus. Their interest was in the rails of the running gear that appeared to be as good as new. Only after Ross had put in a sealed bid of $427 did he learn the story of that machine.

Just before it was last used, it had been completely overhauled at the Anchorage maintenance station. Besides being given a new engine and generator, the whole undercarriage had been rebuilt with new sprockets, idlers, rollers, and rails. It then went out on a job that fall. The very first week of operation it had been left standing mired in mud from Friday noon until the following Monday. By then it was frozen in. The operator tried to free it by pulling out the heavy cable from the Hyster winch on the back of the cat and anchoring it to a large spruce tree. Instead of freeing the cat, that powerful winch split it open at the axles. It was the next summer before they pulled the broken cat out and got it back to the salvage yard for sale. Even though this was bad news for the government, it was wonderful news for us because it meant the salvage parts were in much better condition than we had anticipated. In fact, it was such good news that Harold and Ross were sure that their bid was much too low. Fortunately for us, it was too late to re-submit.

Now we have all the essential parts to make our cat like new. Plus, the really exciting news is that the good new engine they salvaged is powerful enough to run the mill right. The gasoline engine that we have been using isn't really strong enough. This new engine will eliminate some of the problems that they have been experiencing. We thought that we would have to pay a huge chunk for the new power unit the mill needed, but that new engine came along for no more cost than we expected to pay for the parts to repair our cat. Thank goodness! The lack of good cat tracks has certainly slowed them up this fall. The lack of a good power plant for the mill also impeded progress and frustrated the guys. See why this is such a good deal?

I sold my standard typewriter. I got $50.00 for it. I don't know yet just how I'll spend the money. I may try to get an old washing machine, or I may save it to buy supplies for toy making when I get Outside. The typewriter, you know, we left up here last summer for the Miller kids to use in their correspondence work.

One of the courses they were taking was a typing course. In the meantime, I bought this little portable, and since it is so much easier to handle, I've decided to keep it.

Right along now I've been opening cans of food that I canned myself. I made a pie the other day with my canned raspberries. It was delicious. When I got ready to put a piece in Harold's lunch sack the second day, he suggested that I stick in another piece for Ross. That was a compliment, don't you think?

The Millers have their generator working now. The electric lights are really nice. But I'm surprised at how comfortable people can live without electricity. Not that we don't plan to have it as soon as we can. After talking to some of the officials of the RE.A., our hopes for electricity shortly have been somewhat squelched. They had considered it, they say, but it doesn't seem likely for some time yet. So, Harold has been scouting around for a little electric plant for us. He knows where he can get a used one for about a hundred dollars. That's about five hundred cheaper than a new one of this kind would cost. So maybe we'll have our own electric lights before too long.

There was some kind of mix-up on the correspondence

course that had been ordered from Nebraska for Erma Ann and Lewie's high school junior year. They still don't have the materials, and it's well into October. They'll really have to double up on lessons when it does come if they want to get through by spring.

Today is one calendar month short of the baby's scheduled arrival. I suppose that month will go fast since every other month has. It had better go fast, or Harold will never survive. He worries about so many things that could happen while I'm here alone - like falling down. Of course, the school kids play right outside my window at various times during the day, and it's only a step to the school where the teacher has a brand-new car. So, should I need to make a rush trip into Seward, I shouldn't have any trouble at all.

We have one little path that, since fall, has become so slick that I dreaded walking on it. The landlord wasn't interested in the boardwalk that Harold volunteered to make with little strips of rough sawed lumber to improve the traction. So, the other night, he brought a load of sawdust over and sprinkled it liberally on the path. The new sawdust sticks out visually alongside the house, but my, how much easier it is to walk now. The path is perfectly non-skid, and I fairly sail around with my chores.

Alma's little pullets have started to lay eggs. Ours haven't. We've had a little discussion with those pullets about that failure and have placed nests around as gentle hints. As winter continues its inevitable approach, we may have to become even sterner with them if they continue to fail to produce some eggs.

Love,
Your Alaskan daughter, Harriet

Hope, Alaska
October 19, 1953

Dear Mom Walker,

Our pullets have finally come through and have started to lay eggs. We have had about seven eggs to this point. That's no more than one each day, but the last few days we have had only one. It leads us to believe that two pullets are laying on alternate days.

We just finished lunch. Since your son has been working on our place on the hill, he has been coming home for lunch. The funniest thing happened this morning. Just before noon, there was a knock on the door. I went to answer it. There stood your grand-daughter, Linda, with the two little Rucker girls. Linda told me very nicely that since there was no bread for lunches, she was to eat dinner with me. I said that would be OK, but she should go back to the school ground and play until Harold came. Pretty soon there was another knock on the door. This time it was Ross and Linda. Ross asked me if Linda could eat lunch with me. I said, "Surely, and why don't you stay, too." He said Alma would be expecting him home. Later, I found out that Linda was supposed to go home, too, but just cooked it?? up in her own little mind. It didn't matter; I had plenty of food. But what a head full of ideas that kid has. She's surely a bright one.

Oh! I must tell you about the house. We're finally getting started on it in earnest. The road has been punched down to the site, the hole for the cellar is dug. In fact, another hole for an icehouse has been dug, too. This icehouse will be a cooperative venture with Jim Carter. Jim and Harold are going to work together this winter on storing ice. So, you know what that means for us next summer. It means ice cream, maybe an old fashioned ice box, and lots of nice little benefits when cooling is needed. But what really thrills me is that we are finally started.

All this bulldozer work was done in less than two hours with our cat. Sometimes I am amazed at how much can be done that way. That equipment is a very valuable thing to us.

Ross is working this week with the cat on contract jobs around here. Harold is taking time off to work on the house. He won't be drawing wages, but we get a cut on the $15.00 an hour that Ross makes on the cat for our share in its ownership. Ross is a very skilled cat operator. Harold bows to him completely in that. Even so, Harold wishes that he might occasionally get a chance to work with that cat and start learning some of those skills. Seems only fair to me, but I am just an observer in this partnership. Well, that's not true, of course, since our savings got it all started. I mean I am an observer in how the procedure of the partnership works out.

Lumber sales have suddenly stopped. Of course, we knew that would happen as soon as it got too cold to build. We have only rough lumber, and it must be used in basic construction. That's why we wanted a planer so badly. If we could sell a few thousand feet of planed lumber now and then, it would really give us a boost through the winter.

How nice it has been to have good cat tracks. Good equipment is so much more productive. Now we are yearning for that planer. Ross and Harold think they have a deal on one that just can't be beaten. You remember the planer that they found that was just lying idle? Doc said for them to go ahead and take it because the owner had been dead for some time. Well, it's a good thing that they didn't. They have finally traced the owner down. Like Mark Twain, the news of his death had been premature.

The owner will let them have the planer in ex-change for planed lumber in the spring. We haven't closed the deal, but I don't see how we lose anything other than time. If the planer doesn't work, we won't be out anything. But if it does, it'll buy itself. We won't have to pay anything until the planer is in good working order and then we can pay for it with a commodity of which we have plenty. In the meantime, we might be able to sell some finished lumber through the winter and early spring, which would be a big boost to our budget. There may come a time when we can sell the lumber just as fast as we process it. But until that time, every deal that we can make using lumber instead of money is just that much better.

We're going to Seward tomorrow for another checkup. The doctor will be taking an X-ray tomorrow. He says that he routinely takes X-rays at this stage of a baby's development. That should tell him how things are going with the baby's development and prepare him to know if he will need any special equipment. It's probably a very wise precaution. I like this doctor. I think he's very thorough. Granny Clark is going along to see her doctor. Alma is going for a check-up. And the Stainbrooks are going, too. So, we'll have a carload of people to see doctors. Some kind of ambulance service, you know.

I'll bet you are wondering how our passengers will react to the slow traveling speed of our car. When we finally got here last summer, you and I were definitely content to move down the road at less than thirty-five miles an hour, weren't we? But there are a lot of drivers of other cars who are not content with driving behind someone at that tempo. Harold and I have decided just to find it amusing rather than frustrating that cars will stack up behind us on the road thinking that there must be a serious reason for the speed of our big car. There is. But it isn't what they think. There really aren't many places to pull off to let them by. So, we just sort of wait and see how long it will take before someone gets up the nerve to pass our car and unplug the traffic.

The days are getting much shorter, of course. But I sometimes find it hard to realize how much shorter and how fast this is happening. We lose five minutes of daylight a day now, and it doesn't take many days for that to be a half hour. I usually have to light a lamp by five o'clock to finish getting supper. And to think that when you were here this summer, it was almost impossible to find a time when it wasn't daylight. This country is so interesting.

Guess that's about all the news for now. Harold drove over to the mill after some lumber and will stop by for me in a minute. I'll then go up on the hill to see how things are coming along, maybe snap a picture or two, and then have a nice walk back.

Love,
Harriet

∾∿⊃ͤC∽

Hope, Alaska
October 23, 1953

Dear Mother,

I was allowed to see the x-ray of the baby. Very interesting. It wasn't a very flattering picture, but it was quite thrilling. Harold says that now we can be sure it is a baby. Humph! As if there were any doubt. I'd hate to think that this ridiculous figure of mine is purely a coincidence. The good news in the x-ray was that the baby is turned into the correct position and should make its appearance without any dramatic incident.

Harold is really making progress on our house. He has the root cellar nearly finished and counts on only a few hours more to finish that job. Then he can begin to build on the house proper. He's doing a very nice job, I think. The root cellar will have shelves for canned foods, storage space for the root crops, and a nice long stairway. I don't know of anyone else up here that has a stairway. Most people use ladders. Harold has insisted right from the first that we must have a stairway for safety reasons. It will be handier, of course, when I come up with my loads. Still, I don't feel it is at all necessary.

Harold just came tearing into the house. It's getting late, and this is Friday night, church night, but he still has a small order to deliver. "That Ross," he said, "When he gets started on an engine, he wants to work all night." Ross is extremely interested in the cat engine that they got at the auction the other day and can't tear himself away. As you remember me writing before, they bid on the machine because of the rails for the cat tracks. But it turned out to have other important parts

127

that they can use. For instance, this factory-remanufactured engine can really boost the power and capacity of the mill. I hope that is true.

The shower for the Elliot baby that I told you about is tonight and a "surprise" shower for me. I may leave this letter unsealed and tell you about it before I drop the letter in the mail early in the morning.

I think the bonnet and mittens set I made to be my gift for the Elliots is just darling. I made them on the "weave-it" loom out of rose-colored wool. Then I crocheted a little white flower for each side of the bonnet and each of the mittens. To finish it off, I crocheted white lace edging all around. It seems funny that I haven't made anything like that for our baby. All I've done for my own child has been to hem up a sheet and some receiving blankets. I have some crochet thread to put edges on the blankets but may not get it done. I am concentrating on knitting socks, mittens, and hats with such fervor that I have little time for much else. However, I'll have a lifetime to make things for this child, and now I'll just sit back and enjoy what others do.

Our silly pullets are still producing at the rate of one a day. That won't be anywhere near enough to supply us, nor will it begin to pay for the food they consume. I shall surely be tickled the morning that I reach into the nest and pull out more than one egg. It irks me to have to keep buying eggs from Doc when these pullets run around all day and do nothing to earn their keep.

Yesterday, I did my washing over at Millers again.

Won't be doing that very often now before the baby comes. Alma's washing machine is still gasoline engine powered. I mean, they haven't converted it to electricity yet. Of course, I'll be doing my washing at home after the baby comes. But until we get a machine, Harold says he will help me with it. The baby things won't be hard to do anyway. It's just things like sheets and work clothes that are difficult for me to do alone.

The thing that seems to be a joke anymore is my ironing. When I think of the big amounts of clothes that I used to iron, I'm amazed at the little wad of stuff that I need to sprinkle down and iron each week. I don't need to iron dress shirts for Harold anymore, and I just ignore his work shirts. He wears them un-ironed. On the few occasions when he has felt he needed an ironed shirt, he just used one of those that we had brought along from the school days. I then wash it and put it away without ironing. I don't know how long his supply will last, but it is wonderful while it does. That leaves only that little wad I mentioned. It's too hard to stoke up the fire in the stove to get the irons heated. I have heard these implements called both glad irons and sad irons. Most of the time I think of them as "sad." At first, I had trouble getting them heated to just the right stage between scorching and not being hot enough. I admit that Mom Walker's coaching last summer helped and I am learning to recognize just the right sizzling sound when I moisten my finger on my tongue and touch it to the heated iron. I suppose now that I have them more under control and my requisite ironing task is so small, I should consider them to be "glad" irons. I'll hold that thought.

I think I've told you that Erma Ann is going to come over to help me after I return with the baby. She'll do the housework that needs to be done, which shouldn't be too big a job. However, it will be nice to have her around. During those early weeks, Harold wants someone to be with me all day while he's gone. Erma Ann gets to do my housework but also will have a new place to work on her correspondence courses. It seems to be a nice trade-off that will work well for everybody.

The community is having a big get-together for Halloween. I don't suppose I'll attempt anything as futile as trying to disguise myself. Believe me, with my present size and shape it would be futile! But Harold and Lewie are going together as a couple. Lewie is going to be on short stilts to represent a tall man. Harold will likely walk on his knees to represent a short woman. At least those are the present plans. With limited residents, a disguise around here is usually hard to hold. Harold thinks that the switch in relative height should lead to some confusion for a while. H.D. enjoys doing things with Lewie - not only because he misses his contact with high school boys but because Lewie is fun to be with.

Everything that we've opened so far from our summer's canning project has turned out swell. I had one batch of jam, which formed a mold on top -- only one batch. But that's a minor problem. You know how I wish that we could have a gardening opportunity next year like we did last summer. But we'll be attempting a garden in virgin soil. Not only is it virgin, but it is rough soil and not nearly so rich as this land here with the garden Mom Walker so much enjoyed. However, we should still be able to produce enough root crops to help us immensely through the winter and enough fresh stuff to make for good summer eating. If we don't have the berries, we can concentrate more on picking wild berries. Next year Harold will be considered a resident and will be able to do some hunting on his own ticket. If you have meat and potatoes, you can fill out the meal very cheaply.

Harold has been working in the mill today. Poor guy! He's really frustrated because he wants to spend every minute on the house and still he must spend time in the mill. They still have those ties to saw and that money is to see us through the winter unless some miracle brings in some more lumber sales. He is so eager to move into the new house and still eager to make a few dollars. This is surely an interesting experience.

OCTOBER 24, 1953

It's only a few minutes until the P.O. opens and I want to get a money order and send an order off to Montgomery Ward yet this morning. But I can't send this letter off without telling you about the shower. It was really something. It wasn't polished and elaborate like the Mullinville ones, but I thought it was surprisingly nice. After church, Emma Clark, who is Grannie Clark's daughter-in-law and a former nurse, announced that they were going to have a little party to welcome the potential arrival of a couple of big birds seen flying around this area. Then they brought in a box decorated with pink and blue crepe paper and filled with presents. Mrs. Elliott and I opened them together. I mean they would give each of us our gifts from the same donor, and we had quite a little fun not getting ahead of the other, etc. After the gifts were opened -- most of them were wrapped and nicely rib-boned -- refreshments were served. They had banana cake, chocolate cake and your choice of tea, coffee, and punch. Everyone chatted and had a good time.

Old Albert was sitting silently in the corner to add a note of humor to the affair. I'd give a lot to know what was going through his broken mind during the whole affair. The only words he said were to indicate that he preferred punch and that he'd not take another piece of cake, thank-you.

I got amused at the ladies last night. When I told Mrs. Blair, our school teacher, the time I expected the baby, she said in her blunt way that I should have been in Seward days ago. Several of the others seemed shocked that I wasn't packing up to leave right away. But Emma Clark didn't seem to think it was necessary and she's the only one who really needed to worry because she would be called on in an emergency. In fact, I have heard that she has already taken out her instruments used so many years ago and has sterilized them. Also, I've checked at the doctor's office, and I guess that should be more authoritative. Of course, should the weather turn bad, Harold and I will leave right away? We won't wait to get stuck here. But the weather has been wonderful and the roads good. Emma Clark seemed to think that I could easily make it even if labor should start right here in Hope. But I suppose every day I put in around here will cause some sweating by these local people, many of whom still think of getting to Seward by dog sled. In fairness to the local watchers, there hasn't been a baby born to a family in this community for several years. So, it isn't a regular occurrence. There seems to be unanimous consent to the idea that all would breathe easier if I were enduring the final stages of awaiting the baby in Seward.

Anyway, let's get back to the shower. You are aware of our shopping situation here. Most of the people had to get their gifts right out of Doc's store or make them by hand. So there were some quite ingenious ones. Grannie Clark is quite a knitter, so her gift was a knit soaker and a pair of spiral socks which she guarantees the baby will be able to wear for years because they don't have an actual foot knitted in. Marge Carter, who lives across the road from our new house, made a darling little old-fashioned bonnet and crocheted a pair of blue booties. Mrs. Blair, the teacher, in her robust, outspoken way declared that she hadn't known about the shower in time, so she gave me a box containing an adult size native Alaskan bracelet, a native made napkin ring and a very old piece of ivory pickle fork. She gave Mrs. Elliot a pink silk folder for stockings. Mrs. Rucker gave us some clothesline and some clothespins. I think that is clever. Emma Clark gave us a little non-spill drinking cup. Mrs. Stainbrook, our future neighbor on the same side of the road, gave us a dozen diapers and a card of large safety pins. Alma brought in an unwrapped sack. In it were thirteen cans of baby food for each expectant mother.

Guess I'm running out of time and out of space, so I'll stop. Besides, I'm very eager to get down to the P.O. to read my new letter from you.

Love,
Your Alaskan daughter, Harriet

~⟶)⁝(⟵~

Hope, Alaska
October 30, 1953

Dear Mother,
Well, I'm getting to the place where I'm doing a lot of lasts.

For example, tomorrow night will be my last potluck. Tomorrow's mail call will be the last mail I get for some time. You might try sending your next letter to me at Seward, "General Delivery." I'm not positive how long I'll be there. But surely that would catch me, and I'll be very glad to get a letter.

This afternoon, I checked four books out of the little local library that shares space with the post office and tucked them into the baby basket to take along to Seward. What with my knitting, that reading, and some shopping, I should be busy and happy until this little urchin decides to make its appearance.

Oh, here is a piece of news that will interest you. Vince is gone. He just packed his car and left on a Monday morning. He gave no warning except that he had been talking more and more frequently about home. I guess he had received a couple of letters, which really made the homesick bug bite. He and his car will be missed around here.

Tonight is the big Halloween get-together. Church has been called off for this week in deference to the community celebration. Can you imagine it? I can't. Lewie will be coming over in a few minutes to get ready. As I told you, he and Harold are going together as a couple. I'll be going with the preacher's family, the Elliots, who are not costuming either. That way, the two pregnant women can sit together so everyone can better calculate times. I told Harold I would put on a sheet and go as a ghost, but he didn't want me to take the chance of someone's thinking my protrusion was nothing but a pillow and give me a big, hearty punch. So I'll go as myself - should be gruesome enough anyway.

Wednesday night Harold and the local young people went ice-skating. Harold's claim that he ought to go as a sponsor didn't fool me. He had a great time. He loves skating.

That night we also made the big move. We moved from the bedroom into the living room. Our bedroom is cold and can't be heated. That wouldn't be so bad, but when the door is shut that separates it from the warmer part of the house, it is like a refrigerator in there. So, we rearranged the living room and put our bed out there. We plan to use a big wooden rocking chair as a cradle. We'll just plant the baby basket securely on it, and we have an instant cradle. Believe me, getting this main room set up took some doing. We have put up extra shelves that I've gaily decorated for the baby's things. Now we have it all arranged and its ultra-cozy. By cozy, I mean close-together cozy. Yet, we really like it. It'll also be nice for me to have a warm place to lie down during the day. So, we're quite satisfied.

I am so very pleased with the way the baby corner is fixed. It's here in the living room, too. I think it will be handy as well as looking like the newcomer is very, very welcome. I hadn't decided about lining the basket. But when I got the corner fixed, Harold mentioned that it might be nice. He was pleased with what I had done and thought that lining the basket would be the final touch. So maybe I'll get some material and line it while I'm in Seward. I agree that it would be nice.

We have turned the bedroom into a temporary root cellar. It seems at times that poor Harold is fighting a losing battle. He's always just two weeks behind in about everything. For example, could we have started on the house two weeks earlier, we would have had the root crops moved into the cellar up on our home site. Now there have been several nights of heavy freezing. Thus, he is facing the almost impossible task of filling in around the root cellar with the ground frozen. He has to use a pick to break up soil that a week or two earlier would have been easy to shovel into place. But he's sticking with it. Had we been able to move the crops into the new root cellar, he wouldn't have had so much worry and sweat trying to keep them from freezing in the old log house where we had them. Finally, he saw that he wasn't going to succeed at that, so he moved them all into the bedroom. I'm glad to have them in here now because they are an important factor in our winter food plans. This is especially true since our time in Seward having the baby will further delay his efforts. I told him I would stay in Seward by myself like the other pregnant women from the remote areas. He just smiles. He'll be staying with me. I'm really glad, of course.

Well, I shouldn't waste time wishing we were further along in our plans. It just couldn't be done. We tried. So what if our new house isn't done? We have a nice warm house here and are very comfortable. We're multi-lucky. We had our first real snow today. I mean this is the first snow that has fallen enough to cover the ground. It's just beautiful. And it's not really very early either. I remember a couple of years ago when it snowed the weekend of Halloween and Kansas State Teacher's meeting. So living in Alaska isn't so different.

We've been eating like kings. Honestly, Mother, this moose meat is delicious. I hope that Harold gets a moose on his own next year. We could give lots away and still have plenty to last us a whole year. The moose meat that we got this fall we've been using lavishly ... a pound and a half to two pounds a day ... and it still will last us for several weeks. But Harold does need that good hearty food ... meat, potatoes, and gravy. And my, the work he can do on a meal of it. He's not gaining weight, but he is strong and healthy.

I hope the little character puts in its appearance right on schedule. After all, it might as well learn to be on time now as ever. Besides, the days for me to recuperate before our trip Outside are numbered and each day of delay will keep Harold from important things. Then, in spite of the generous offer of a place to stay, there's always added expenses involved with staying in Seward. But I suppose I'll find it in my heart to forgive the kid no matter when it arrives if it will do so in a healthy condition.

I've typed to the end of this sheet of paper so I will quit now. If I get a chance, I'll tuck another page in tomorrow to tell you about how the big Halloween celebration tonight comes out. I love you and will be sending you some very good news before too long. We're all ready. We even have the two requisite names picked.

OCTOBER 31, 1953

Last night at the Halloween party Harold and Lewie were really a hit. They had kept their plans a complete secret, so no one else in the Miller family even knew. Lewie built small stilts into a pair of old overshoes and went as Digger O'Dell, the Friendly Undertaker. He had on a black coat and black hat, a terrible rubber mask, a white shirt with black bow tie, and carried a shovel. His stilts made him deceptively tall and caused his gait to be stiff and most effective. Harold padded himself with pillows across his shoulders and stomach to make himself very hunched and stooped. Then he squatted down and wobbled in a way that made him appear to be only about four feet tall. He had a blanket thrown over his shoulders and another smaller one for a shawl over his head. He was a perfect ghoul. They really made quite a couple.

Of course, in a village this size, the process of elimination soon revealed who these two were. But even Alma didn't know which was which. Consequently, when they went to give out the prizes, Lewie got Harold's, and Harold got Lewie's. Alma just knew that Lewie wasn't that tall. Boy, she was surprised. Harold's prize was a cigarette lighter. First one he's ever owned, you know. He will not be taking up smoking just to put it to use. Linda was dressed very cutely as a little Indian maiden. Alma really did a clever job on her. Linda, therefore, received one of the children's prizes.

Well, I guess I'd better get this to the post office before the mail goes out.

Love,
Your Alaskan daughter, Harriet

CHAPTER 6

November 1953: A New Alaskan

*D*ear Karen,
    In the next series of letters, we are covering the time of your father's birth, so I want to carefully answer the questions relating to that big event. But first, let me get at a couple of questions that have shorter answers. You asked about where people went ice-skating. There were not any actual skating rinks. Out on the tide flats, freshwater springs would create large pools in shallow depressions in the relatively level ground. In cold weather, these pools would freeze over quickly leaving fine smooth ice just begging for a blade to cut figures. That's where Harold, Doc, and the community youth would hold their skating parties.

I'm glad you expressed more interest in Albert and his relationship to the Hope community. That doesn't come out as clearly in the letters as it perhaps should. Albert's life was clearly limited by his mental disability, but he was a stable fixture of village life. He was cared for by the community, and he would contribute back in whatever ways he could. An example of his civic service occurred when the salmon were running up Bear Creek. Many people would turn out at that time to snag salmon for canning or smoking. As they pulled in the fish, they would lay them in individual piles, which would offer a tempting array for the village dogs. Albert would de-

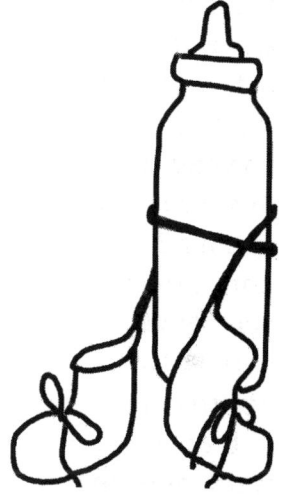

vote all his time to catching fish to feed the dogs to distract them from robbing the fish intended for future meals of other members of the Hope community.

Well, once again, your questions have forced me to stretch my memory back many, many years to the time of your father's birth. I don't remember that Harold and I had any qualms about having a baby in a remote section of Alaska. At my present stage of life thinking back to the naive and unfounded confidence that we possessed in those days gives me pause. Our thinking ran along these lines. We were college graduates. We had read the books. We had checked the calendar and had counted the weeks. I had been under a doctor's care both in Kansas and Alaska. What could go wrong? That overweening confidence was ours alone. It was not shared by everyone either inside Alaska or Outside.

For women who lived in remote areas planning to give birth in the Seward hospital, it was the custom to go into Seward well ahead of the due date. A waiting period that ran into several weeks was not uncommon. There were homes throughout Seward with room and board arrangements for this very purpose. At a comfortable time before her expected delivery, her husband or a neighbor would take a woman into Seward. She would then have easy access to the hospital and spend those weeks in relaxed anticipation. After the baby arrived and the mother was ready to come home with the newborn, the father would be notified.

Although we could see the rationale to this pattern, it was not a pattern that Harold and I intended to follow. Harold intended to stay with me in Seward and be there for the birth of our child. We would be together all the way through. But this meant that we didn't want to go into Seward until the last reasonable moment. The days away from work for Harold would be costly. Fortunately for us, Alma had asked some good friends in Seward if we could stay in their home when we went in for the birth. The Boe family agreed, and this dramatically eased our concern over this situation. We didn't have to go into Seward too far ahead of time to seek a place to stay, because we knew we had a place. Therefore we could stay in Hope where Harold could keep working as long as possible.

However, our smug self-assurance that all was well and would be handled in proper order at the appointed time was not shared by some of the Hope residents. There was a general concern among the women that I should be departing for Seward for the waiting period. In fact, there was the opinion that I should have left long before I actually did. In the end, two or three elements came together to propel us to Seward. About eight days before the baby was due we were at Alma's house for a Sunday night meal. George Windle, who had driven his jeep up from Seward to spend the weekend, was sharing that meal with us. Under the usual interrogation, we carefully explained to Alma and Ross that we would be leaving midweek to be sure to be there in plenty of time. I distinctly remember the look that passed between the two of them.

Well, as it happened, when I went out the back door to toss the rinse water, I slipped on the Miller's back step and took a little tumble. There was an instant reaction. Brooking no negatives from us, Alma had us back to our cottage and packing for the trip to Seward with George. I could see the relief on this good sister's face as we rode off with our suitcase and the baby basket in George's very reliable vehicle while our own balky Buick remained behind sitting stolidly in front of our cottage.

Homer and Augustine Boe had a large home that easily accommodated their teenage son and daughter and two schoolteachers who were rooming with them at that time. In the basement, there was a shower and a small sleeping room. This became our headquarters while in Seward. Seward was a very friendly seaport town. Since we were afoot there, Harold and I did a lot of walking around town.

You asked about the Seward hospital. As a small but efficient hospital, it served a large geographical area and often had patients coming from very remote locations. Since the road through to Anchorage had been opened up only within the last year or so, this hospital had always been a destination hospital. The Methodist church had established it and serving on its staff were people involved in the Methodist U2 Volunteer Mission Program.

Well, there is no need to tell all of it in this e-mail. The letters from November 1953, speak for themselves. They tell the story of your father's birth

> *Love,*
> *Grandma*

⌒◟◞⌒

Seward, Alaska
November 10, 1953

Dear Mother (and brand-new grandmother),

You've no idea what a sweet baby your new little grandson is. I know most new mothers think their babies are darling, but most of them have much less reason for thinking so than do I. It's about time I got around to writing you to tell you about the big event. The telegram Harold sent to you had the important facts. But I am sure you are eager to hear the details that surround the entry into the world of our new little one.

With our son sleeping under the watchful eyes of the nurses I have plenty of leisure, so I am going to back-track and tell you step-by-step how it all happened. I regret that you'll have to read a long hand-written letter, but I am actually savoring the intimacy of writing to you without the familiar and much speedier typing.

Last Sunday evening, November 1, we were at Alma's for supper. I slipped on the back step and took a tumble. Alma immediately decided that we must go right on into Seward. Neither Harold nor I felt this necessary, but she was so insistent that she persuaded us. We came in with George Windle who was visiting Hope for the weekend. Our car is still acting up quite a bit, and George's new jeep station wagon seemed like the best idea. We drove back from Alma's place to ours. We picked up the baby basket, which had so long held the necessities. Well, I guess it wasn't meant to hold that many necessities because one of the handles cracked when it was lifted up. Harold assured me that this was a minor matter and could easily be fixed. So, we loaded into the jeep and took off down the road to Seward.

Well, my fall brought nothing on. So, we waited in Seward. Since we had arrived in George's jeep, we were afoot for a week. Every day with Harold's firm grip on my arm we trudged downtown. One of the main department stores in Seward is McMullen's. I know that they got awfully tired of seeing us come in. I did my Christmas shopping then -- one item at a time. One day I bought the paper. The next day I bought ribbon. The next day I bought stickers. Do you get the picture? Probably no one in Seward was happier when our baby finally came than the staff at McMullen's.

No ships were in the harbor, so Harold didn't get in any of the stints of long shoring that we had counted on. He helped a friend of Boes who was working on a boat and enjoyed that experience. And, as you might guess, he gravitated over to the high school gym where our hosts' son, Gene, and the rest of the high school team were practicing basketball. By some quirk of fate, he found himself being asked to referee the high school game Friday night.

Friday morning, I woke up and got up at the usual time. But something strange had happened. My water broke and was coming in little dribbles. Mrs. Boe con-firmed my suspicions that the long-awaited time was near. She, of course, asked me to get in touch with Dr. Hall. He said to wait until the contractions were ten minutes apart and then to check into the hospital. The staff there would notify him.

I braced myself for the pains, but they didn't come. Friday was actually a boring day because nothing happened after my water broke. Finally, toward evening, about 3:30 pm, which is well into evening twilight this time of year, I started having light cramps. But even then, I wasn't sure that they were the real things.

Now I know this is going to seem foolish to you, mother, but I went with the Boe family to the basketball game. It seemed like a good way to get my mind off the fact that nothing seemed to be happening. Well, it certainly achieved that purpose. Unfortunately, Gene Boe, our host's son, not only is the star of the Seward team, but he is prone to fouling. Thus, it was an evening of high drama. There I sat while my contractions intensified and Harold called foul after foul. I knew that once he was refereeing, he wouldn't even be aware of the mounting number of fouls charged to an individual player. And, of course, he shouldn't be. Watching the scoreboard and timing my contractions added a truly unique element to the drama. I was miserable in more ways than one when Gene finally did foul out with Harold on the whistle.

After the game, we all went back home. Then the Boe family left for an after-game dance. At that time the contractions were still fairly light and not yet 10 minutes apart, so Harold and I decided to go to bed. Actually, I should make a point that Harold, the baby and I decided to go to bed. We had been staying in a three-quarter bed in the Boe basement. It had indeed been a bit crowded and required more than usual cooperation when one wants to turn over. But, oh we have been so grateful that the Boe family took us so warmly into their home.

About 12:30 we decided to go to the hospital. The Boe teenagers were still out, and Gene had the family car. Fortunately, however, their friends, the Bristols, were visiting the Boes for coffee and a chat. Mr. Bristol was the one who obligingly took us to the hospital.

The nurse checked me in, did the usual preparation, and then allowed Harold to come down to my room to wait. My contractions were getting more frequent and of longer duration very rapidly, so we both thought we'd get this project over soon. H.D. sat with his watch in hand. We laughed about his coaching instinct--timing the "human" race--and said he should have a stopwatch for greater accuracy.

What folly, because about then something happened. I hadn't had a drug or anything, but my contractions slowed down, and I had to start practically all over again. A roommate was admitted about 5:30 A.M. and was delivered of a son around 1:45 P.M. The nurse and the doctor checkups all seemed to indicate that my baby was just about here. But apparently, he didn't know it.

I thought back to the concern of the women in Hope about getting me into Seward ahead of time. I believe I could have crawled in on hands and knees from Hope and made it in plenty of time. Well, maybe I should say that we could have made it in time driving our non-speedy highway vehicle. Anyway, the nurses took me into the delivery room around 3:00 P.M. Harold stayed in there with me almost to the end. This intrigued the hospital staff because most husbands stayed away or sat reading magazines in the waiting room as so often depicted in movies.

I was very tired by the time the baby got here but was conscious the whole time. When it dragged out so long at the end, I was given a little bit of something... ether, I think, but it didn't put me out. So I was on hand to thrill at the lusty squall of Thomas Hayes when he arrived on the scene at 6:30 P.M.

He really is a sweet baby. I'm so happy about him. He doesn't cry much, and I'm sure he is going to have his father's sweet disposition. I may get a rude awakening when I get him home, but so far, he has been adorable. His little nursery roommate bellows and bellows but even when he's awake our son will just lie there quietly.

He has amazingly large hands and feet, I think, but his fingers are long and slender. He also has a long, distinct nose, not just a button. A mass of black hair covers his head. He even has a decidedly receding hairline just like his father's. His head was a little out of shape--long toward the back but is already shaping up as Dr. said it would. Perhaps the best part is that his complexion is clear--not the fire engine red of so many newborns. Well, that's enough of my gushing.

Sunday morning, I walked to the bathroom and have been up and around ever since. I sit up quite a bit so I shouldn't have too much trouble. I really do feel fine and plan to take it easy, so I'll continue to feel fine.

Sunday evening Harold got George to take him back to Hope for the car. He plans to work a couple of days and return to Seward this afternoon. I hope to go home tomorrow, but the doctor keeps mentioning Friday so I may have to wait another day. I wish Harold could have been with me these past few days basking in the joy of our baby, but I understand his need to go home, and I will never get over being grateful that he was here with me right through until our little Thomas Hayes came. All during our five-day stay in Seward before the baby came, my conscience hurt me that I was so privileged. Because it really is the custom here for the wives to come into Seward, wait for their babies and have them by themselves, Harold was kidded some. Bea Davis wanted to know why he was here. "Taking advantage of a chance for a vacation? You can't do anything. This is your wife's show." Harold wasn't a bit bothered by it.

I've had a surprising number of visitors. I had supposed I would be virtual without visitors since I am so unknown. However, even people whom I considered just casual acquaintances have stopped in-several with gifts. It's been quite touching. A lady just came in to see me with a lovely pair of cowboy booties. I had a terrible minute while I tried to figure out who she was. She was the wife of the man for whom Harold and Ross worked for those few weeks way last summer. Imagine!

Got your letter this afternoon. I really enjoyed it. I'm eager to see Harold again. He'll have last week's mail with an earlier letter from you, which I shall also enjoy very much as well even though it will be a chronological anomaly to read it. And I'll also be glad to hear his report on how our chickens, etc., survived our absence.

Did I ever tell you that I got the package? The sheets are plenty big. I have one on the basket now. I'll try to get a thank-you note off to Mrs. Hursh tomorrow. After Harold left, I had a little trouble getting the announcements mailed but reckon a delay of a day or so won't matter. By the way, we didn't have any extra announcements. Do you suppose Evelyn or Jean would save hers for me to use in the baby book?

Guess I'll stop ... could ramble on forever

Love,

Your Alaskan daughter, Harriet, and grandson, Thomas Hayes

⟨~⟩⟨~⟩

Hope, Alaska
November 15, 1953

Dear Mother,

I will write you a short note tonight because if I wait until next week, it'll be too long between letters. Well, we're home! We left the hospital yesterday and got home last evening around 6:00. The baby and I stayed in the heated car while Harold got the house cozy.

Tommy was restless some last night but has been just perfect all day. I hope he has a good night tonight.

I was surprisingly tired last night but have had several short naps today and am feeling very good this evening. I suspect that I shall be slow in recovering my strength. In the meantime, I'm being very good about "taking it easy." Of course, I don't know yet if I shall be able to nurse the baby completely. Before we left the hospital, they had stopped his supplementary feedings. But last night we did give him a little formula ... I suppose the trip tired me enough to affect my supply. However, he hasn't had any formula again today, so I'm hopeful.

Of course, Harold has been a wonderful help, and I think Erma Ann is going to work out very nicely as an assistant.

Here are the gifts I received while in the hospital: a kimono, "creeperalls" and a tee shirt, flannel sleeper bag, a pair of cowboy booties, sweater set, a pair of boxing gloves (toy), baby hangers, flowers, candy, diaper bag, towel and washcloth set.

How about all that? Our baby is surely overly supplied. But I am going to save many of these things back so that little number two will have some pretty new things. Nothing shall be wasted, I'm sure.

I smile about our baby's name. I know how to set you are against nicknames and "shorts" but we wanted to use the name Thomas, and it's much too dignified for the little character. Somehow Tommy is just right for him. Bet you're already used to thinking of him as such. Strangely enough, Harold had wanted to name his first son after his boyhood chum, Thomas Mizel who was best man at our wedding. And way back when I was just Harriet Thomas, I wanted my first son to carry our family name. Isn't that a beautiful coincidence? And you can readily understand why he has the name Hayes after Harold's father. Through Harold, I am beginning to learn what a godly man Hayes Walker was. I wish I could have known him. We pray that little Thomas Hayes will honor the heritage of his grandfathers.

Harold and I have had a little bad luck as a result of the early cold spell. Guess it usually gets cold early but the extreme cold so early this year is very abnormal. We fear that we've lost our potatoes. Also, Harold's work on building our house was prolonged because the ground froze early. This cost us time from work, which means we won't receive as much money from the company.

You've probably guessed the point of the above paragraph. It looks like our Christmas reunion may have to wait until Valentines. I'm very disappointed, of course, and know you will be, but it may be all for the best. We have some obligations, like our pledge to York College, which is due before the end of the year. We're surely a bit behind schedule financially. Anyway, we want you to know that no matter if it is delayed, the trip is on the schedule.

Thank you, Mother, for suggesting that you write to the Boes. I think it's a terrific idea. They were so wonderful to us-- just took us right in though they really know us only through

Alma. They fed us, roomed us, and wouldn't hear of pay. Harold and I enjoyed the contact with their teenagers. Harold does miss that aspect of our former life. Being with the Boes was a good stay for which we are grateful. We can't afford to give them an appropriate gift, so will take eggs to them when we go into Seward. Your note would help them to know how much our whole family appreciates their aid.

Mother, I think Tommy is going to have your dimple. I can't be sure, but I'm beginning to suspect that I see one popping in and out. Well, guess I'd better close this now. Just want you to know that we are well and very happy. God has certainly been good to us this year.

Love,
Your Alaskan daughter, Harriet

Hope, Alaska
November 21, 1953

Dear Clarke and Evelyn,

I know that Mother has been keeping the two of you up on developments here in Alaska, but I wanted to fill you in on some details and send along photos from the first set of pictures we have of your new nephew. Please excuse the carbons but I am very pressed for time at the moment, and I would have written pretty much the same thing to each of you anyway.

I'm sure mother filled both of you in on the incidents that lead to my precipitous trip to Seward and the events that transpired in the week we waited for Tommy to put in his appearance. So, let me start at the point that we actually got to meet our new son. It was incredibly exciting to get my first glimpse of Tommy when the doctor brought him to my bedside. I can remember feeling slightly giddy and being rudely jolted to reality by the doctor's attempt to reassure me. "His head will straighten out nicely. It will just take time," he said kindly.

So, I took another look at that beautiful object he held. It was true that his head was all drawn back into a point. But my chance to examine him was very short. Wrapped up in one of those coarse looking very sterile blankets, the nurses whisked him into the nursery for his first introduction to this world of cleanliness. Harold stood outside the nursery window and mentally supervised the process. He told me later that Tommy had beautiful big, blue eyes and was truly a very handsome creature.

Later that night the nurse asked me casually, almost as if it were an afterthought if I would like to look him over. Equally as casually I answered that I would if it weren't too much trouble. So "the lump" as he soon came to be known to me was brought in. A new baby is composed of two main parts - ahead and a stomach. All the other parts are necessary only to hold these two together or to be stuck on for interest and to confirm the hope that this new mortal will eventually be human. When I could get his legs uncurled long enough to look at them, I noticed that they were very bowed. The nurse assured me that all new babies had bowed legs, but I couldn't help harboring the opinion that this was part of his heritage, Harold's legs being what they are. Although his color was the pride and joy of my maternal heart, his skin still lacks some elements of being perfect. For example, it looked like he had been tucked into it at the last minute with no time for alterations. Frankly, it didn't fit.

His arms were short. In fact, when he'd stretch and yawn, only his hands extended above his head. Check yours when you stretch. See what I mean? He kept his arms and legs doubled up against himself most of the time. His little back was bowed around, and his head tucked in. It was some time before he realized that he had left the cramped little world where had lived so long and was now living in roomier quarters.

But perhaps the most striking thing was the little, old man

look on his face. Rarely in my lifetime have I seen a face that so clearly portrayed the word "wisdom." Who says that a new-born babe looks innocent? That look was yet to come. He just looked wise and perhaps a little sad at the burden of so much knowledge.

You think I was very objective and impersonal. No, I wasn't. I thought I was, but it wasn't until I brought Tommy home and watched the faces of his first visitors that I realized that I was just another adoring mother. I expected them to express somehow my adoration, but instead, my shocked ears heard the same words, which I had used so often in talking about a new baby. "Isn't he small? ... Look at those tiny hands." Then I knew. Only to us was he so wonderful and special.

It was a very clever move on the part of nature to send us our babies completely stripped of any endearing personal qualities. They respond in no way at all. No smile. No cooing. No gurgling. There is just stoic attention to the business of keeping alive and a noisy reminder when you fail to help them in this job. Thus their only claim to your fierce, protective love is their minute perfection and the price you paid.

I can imagine that it's in the unfolding of their personalities that this original situation shows its wisdom. Each little development such as a toothless grin or a little chuckle or again a sigh of contentment blossoming where none was before takes on tremendous importance and clutches at your heart.

Harold has tried to capture on camera the fact that Tommy is getting more darling, adorable, precious, cute, clever, etc., by the minute. Harold just took some more pictures of him in his little terry cloth pajamas. They are something new in the way of baby clothes and are they nice! I think another time I'd get them instead of the traditional long baby gowns that were on my suggested list. In this outfit, he has all kinds of freedom to kick and still be covered. That's not true with the gowns I bought. So, I put the pajamas on in the daytime because he just kicks and kicks and I don't like to have him uncovered completely. Anyway, these pajamas are blue and match his eyes.

I rely on Harold to take the pictures. He's tried to coach me to use our camera. Maybe, maybe sometime I will master that ability. Right now, I do hate to take the chance that I might waste a lot of precious film and still not capture some precious moments. Often, I have wished that we didn't have this wonderful camera with all its potential for success when handled by Harold and potential for failure when in my hands. The camera is a 35 mm one. It requires a light meter to get a reading on how bright the daylight is. Then depending upon the emulsion speed on the film being used, the light meter reading indicates which shutter speed and "f" stop combinations would be appropriate. Let just one of those adjustments be off... It's too much for me.

We should have these latest pictures that Harold took back in plenty of time to show off with the model. Right now, I am sending out some pictures we took of him at birth. We had hoped to bring all our pictures

along and show them in person at Christmas, but now those plans have fallen through. So, our next target for getting Outside to show off our son is sometime in February. We will fill you in on our plans as we get them firmed up.

Well, I need to get this sealed up and down to the post office before the mail goes.

Love,
Harriet

Hope, Alaska
November 28, 1953

Dear Mother and Mom Walker,
I know that you will understand why I am going back to using carbons and writing the same letter to both of you. I have so much to visit with you about and don't have the same leisure to do it that I have had before. I was writing much

the same thing to each of you anyway. I suppose the main difference is that I start the letters individually and that you, Mom, have already been here and are more familiar with what I discuss. I know that you two shared things when you were in college together, and I have no hesitation to let you share these letters now. I'll take turns with which one of you gets the carbon copy and which one gets the original. How does that sound?

What a haul we got in the way of mail today: letters from both of you including some that had been forwarded up from Seward. We heard from several Mullinville people, and we even got cards from a couple of Harold's ex-students and one of mine. Imagine!

I am sorry to have to announce that we will NOT be coming Outside at Christmas as we planned. Several factors go into this decision. My health is coming back but is slower in returning than hoped. Dealing with a newborn is exhausting at home; it's hard to imagine how we could cope with it while traveling. Higher travel costs over the holiday are the final and decisive kicker. It seems too much to pay just to make a Christmas gathering possible. I heartily blame myself for setting up this disappointment for us all. I wanted it so badly that I kept hoping too long. Harold has been a little skeptical about that possibility for some time now, but he was willing to do everything he could to make it happen. However, I have decided for both of us that it would be foolish to pay such a high price for sentiment. I just knew that if you were here and talking this over with us, each of you would advise us to wait for a little. So that's what we will do.

I am pleased with your responses about the baby's name. I agree with you, Mother, that Thomas should be his grown-up name. That's his name, anyway, no matter what he's called. Nicknames may be O.K., but there's nothing like having a good American name for legal purposes, etc. Your response, Mom, about our giving him Dad Walker's name for a middle name, was gratifying. Your reaction was beautifully worded. Harold and I have a rich heritage. What's important, I think, is that we realize it.

Talk about the 2:00 feedings. You should meet your grandson. He's on no schedule and intends to get on none. I'm using the new system of "on demand feeding" That is it's new to modern America, I guess. Primitive people have been using it for ages. I don't seem to have an abundance of milk, and it's a bitter disappointment to me, but that's the way it is. I nurse him as much as I can and then supplement when necessary. I keep hoping that more frequent nursing will stimulate my "dairy" as the book suggests. I let him get what he can and then feed him again when he is hungry. So, he eats at all hours. However, since I have nothing else drastically important to do, I don't mind the irregularity at all. Furthermore, this method seems to be cutting way down on the amount of supplement required.

His navel has healed nicely, I think, and he is gaining weight right along. He's not awfully heavy yet, 7 lbs. 10 oz., but he is coming along. He has a slight case of diaper rash, so we've added a period of boiling the diapers to the washing process. Harold has been doing the washings since we brought him home. Harold puts the big tub on the stove after supper and then scrub! Scrub! I hope that I can take over the washing of at least the baby things before long. The new daddy thinks it's wise not to rush it; and, of course, the new mommy concurs.

My heart failed me when Harold told me that my assignment for the community Thanksgiving dinner was three pies and a salad. I've made lots of pies by now, of course, but I always make them fast and not fancy. Even then it still seems like a terrific project to turn out more than one. But dear Alma came to my rescue. She said she was making several pies anyway and wouldn't even notice three more. She said she'd just as soon do it while she was in the business if I would make her salad. So that's what I did. I furnished the stuff for my share of the pies and also for her salad. But I didn't mind because I got out of a lot of work.

The big dinner was at four o'clock Thursday afternoon and was quite a spread. Elsie and Dave had driven down for the occasion and brought a ten-gallon container of fresh milk from their dairy. That milk was really a hit since there are no cows here and fresh milk is rarely available. This is a community of canned milk consumers. The fresh milk was perhaps the best-appreciated part of the whole meal. It is surprising how much milk ten gallons is. Since that meal, we have made ice cream, cottage cheese, and are just finishing the last of it now in delicious milk and cookie snacks.

For the Thanksgiving meal, I dressed Tommy up in a little blue kimono and the little blue booties of Mrs. Hursch's, wrapped him in a yellow blanket and tucked him into his basket. He slept practically the whole time he was there.

He had his second public appearance the very next day. We had our "family" Thanksgiving dinner over at Millers on Friday. We had goose, salad, ice cream, pies, sweet potatoes, dressing -- the works. Alma makes a pumpkin pie out of carrots. I can't tell the difference. It is amazing. And carrots really are cheap food up here. Hope we have just scads next year.

Elsie and Dave left in the middle of the afternoon, then, to go back home. Elsie brought over a beautifully knitted sweater for the baby. I think of myself as a knitter until I am around her and see the results of her efforts. My knitting is so plain -just socks and mittens and boring, very long stocking caps.

Harold got an offer in the mail today to teach sixth grade in the Seward schools. They surely have trouble down there keeping up with the population. They have their fourth graders so crowded that they are going to have to divide those rooms up too. I don't think that he is interested. He really wants to stick with our plans about getting the mill project going.

Harold and Ross spent the day at Portage, which is halfway between here and Anchorage. They were jacking up the planer that they bought and taking it apart. They'll have to make another trip to get it out. The ground wasn't quite frozen enough to bring a loaded truck over. They are thrilled about the planer. It's a good deal. It has all the knives and takes lumber up to eight inches thick by twenty inches wide. Best of all it is in excellent condition. Harold wanted me to explain this to you. He and Ross did get a superior bargain on the planer by being able to buy it with lumber. It's better than we'd ever dreamed. We're making good progress on getting the mill equipped, but the business of taking advantage of bargains has really cut into our company capital. Of course, it'll pay off in the end.

You should both be here now. Harold is tending the baby. He's trying to get him to burp. It's really funny to hear all the instructions he is giving his son. Tommy keeps rearing his head back to look around, and in so doing he scratches his face on Harold's stubbly unshaved chin. His reaction brings a smile to me. New babies never have interested Harold, and I was so afraid he'd just wait until this one got to have some "personality" before he took an interest. But even when I was in the hospital, I could see him standing in the hall looking into the nursery and reacting to the baby's facial expression. I'm glad because it does make it so much more fun for me and it will be wonderful for our new little son.

We really do enjoy your letters. You two certainly lead terrifically busy lives. I don't think I could keep up with you. But please don't do so much that you can't keep up with yourselves!

Love,
Harriet

CHAPTER 7

December 1953: Alaskan
Christmas

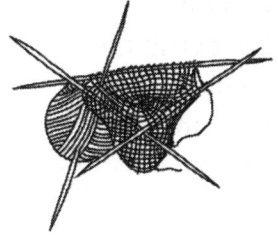

*D*ear Karen,

    By the first of December, the aura of the Christmas Season had already been with us for some weeks. One could not help thinking of Christmas in this land of Christmas card beauty. Even when we were in Seward awaiting the birth of our little one, my thoughts turned to a young woman two thousand years before who had been a traveler living in a borrowed shelter awaiting the birth of her son. So we found ourselves in the actual Christmas Season gratefully aware that this year we were free to savor the beauty of the season without the almost frenetic community, school, and church activities that used to be part of December in Kansas.

    Coincidentally, Karen, your question about the role and purpose of longshoring fits right in with the December letters. A longshoremen's strike played a part in the Christmas preparations for that year. During previous summers Harold earned good money loading and unloading ships as a longshoreman. However, the longshoremen's strike that so affected our Christmas season of '53 took place on the docks of Seattle preventing the loading of ships headed for Alaska.

We had originally hoped to be with our families in the States at Christmas time showing off our new son. But once we realized that this was not to be, a sort of peaceful acceptance settled over us. With effort our little cottage could be kept warm, the water buckets could be filled, meals prepared. We were comfortable in the one main room of the house with Tommy in his moveable basket bed. Beautiful clear static-free music entered our home via the radio. I had a goodly supply of yarn for my knitting projects. Yes, I was learning the meaning of the word, contentment.

Love, Grandma

Hope, Alaska
December 5, 1953

Dear Mother and Mom Walker,

It's a little after two thirty in the afternoon, so I should have about twenty minutes or so before I have to light the lamp. Of course, it won't be completely dark outside by then so the fellows will get to work a little longer, but darkness will send Harold home long before five.

Well, our son tipped the scales at a fraction over eight pounds today. Being so far from a doctor, I do appreciate these scales borrowed from Emma Clark. She used to be a nurse and has been handy with advice. The baby's gaining steadily sleeps a lot, eats heartily with much noise, and seems to be a happy character. Harold is determined that he shall turn out to be a great physical specimen. He keeps a tab on whether he sleeps too much on one side, the strength of his legs, and the grip of his fingers. So far he is content with progress in all categories.

Harold, however, is not going to be any help at all in my careful discipline. Last night I decided that Tommy had had plenty to eat, he wasn't wet, and therefore, as I had been counseled, I was going to ignore baby cries. Such a strong character I am! After just a few minutes, Harold announced the firm conviction that the baby was hungry, even if he had eaten recently. Who wants a baby to stay on schedule anyway?

"He can't be hungry!" I assured him. But my son proved me wrong. Harold warmed up a little formula and Tommy promptly made a liar out of me by noisily gulping it and then quietly going to sleep. Harold sat back very smugly after having so satisfactorily quieted his gluttonous boy. It'll be some time before we get over that victory. I've also caught him peering down into the basket, talking and playing with Tommy when he is supposed to be going to sleep (Tommy, not Harold). He always looks guilty about it too. Goodness, the two of them are really becoming a problem.

Last year I purchased a string of electric Christmas lights, which we brought up here with us. Looks like we won't have our electricity until after Christmas now, so I'm going to loan them to the Millers. They can hook them up to their little plant. It'll be the first electric ones they have ever had. I'll likely enjoy having them there more than I would if I used them myself this year. Harold is going to get me a tiny little tree, which I'm going to decorate for us and set on the worthless sewing machine cabinet. We are so packed into this one room that a tree with any size to it would be absurd. Besides, I have just enough ornaments for a cute little tree. Funny, too, because up here we could have the largest and most beautiful Christmas tree around just for the taking. Since I've mailed out the presents, I won't have any to speak of under the tree. But I have lots of wrapping paper, and there may be some just plain little boxes wrapped and gracing our tree. Who knows?

I guess there are two times a year up here when new clothes are a "must." Fourth of July and Christmas. The Christmas dresses that Alma and Erma Ann ordered by catalog came the other day. They are pleased with them. They feel very fortunate to get them at all because there is a longshoreman strike on the docks in Seattle. This will soon be holding up package delivery everywhere in Alaska if it's not ended soon. We certainly hope that the strike is resolved in time for the Millers to order the gifts that they have planned. I will be getting along without a new dress for Christmas. However, no one will notice if things go as planned and I'm able to get into one that I already had, instead of maternity clothes. I'm keeping my fingers crossed.

We had a nice trip to Seward Monday. We didn't slip once on the icy road. One thing about our poor crippled car, it really holds to the road nicely. One could say that it is slow but sure-footed. We got to Seward in time to get Tommy's doctor examination over early -- just before noon. That way we didn't have to wait until the doctor's office opened in the afternoon. I stayed at Boe's then with Tommy while Harold did the shopping and ran errands for the business. You really have to rush around to get anything done in the daylight now, and we didn't want to be on the road too long after dark.

Since we were making the trip, Alma and Ross asked Harold to be on the lookout for gifts they could give to their children. Harold ran across a real bargain for Lewie's Christmas present. He found a pair of second-hand skis that was practically new. He got them at half price. He's thrilled over them, and we do hope that Lewie will be pleased. Harold did not find anything for Erma Ann. Linda's requests are so frequent and so varied that what she gets will depend merely on what minute her parents decide to get it.

It was a beautiful trip. The snow lies so thick and velvety all around. There have been very few actual snows, but we haven't been without snow on the ground since Halloween. It just lies there peacefully day after day because the temperature is right and there's no wind. We saw many scenes of breathtaking beauty. The mountains, trees, the streams with floating ice and black, black water. Even the telephone lines near Seward, which could mar the natural beauty, redeemed themselves in this winter scene. I couldn't help remarking to Harold, "Look, they have their Christmas decorations up already!" as we drove along and saw the lines covered with fuzzy snow, encrusted with sparkling, shimmering ice particles.

Lovely.

Alma was over just the other day for some blouse material, which I said Erma could have for her sewing course if she wanted it. And then yesterday she told me that Erma had her blouse finished. She's really concentrating on that one school subject, it seems. That's often the way she does her work. When she was working over here for me, she was concentrating on American History. She did about two weeks work in the few days that she was here.

The preacher's station wagon just drove in. I can see it from the window where I am. I see that he is alone. I suppose it will be some time before his wife will be making the trip with their new daughter. Boy, will she and I ever be comparing notes come summer! I think I'll go to church tonight and leave Harold home to spoil the baby. For a while yet, we'll take turns about going to church. If it were in the daytime, it would be different, and we'd likely take Tommy and go as a family. But it gets really cold at night, and we don't want to risk it.

Now that Tommy is sleeping longer intervals at night, a new problem has arisen. We sometimes let the fire go out. When we first had him, he woke up often enough to keep us reminded to keep the fire stoked up. What we really need is a heating stove that could be banked or even a bigger range, which could last all night. But we do our heating with our cook stove, and its firebox just isn't big enough to last very long. We may be the only people around who don't have a true heating stove. This house was really only built for summer occupancy.

So, to avoid letting the house get cold, while we blissfully sleep the night away, we have had to start setting the alarm clock. One of our purchases in preparation for the baby was a thermometer. We keep it right by his basket and that way by controlling the fire and shifting his basket to warmer and cooler spots, we've managed to maintain a constant temperature for him. Being able to know is a great comfort. That basket you gave us, Mother, has proved to be such a blessing.

Sometimes it is situated on the rocking chair as a sort of cradle. Then if Harold wants to sit in the rocker, the basket goes nicely onto the counter. It can be easily moved into the kitchen nearer the stove. It has even on occasion resided on the opened-out oven door. We really appreciate the versatility that it gives us.

Another sign that our little house wasn't built correctly for occupancy during an Alaskan winter is that the walls sweat. I guess it isn't insulated properly or something, but anyway, we have water running down the walls and onto our floor. It's quite disconcerting. At least we have no worries about whether the air is too dry or not. The door also sweats, and the other morning it was frozen shut. But solid! Poor Harold had to work twenty minutes of careful chipping so as not to damage the door or sills before he could get out of the house. Before he left, he showed me how to use hot water from the teakettle to open the door in an emergency.

Our little chickens are a real delight to us now. Fourteen eggs they gave us yesterday. Now we are going to have to look around for a market for the eggs. But what a joy it is to have all the fresh eggs that we can use. Custards, jelly rolls, cream puffs ... mm! We saved three-dozen to take to the Boes last week. They wouldn't take any money for all their hospitality, so we'll do this once in a while. Harold says that boat eggs were selling in Seward for $1.15 and that fresh eggs were $1.35 and seldom available. So, we are living high!

Harold and Ross have been working a couple of days for a man who wants to get some pipe out of an old mine. They're just doing hourly labor although they are using our truck. This is a cash job, and it will really be nice to have some extra money. Ironically the job is going faster than Ross had estimated and now he wishes he had just bid the job instead of working by the hour. It's going to cost that old miner much less than what had been estimated. I don't understand all that Harold tells me about this interesting project but here's what I remember.

The pipe was put in to bring water far down the mountainside to build up enough pressure to scour away banks of clay, gravel and even small boulders. Oddly, because it uses water pressure to remove unwanted materials, this is called placer mining. When I hear that term, I think of standing in a gently flowing stream with a gold pan not the violence of high-pressure water digging up the earth. This pipe is made of spring steel, which makes it thin walled but strong. The uppermost part of the pipe is huge to accept a large volume of water. Then as it plunges down, the size of the pipe is reduced to build up the pressure. While our guys are wrestling 20 ft sections down the hill, they are amazed at the industry of those earlier gold-seeking men who had to drag all that pipe up the side of the mountain. I believe that there are over seventy sections of pipe to be hauled out like hollow logs on our logging truck. By stacking them in tiers separated by wooden cross pieces and then nesting the smaller pipes in the larger ones, the fellows think they can get it all done in three trips.

Harold was offered a teaching contract in Seward. Homer and Augustine Boe just couldn't believe that Harold wouldn't jump at the chance. They thought that now in the pinch of winter is when he'd see his "mistake" in trying to stick it out in Hope. But he and Ross are very optimistic about how things are coming along. True, we're very short of cash. But we are about a year ahead of schedule in acquiring essential equipment for the mill. Actually, by spring if the weather holds, we'll have the mill equipped for full production. Also, Harold and I will have a house worth at least $2,000. When we get the interior done, it'll be worth easily twice that. Really, that's not bad for a year's work when you have your living besides.

The baby fascinates Linda. When we were over there for Thanksgiving dinner-the-day-after, she just watched him and watched him. Now, Alma informs me that Linda has become quite the little mama. She has to dress, bathe, feed her doll. Gets to be quite a nuisance at times, I understand. The other day when she was too busy with the baby to take time to eat

Ross finally had to tell her, "Well, you're my baby, and I want to take care of you and see that you eat." Just goes to show how children imitate adults. She never has played with dolls before. But come to think of it, why should she? She never saw anyone doing the things with babies that lead other little girls to play with dolls.

Alma comes by two or three times a week to visit me. She stops in when she walks over with Linda to school. She's so early that it keeps me hustling to get my house straightened up before she gets here. But, then I know she doesn't have her morning work done yet either so why I should worry?

Well, the diapers I'm boiling are spitting and sputtering on the stove, so I better tend to them. Harold does the actual washing, bless his heart.

Love,
Harriet

Hope, Alaska
December 11, 1953

Dear Mom Walker,
I wasn't feeling very energetic Monday morning, so Harold asked Erma to come over and help me for the day. It was surely a stroke of good luck that she did because we had a chimney fire that day. It wasn't too bad at first, but it kept getting worse. The roar of the fire in the chimney was terrible. So Erma went and asked the neighbors what to do. They said to close the damper down completely, and it would go out by itself. I guess it was a rather severe fire for a chimney fire. No damage was done to the house, and the fire burned itself out in time. However, part of the chimney cracked. The damage happened to asbestos stuff near the roof. The neighbor said that fire shouldn't be started in it again until that part was replaced. Erma Ann and I packed up and went over to Millers for

the day. We padded the inside of the basket with diapers and covered Tommy up well. I put on the long underwear you lent me (thank you). Then we hiked across the flat to Millers. Erma carried the basket all the way. It was quite an awkward load to carry, and she was a little sore from it the next day. When Harold came in that evening, he and Ross went to survey the situation. They bought and installed all new pipe, so now that danger is removed.

We now have about six dozen eggs to sell. We plan to sell them for a dollar a dozen locally. We don't have a large quantity, so we're not trying to establish a market in Seward or Anchorage. The local people aren't willing to pay big market prices for them. Still, a dollar a dozen is about the price that Doc is asking for boat eggs. At that rate we should be able to get rid of all we have to sell. And the extra money will surely help. We've already started to sell them. Rev. Elliott has placed an order for two dozen each week. He is sure that we could get rid of as many more as we could care to sell. The Ruckers also took a dozen. The little Rucker girl was so excited and said that she had forgotten what fresh eggs were like. They use powdered eggs most of the time.

Harold and Ross are still working for Eddy Nash, the old miner I told you about last week. The pipe removal went so well that he had another job for them. They are working up Sunrise Creek. Although Harold and Ross are making good wages, they hate to spend the time doing work for someone else. The Sunrise Creek job is moving right along, but the temperature has really dropped, which has complicated the work. Harold says that he has a hard time staying on task because nature's battle with itself is so fascinating. The creek is trying to freeze, but the water is of sufficient volume and moving too fast to freeze. It is crystal clear, and it's easy to see slush build up behind rocks on the bottom and then to see that slush break away and float down the stream becoming liquid again. That running water is supercooled, and if dipped out in a tin cup and let to sit a very short while in the frigid air, you can watch it freeze solid in a couple of minutes. That is if Harold isn't pulling my leg.

The radio announcer just said that sunset was at 2:43 P.M. How about that? Of course, it doesn't get dark for a little while after that, but I have to light the lamp in the house about that time. Seems funny to lie down for a nap after lunch and wake up to a pitch-black house. That makes you feel like you've slept and slept on into the night.

I'll really have to step lively now if I am going to get Harold's mittens done by Christmas. And I intend to. Harold still has some raggedy shooting mittens left from his military days. Those mittens have a knit-in trigger finger separation. I have mended and mended them for his hunting excursions. Recently they have started to wear out rapidly because he needs to use them with the chain saw. Of course, he does switch the mittens around from one hand to the other so that the wear is more evenly distributed. I have wanted to make him a new pair. Alma and I talked it over, and we believe that I can use the same procedure for knitting the separate trigger finger that I use for the thumb separation. If I can pull it off, we will soon have a new pair of warm hunting mittens. It's taken a few hours of trial and error, but it's going to work.

I guess I will close and get a letter off to the other grandmother.

Love, Harriet

Hope, Alaska
December 11, 1953

Dear Mother,
We have really had a beautiful snowfall this week. The nearest thing to this kind of weather I've ever seen was the snow when we visited you in Nebraska last winter. It really is beautiful. We've had about two feet of snow. Out here in the coun-

try there is nothing to contaminate it with black soot and the light traffic leaves it pristine without the slushy mess I'm used to. All the fence posts are holding beautiful big white angel food cakes, and the houses are frosted within an inch of their lives. In a word, it is lovely.

We are really enjoying the eggs. Twice this week I've had scrambled eggs for lunch. This is an unheard-of luxury when you also can have eggs for breakfast. I've made custard twice and plan to make cream puffs tomorrow. We are getting ahead on eggs. We think that we'll have about five dozen to sell each week if they keep up at their present rate. I'm already calculating how I'll spend it.

Ross and Harold are really optimistic about logging prospects. All along Harold has wanted them to stockpile logs in the wintertime when logging is good. Winter logging enables them to easily skid logs over the snow. Also, the work is free from annoying, biting insects. He hoped that they could concentrate on doing the milling in the summer when they don't have the difficulty of sawing frozen logs that push mill blade out of alignment, producing inaccurate dimensions in the lumber. Harold feels that this plan would really utilize the weather and manpower best. But there has been some difference in philosophy here. This first year Ross is concerned about indebtedness and so has felt all along that they had to keep sawing to pay expenses.

Today they made the big decision to try to get as many logs laid away as possible. The change that caused this shift to Harold's preferred plan is that they just got a nice order for house logs. Since we will get paid for the house logs right away and since the men can just as well cut the other trees around the highly select house logs, the focus has now shifted to stockpiling logs. There is a catch to this plan. It will cut us really close on money until summer. Especially since the Forest Service now requires that we pay for the timber up front. Harold thinks that there will be enough money for groceries, baby expenses, and this spring's work on the new house, but not much more.

Therefore, we were wondering if you had any money available to lend us for a trip outside. We'd borrow it on the same basis as we have the other loans, of course. We feel a little awkward about asking because the mill has really done well. We'd have plenty to spend if we weren't pouring it all back into the mill. I guess we just need to keep thinking about the long-term goals. Harold says that our being here and working has increased the value of the mill much more than we could have possibly saved by both of us teaching two jobs outside. The real bonus then is this wonderful experience we have as a family with me at home for Tommy.

It does seem funny not to have any cash in the house at times and none in the bank for check writing. Of course, we have credit at the grocery store, so existence is never in question. Another thing is that I'm learning that many of life's little necessities aren't necessary at all. If I had known last spring that we wouldn't have electricity by now, I might have balked. Now it doesn't even seem important. It gives one a very valuable sense of self-sufficiency to live like this. The only time I really long to be modern again is when it comes to washing clothes.

Aside from missing the holidays with all of you, I'm rather glad that we aren't going outside just yet. Tommy really is so small. Maybe he'll always seem small, but I'm sure I'll feel better about it all later. Two weeks from today is Christmas! Is that possible? The Seattle longshoremen's strike still holds. The Millers are beginning to be concerned about gifts -- especially those ordered for Linda.

We have had some splendid radio programs this Christmas season. I'm wondering if they're just better up here or is it that every previous Christmas I've been too busy with the hustle and bustle of civilization to appreciate them. I'm really enjoying the peacefulness of the Christmas season here. There is none of the frantic rush, which I've always associated with Christmas and always rather enjoyed. But this is refreshing for a change.

Love,
Your Alaskan daughter, Harriet

~~)☀C~~

Hope, Alaska
December 19, 1953

Dear Mother,

Since tonight was the Christmas program, our whole family went to church. Tommy behaved himself like a veteran, and we were very proud of him. The service was very simple. There was a very small decorated tree, a reading of the Christmas story, carols, and the traditional sermon. Then after the service, the minister gave out candy and showed a small film, which he had ordered for the children.

Our son is really growing. He's pushing ten pounds now. I guess he must be healthy or he wouldn't gain so well. But the tragic thing is that he is losing his hair. He must have heard his parents discussing his chances for baldness. If it is carried down the maternal side as popular opinion has it, he has a fifty percent chance of keeping his hair. But if both lines must be considered, his chances are very, very thin. Whatever the cause, his receding hairline is getting more receding and his scalp more evident. However, by some magic, he suddenly got on a schedule and has been staying on it nicely for several days. It is nice in that it helps me plan my day.

For four days in a row now we have gotten nine-teen eggs. I would say that was doing pretty good for twenty-one chickens. Wouldn't you? But Harold says, "A couple of those chickens aren't pulling their share. They are courting the stew pot." It won't keep up, but it must be some kind of a record.

Monday will be quite a red-letter day. What makes Monday so important is that it is the shortest day in the year and up here that's saying something. I usually don't turn out my lamp in the morning until 9:30 and have to light it again soon after 2:30 pm. Funny, though, you get used to it, and it doesn't seem a bit strange at all. It is not nearly as depressing as I thought it would be either. I've gotten to where I put off my naps until dark so that I can utilize every minute of daylight. Lying down at 2:30 or 3:00 isn't really so late for a nap, though, is it? The early darkness has a big advantage in that the fellows have to quit work early. Harold and I have nice long evenings together. But as I said, the 21st of December is the dividing point. After Monday the days start getting longer. I understand that the daylight increases five minutes a day. It's hard to imagine how that will add up to endless summer daylight. But add up it must. I guess it won't be obvious at first, but it will be interesting to watch the days get longer and longer instead of shorter.

Now we will have a weather report. According to the radio, Georgia reported weather of 17 degrees yesterday and the temperature in Minnesota was 22 below zero. Here in warm, tropical Alaska, the temperature was 36. Yeah, that's what I said, 36 degrees above zero. The problem is that I'm getting to be Alaskan enough that I don't trust the warm weather. If it stays this warm, we won't go to Seward on Monday the way we planned. Isn't it strange to be worrying about the weather being too warm in the winter? Just to be safe, I'm mailing this letter now instead of waiting until we get to Seward as I would normally do. You see, this warm weather causes complications. The roads become dangerous. Any slight rain and they are iced over. Then the melting and freezing keep them treacherous.

But the unseasonable warmth has some interesting aesthetics. It seems to me that the whole landscape is changed from cotton and marshmallow to beautiful, gleaming glass. Crystal trees overlook the crystal ribbon of the highway. Children slide gleefully upside down as often as not. Cars creep along with their chains rattling. Adults don "creepers" (little, spiked affairs that fasten onto shoes) and all sit back wondering if the snow will leave us completely and rob us of a "white

Christmas."

Harold isn't at all perturbed by the weather. He has perfect traction because of the spiked "caulks" in his logging boots. The other night he beguiled me into getting onto a sled, after dark, in the moonlight, and pulled me up and down the road. It was really fun.

A week from today is Christmas. Is it possible? The long-shoremen's strike still has not been negotiated satisfactorily. Likely we'll be doing some "emergency" shopping at least for Linda when we go into Seward on Monday. All these adults and almost adults around here are becoming increasingly concerned about Linda's Christmas experience.

The community has been planning our Christmas get-to-gether. It will include a big feed, a movie powered by our storekeeper's power plant and then square dancing. Some of the married women will make pies as gifts for all the old bach-elors who in turn will buy candy for the local children. There surely is something magic about the Christmas spirit.

Really, there has been nothing this year to push the season upon us as has been true in past Christmases. It has just stolen quietly in. Even though I've usually enjoyed all the activity of Christmas preparation in the past, I certainly do not miss the frantic rush that usually accompanies it. I'm learning a new feeling of Christmas, which I shall ever strive to keep. The music, the magazines, time to meditate on the real meaning of Christmas. Likely in years to come, I'll be back to the same rush as before, but I hope I can always keep some of this calm-ness.

Do you hear that sputtering, grumbling sound? Your grand-son is in the process of waking up. No telling how much far-ther I shall be able to go in this letter before I stop to tend him.

I've been thinking about how I can put letters together to form words to attempt to convey my message of love to you ... to all of you, my family, this Christmas. Somehow my thoughts wander back over the many Christmas seasons we've shared in Africa, Coffeyville, Topeka, and Lincoln. They've been wonderful. I have a warm glow around my heart when I think of them. Then I look over at my son in his basket, and I know that I could wish nothing more for his Yuletides than the family-kind of Christmases that I've known. If simple gifts, creative giving, shared tasks, and love are the keys to it, then we'll use them to unlock the door for him. May God bless you and all we love this season!!

Love,
Your Alaskan daughter, Harriet

Hope, Alaska
December 24, 1953

Dear Mother,

Well, this has been a real old-fashioned Christmas around here. We didn't make our trip to Seward. The roads were really bad. The highway is all right, but the seventeen-mile stretch between here and the main highway isn't passable. Ross and Harold have been busy pulling people out of the ditch who do attempt it. Since we didn't get to Seward, Alma didn't get a chance to do that Christmas shopping for Linda and Erma Ann. How fortunate we had bought skis for Lewie on a previous trip. Erma Ann says that she doesn't mind waiting for the strike to be over, but that would never do for Linda. So just like an old-fashioned Christmas, we've all been making things so that she will have gifts under the tree. I had a little old tin box, which Harold is fixing up into a "treasure chest." Lewie is making her a little hobbyhorse. Harold plans to make her a pair of short stilts. Alma is making a big stuffed rabbit. She also started a pair of twin cloth dolls, which I am stuffing, sewing together, and fixing the hair on. Anyway, in spite of the roads and the strike, we are making sure that our little Linda will have a merry Christmas.

We have our tree up. It's a little one, and I have it all decorated with tiny ornaments. We're surely pleased with it. We couldn't have turned around in our living room if we had had the big kind so typical in this land of Christmas trees, and anyway, it's really for Tommy, and he's such a tiny guy; he needs a tiny tree.

Last night we went to the school Christmas program. It really is an all community affair. We took Tommy. His good behavior made his proud parents even prouder. Not a "squawk" out of him. The program itself was quite an experience. Harold says that it was very typical of a small community program, but I guess I hadn't seen any of that kind. It didn't take me long to get over the unprofessional, relaxed air of it all and really enjoy it. Linda and the other first-grade girl, Margie Rucker, sang a duet. They were too cute for words. Margie is blond and fair and such a contrast to dark-haired Linda.

You would not believe the gifts! I'm not kidding when I say that most of the children came to the program with shopping bags and went home with their faith rewarded. I guess lots of people gave each child a gift. Linda must have received seven or eight. But what amazes me the most is that every year, for years and years, Grannie Clark has knitted a pair of mittens for each child in Hope. She says this is absolutely the very last year. This year she knitted about two-dozen pairs of all sizes. They were all wrapped up and under the tree along with numerous other gifts for the local young people. Alma received special permission from Grannie to let the children open their "Grannie mittens" so that she could get a picture of it all. They lined up and held their mitten hands up in the air. From the littlest Crosby girl to the teenagers, all had new Grannie mittens. There were mittens, mittens, mittens, and every one different. It really was an astounding array.

Last week in the mail I got four or five packages for Tommy. They were wrapped in baby gift paper, but they went right under the tree unopened. So, they'll be a big surprise tomorrow when we open our presents. They really make it look like Santa is especially fond of the Walkers. And speaking of Santa,

I still have to finish up those mittens for Harold. I have them all done but the thumb on one. I've been rather sidetracked by dolls, etc., you know.

Our Christmas day tomorrow will go something like this. I'll do up my morning work first, then we'll open our presents. At four o'clock we'll go over to the big community dinner. Isn't that the funniest hour for a meal? Makes you wonder when to eat the other meals. I guess there's always enough left for another big meal the next day. So likely we'll be eating Christmas dinner again Saturday evening.

The mail truck just drove in. I know that the mailman1 usually has quite a few deliveries around town, so I am going to chance writing yet a little more. I know that you have been aware of my disappointment that I would not be in the States for Christmas. I know that I have the gift of your understanding in that realm. So, I want to give you a gift in exchange. You won't get it in time for Christmas, but you will know that I am sending it at the right time. Here is the gift:

A couple of days ago when Harold got home from work, I decided to walk down to the store to get an item or two. I dressed warmly, grabbed the flashlight and soon had accomplished my mission. On the way back from Doc's I was suddenly aware of the ethereal beauty around me. Even though it was only late afternoon, the moon was out. The snow crunched crisply under my feet as I walked. I passed our little church, just a dark shape in the moonlight. In the moon glow, the snow on the road was a field of diamonds. My flashlight's beam was pale and completely unnecessary to illumine my path.

As I passed the dark empty schoolhouse, which neighbors our little house, I could see the glow of lamplight from our cottage window. It spilled out, a softly flickering yellow reflection on the snow. I could hear the subdued radio sound of violins interpreting a familiar Christmas carol. This background music told me that Harold would be sitting in the big old wooden rocker reading. Likely he would have Tommy covered up nicely and asleep on his lap.

My warm little cottage. Food in the pantry, the tea-kettle steaming on the stove, the brave little Christmas tree. My husband. Our baby. As I crunched the final steps to our house, I thought in surprise. "This is my home. I will be home for Christmas after all."

Love,
Your Alaskan daughter, Harriet

CHAPTER 8

January 1954: A New Year

D ear Karen,

I am going to try to anticipate some of your questions for this set of letters. In the January 16th letter, I mention the difficulty of getting the planer out because of all the muskeg around it. When you look at a field of muskeg, it appears to be a plain of vegetation on the solid ground, but it is actually a mass of peat like growth covering water. The thickness of the muskeg and the degree of weight it will sustain varies from one bog to the next, but none of it will hold up machinery. In the instance described in the letter, Ross and Harold were waiting for a deep freeze so that they could take the truck over the muskeg to get the planer. That plan would work only if the freeze came before a snow cover, which would insulate the muskeg enough to prevent freezing. As it happened, the snow came first, so there was no possibility of the muskeg supporting the truck. However, the cold did freeze up the little creek that ran by the old mill where the planer was located. This creek ran all the way down to the road. The men built a sturdy sled out of rough lumber, took the planer apart, and skidded the dismantled planer down the frozen creek piece by piece to be loaded on the truck.

Another issue important to this series of letters is the informal nature of mail service and the special role of Bill Brattain, our mailman. You recall from the letters around Christmas that he changed mail delivery dates. Well, he did that again around New Years without my finding out until too late to get a letter ready for Mother. You'll see how we dealt with this in the first letter. Nevertheless, you now realize how much importance we placed upon his delivery of the mail. However, Bill Brattain's mail service was also a delivery system for all kinds of things. Villagers could place orders with him for items that he could pick up for them in Seward and bring out the following week on his regular route. He charged for this service, of course, but on balance, this charge often proved to be a good investment

When I think of those months in Alaska, strong in my memory is the radio program, Mukluk Telegraph. You have already read about how this program broadcast personal messages all over the territory. I have never felt that I could describe adequately what this single daily broadcast meant to those of us in remote areas with once-a-week mail service and no telephones. As winter closed in and the dark came early and stayed long, the Mukluk Telegraph program became more and more a cause unto itself. We planned around it. In the deep dark of an Alaskan winter night, that calm, almost bored, voice of the radio announcer was a reminder that all over the territory there were people like us who could indeed be contacted if there were a need or if we could be of service to a stranded neighbor. The night a message did come through of import to our family was one of the rare times that we had missed listening to the Mukluk Telegraph. However, as you will see, there were other listening ears in our village, and the message was delivered.

Love,
Grandma

Hope, Alaska
January 5, 1954

Dear Mother,

We finally got into Seward for Tommy's checkup at the doctor's office. It turned out to be more complicated than expected. You remember George Windle. He is the one who took Harold and me into Seward when Tommy was about to be born. George came up to visit Millers both for Christmas and again for New Years. I do think it is wonderful the way Alma takes those fellows in and just makes them part of her family. Her family enjoys these fellows too. Lewie had a great time being pulled on his "new" skis behind George's jeep.

Anyway, Sunday night Alma and I came back down to Seward with George in the jeep. We stayed all night with Augustine Boe. I took the baby to the doctor and did the shopping and business the next day. Then Harold came in last night after work. This way we can get quite a bit done, and he won't miss much work. We'll be leaving now in a few minutes. I'll be able to drop this letter in the mail as we leave, which is fortunate because Bill Brattain brought the mail up early again last week because of New Year's Day. But this time I had had no warning. So, it is very lucky that we came to Seward so you can still get a letter this week.

The mail worked perfectly for getting your gifts to us at just the right time. I brought your big package back from the post office Christmas Eve, but knowing your aversion to wrapping packages, I waited until Harold came home to unwrap even the big outside wrapping. I should never have doubted you, Mother. The gifts were all individually wrapped. We had so much fun digging the gifts out and putting them under the tree. Harold was quite touched that you have gone to so much work to make a nice Christmas for us.

Thank you for all those lovely gifts. Harold told me this morning that he used the trouble light you gave him on the way down here to Seward last night. He had forgotten a flashlight, an unforgivable sin around here. Then he remembered the trouble light. It was swell. I'm glad about that because it will stay in the car and we won't be caught without a light in this country of night. The gift of $10.00 we have decided to spend on some little household articles that we will need in our new house. We're using the landlord's stuff now and will need to leave it behind when we move. These articles will be a dishpan, water buckets, and teakettle. I'm very pleased with the hat. At first, I thought I couldn't wear it with my hair this length, but it looks cute, and even my critical husband approves. The cobbler's apron is a little large (thank goodness), but very welcome.

Tommy's gifts were wonderful too! I hope you have kept a pattern of the little soap gift. The wash-cloth wrapped around it in such a way as to make a cute little animal might be something that I can make when I'm outside to give as hostess gifts. Wouldn't that be nice? When you told me, you were making a stuffed toy for Tommy, I envisioned some big animal to sit on the shelf, but the little toy you sent is so cute and will be just the right size for our little boy to love. And of course, he'll look darling in his creepers, as you shall see. The little, knitted hat is a bit too long in the back, but as it stretches to fit his head, it'll come down.

Of course, it pleases me ... so masculine and warm. Not a feminine bonnet for this lad. I could tell you the same thing I told Grannie Clark about Tommy's response to the gifts. Grannie mittens were knit without thumbs; convenient for the mother of one whose thumbs are too tiny to tuck into mitten thumbs anyway. When I told Grannie that Tommy was "speechless" with delight, she thought that was so funny that I think she's told everyone in Hope at least twice. It rather embarrasses me anymore.

As you probably know, we can hardly wait until he becomes interested in toys. But he's not there yet. Harold has patiently folded his little hands over the rattle that Clarke and Jean sent us. H.D. assures me that he is encouraging him. The last time Tommy kept hold for quite a while and looked so sweet. Then the first thing we knew he bonged himself on the head. He was startled. For that matter, so were his parents.

Well, you can see that we appreciated the gifts - all of them including the little ones not mentioned but already put into use, too. And you'd be surprised how handy some of the wrappings are. Thanks very much for our nice Christmas.

We put Tommy to bed Christmas morning while we opened presents. We won't get by with that in future years, I bet. He got a cute present from Linda. She decided what she was going to give him, announced it to the family, and asked Erma Ann and Lewie to join her in giving it. They told her that they wouldn't want their names attached to such a silly gift. Linda was undeterred. Just before Christmas Harold came home carrying it -- a long gray wool sock stuffed with two cans of milk in the bottom, two oranges on top of that, and two prunes on the very top. Each item was wrapped carefully and labeled, "From Linda to Tommy."

The community Christmas meal was very nice too. We took Tommy there in royal style on the wonderful push sled that Harold gave me for Christmas. I knew that he was spending a lot of time over at Millers working on gifts for Linda. I never imagined that he was building something for me. So, the push sled was truly a surprise. It is long handled to be pushed like a baby buggy. So, we have combined two, sled and buggy, to call it the "sleggy."

At the community meal, there was ample food, and everyone enjoyed it. I mention ample food because that is not always the case. The potlucks here are so different from the ones that we grew up within the Midwest where the tables were burdened down with so much food that everyone overate, and there was still food left over to take home. Here the quantity and quality of food vary drastically with the economy. But people must have saved and planned for their contributions to this Christmas meal. It was festive and plenteous enough so that we could just relax and enjoy it.

Tommy enjoyed it by sleeping right through the entire event. We had several people comment on what a sweet baby he was. We recognized their insight graciously. We then went over to Speckings for a relaxing visit. It was a very good

Christmas.

You may put a circle around February because that's when we are coming out. I don't know just when in the month. I may come out a little ahead of Harold if he can't take time off from work to give me more than a couple of days in York. I want about two weeks there. After all, you and I have a lot of visiting to do. Harold needs to mail this letter so that we can get started back to Hope. So, I'll ring off. Thanks again for the wonderful Christmas.

Love,
Your Alaskan Daughter, Harriet

Hope, Alaska
January 8, 1954

Dear Mother,

I have just returned from a nice long walk through our Alaskan countryside. On everything, the snow is heavy and lovely. There is no man-made soot to dull its purity, and the lack of wind allows it to lie undisturbed as it falls. It is all very invigorating. I was torn between the desire to run wild through some of those lovely unmarked fields of white, just like a beautifully iced cake frequently makes my fingers itch to mar its surface and to stand guard with the resolution to shoot on the spot anyone who tries it.

I've been enjoying my sleggy more and more. You remember that is the name we gave to the half sled, half baby buggy contraption Harold built for me as a Christmas gift. Getting out and taking walks is very good for my constitution. I had been fastening the baby basket onto the sled for some weeks now. That was handy for short trips like to the store. But controlling the sled was another thing. If I tried to walk briskly, the sled would tend to glide right up on my heels and bump my ankles. The sleggy puts me in control. I can move right along, have the baby in the basket in front of me where I can see him, and have control of the speed of the sleggy.

I have been giving Tommy Pablum. He loves it. Well, he loves it now. Boy, did he ever look startled when I stuck the first bit of that cereal into his mouth. It must have tasted and felt so different from milk, I suppose. He wasn't too happy during the first feeding, but from the second time on he has been crazy about the stuff. The trouble is that he can't understand that a spoon has to be returned to the dish to be refilled. He's used to a never-ending supply of milk just ready for his swallowing. He gets stiff with apprehension between bites. Guess he thinks each time that's all he's going to get. He eats in a very neat and gentlemanlike manner if his mother pays strict attention to business and keeps both arms pinned down. But let one get loose or let her look away for a minute and whish! Pablum everywhere!

I don't think he's going to be a feeding problem. I'll be giving him vegetables and fruit before too long now. The Elliott's baby has already been eating meat, and she's younger than Tommy. But her gain hasn't been as great or as steady as Tommy. In fact, I think he has caught up in weight with her, and she started out about three pounds heavier.

Tommy is getting so he laughs and responds so delightfully. Harold was rocking him tonight, and he just laughed and laughed. He would just throw his head back and laugh the biggest crinkly-eyed toothless laugh you ever saw. Harold is so eager for him to start playing. He keeps checking to see if he is ready. He spent several minutes last night trying to get him interested in a game of peek-a-boo. But Tommy just lay there wisely and patiently watching his father's antics. I'm getting so eager for you to see him, but that brings us to some very sad news.

Last night we heard a knock on the door just as we were preparing for bed. I admitted Mrs. Blair who asked if we had heard last night's Mukluk Telegraph. We hadn't. So, she gave us the message. Ross's father died, and the funeral was planned for this weekend. If Ross wanted to come Outside for the funeral, they would hold things until he got there. His mother wanted him to telegraph his plans. Harold started over to their place with the message but met Bob DeFrance who was returning from there. He, too, had heard the Mukluk Telegraph and had already contacted Ross.

I was worried that Alma wasn't able to be with Ross last night. That isn't the sort of news one should have to receive alone. Alma is still in Seward staying with the Boes, getting some dental work done. It's true that Erma Ann and Lewie are both responsible and efficient, so the family is getting along fine when Alma went. But it just seems like being together with Ross when he gets this kind of news would have been a comfort.

Harold and Ross drove about thirty miles or so to Portage today to send a telegram to Ross' s Mother. Ross won't try to get Outside just now to be with his family but will plan to go later when the slack season hits. This brings us to the rest of the bad news that I need to tell you. This decision means that we probably won't be able to come Outside in February as I told you last week.

To prepare for both to be gone from the business, the fellows are going to work in the woods every daylight minute. This is ideal logging weather, and they are trying very hard to get a stockpile of logs laid ahead so that this summer they can run the mill full-blast. The best logging weather should last until late March. Then comes the slack season that is known as "break-up." Isn't that an interesting term? It refers to the ice going out of the ground and leaving behind deep and, in some places, bottomless mud. I rather think that will be when we plan to come Outside. I'm starting to wonder if it is safe to make any projections. Maybe I should say, "Don't look for us until you see us." But this can't be helped. Don't worry, I'm stashing the loan money away carefully, and you'll see this little grandson of yours before too long.

I was so disappointed about the further delay in our trip. I moaned to Harold that Tommy was so cute now. But I guess he'll just keep on getting cuter. It hardly seems possible. It's wonderful that babies come to you with no really endearing traits except their helplessness and their miniature perfection. Thus, each new step in the development of their personalities is surely a thrill.

Our hens have been coming right along. They about outdid themselves one day when the twenty-one of them produced twenty eggs. That scared them to the point that they have cut their production down to eighteen a day for a while now. We are going to have to get out and sell eggs. We have a steady market now for seven-dozen eggs a week. Boy am I ever shopping in the catalog with all that money I'm going to have. (Don't count your chickens?).

One of the most exciting things about our egg business is that it has enabled us to obtain a washing machine. We bought it from the Elliott's for ten-dozen eggs, which we will deliver to them at the rate of two-dozen a week. It doesn't have an engine, but we have one that can be used. Harold has been working on it. If it works, I'll be very happy. I realize that it will be noisy and venting the fumes outside is a nuisance, but what luxury. I suppose it will be some time before we'll be able to use it. Right now, I don't know if I can clear enough space to set it up in this house anyway with us living in just one room during the winter. Even when it gets working, I'll likely continue to do most of the baby's washing by hand. Hauling water to fill the machine and rinsing tubs is really a big job. We'll probably do a big washing only once a week, which isn't often enough for Tommy's things. Besides, I've got his washing down to such a smooth pattern that it doesn't take me long. I don't mind at all.

I just asked Harold if there was anything, he thought I should mention to you. He went through what he considered a long list of things, but I'd already written them all. So, he said that I'd said everything and had better stop. If nothing else I'm a dutiful wife.

Love,
Your Alaskan Daughter, Harriet

Hope, Alaska
January 16, 1954

Dear Clarke,

It's always a bit of a game with me when I begin a letter as to what date I should put in the heading. You see, no matter what day during the week I choose to write the letter, it still does not depart from Hope until Saturday. Therefore, I frequently use the departure date so that there will not be such a lapse between the day of writing and the day the letter is received. I believe this improves morale and reduces people's perception of Alaska's remoteness. Sometimes, of course, that leads to confusion. I might mention that church is tonight if I happen to write a letter on Friday and get myself all bothered because I addressed the letter for the next day. I was sorely tempted to head this letter with the date of your birth, the eleventh of January, but I shan't allow myself that little deceit. No, it really is after your birthday when I am writing. It does console me slightly that even if I had written this on your birthday, you would have gotten it no sooner than you will now. The point of all this verbiage is to wish you a happy birthday and so I will. Happy Birthday!

Just so you don't get the impression that we are completely beyond the reach of the modern world, let me tell you about Tuesday night. That was our night to be favored by invitation to the Mitchells' home for a television evening. They have had a television set since Christmas and have been busily seeing to it that everyone gets a chance to view it. It does seem funny to me that we should have a television set in Hope when you can count the modern bathrooms on the one hand. It would take fewer fingers to count those who have electrical generators. But now, the television has now arrived in Hope. That puts us in the same class as other great cities. It is ironic that Seward, conceited, self-satisfied Seward, can't get television. Don't think for a minute that it doesn't gall folks in Seward to realize that we Hope dwellers can view this marvel when they can't. When pressed about the issue they admit condescendingly that it is nice for us out in the sticks to be able to get television, because it gives us something to do on long winter evenings.

Of course, we have only one set in town. No one else can afford it. Mrs. Mitchell is the postmistress here, and Mr. Mitchell works for the Territory on roads. So, they are comfortably fixed-wealthy by our standards. Their generous sharing, however, spreads the benefit to the entire community. So, we all hold our heads up as participants in this metropolitan marvel.

Television reception here is possible because we are right across Turnagain Arm from Anchorage. Anchorage has recently acquired two television-broadcasting centers and enough television sets, judging from the radio announcements, to supply every individual in town and have some left over. But Seward is separated from Anchorage by mountains, so they don't receive the benefit of this new invention.

Aside from our very pleasant foray into the realm of entertainment technology, we have been living a life full of attention to bare essentials. It has been a real education. Here, one's chief concern is to see that the water buckets are filled, the wood box stuffed and that some cans of food sit on the shelf. So many problems that baffle the society in which we've lived before are just nonexistent to us right now. Hope is a town where there is virtually no way to make a living. Roadwork provides for one family. A couple of families make a living by fishing away from here in the summer. Doc runs the store and supplies everyone with almost unlimited credit. Then he scurries around getting orders from the railroad for hand-hewn ties so that people will have a way of paying him back. There are a couple of families living on pensions. There are a couple of families living off savings and small real estate investment. Then there are a couple of families living off the promise of a small sawmill.

Actually, as I see it, we are the only folks who have a real promising means of making a living. But so far it has been most promising. Therefore we, too, know what it is to run up a bill at Doc's store for groceries. We know what it is to be completely without a cent in the house. And it has been an experience that I wouldn't trade for the world.

I'm not heroic, and if things were truly as they seemed, I'd be discouraged to the point of quitting. But, take our millwork, for example. We have enough work done and on the books for over twelve hundred dollars. That is due any time, and we expect it in about the next mail. We could live plush at three hundred dollars a month for the two families. So, you see what a big sum like that could do. Then we have orders for about seventeen hundred dollars' worth of work, which will be done before spring. Besides this, we have bought about two thousand dollars' worth of equipment mostly by barter, it's true, but worth that nevertheless. So, it's a matter of living from season to season as farmers do rather than from pay check to pay check as has been our custom. Spring is not far off. We're going to be able to sell finished lumber this year. The market is increasing. Our equipment is infinitely better. This should be a good year.

I don't know if I ever told you about Harold's brother, Willard, who was up here last summer. He wrote to us and asked if he could be a partner in the operations too. This was really a tribute to the potential of the mill as far as I was concerned. He'll be a real asset. He's a skilled mechanic. In fact, he is the head mechanic in the night shift at the giant Leslie Salt Company in Newark, California. His partnership obviously improves the outlook for our venture.

Harold and Ross are two men cut to different patterns. Ross is the conservative one feeling his way cautiously. Harold believes that Ross actually wastes time and money in trying to be too saving. Harold is the impatient dreamer. He wants to live five lives in the one short lifetime allotted him. He must get things done and move on. He is so eager to go into this logging and milling operation on a big scale while the opportunity is so ripe. Selfishly, we need this to facilitate our next stage of law school preparation.

Now with Willard coming into the partnership, there'll be another who knows how things can operate on a big scale to swing the balance a little that way. I'm sure that in many ways he is more practical than Harold, so it should be healthy all the way around. One thing for sure with Willard coming in, the mill will be whisked to maximum production as fast as possible. So, in spite of our presently constricted budget, we believe our outlook is very bright.

The presently constricted budget has been a determining factor in several areas of our lives. My one major disappointment this year is that I showed the lack of wisdom twice in setting a date for our trip out to visit Mother and the rest of you only to have to withdraw the commitment both times. I was braver just before Tommy's birth than I was after it. I didn't feel it too wise to attempt the trip for Christmas. We didn't have the money. Harold and I then decided that the best time would be in February and that we had best commit ourselves so that we'd be sure to do it. Then came the blow of the death of Ross' s father and another shift in plans. Now I hesitate to set a date. It would be much wiser financially for us not to come out at all this winter. We have rarely let anything like prudence guide us so why should we now? We will be coming Outside. But I'm not sure just when.

In the meantime, we will be content with the lifeline of communication provided by the U.S. mail service. On that subject, I want you to know that we received our gifts from you the day before New Year's. Although it was a week later than you perhaps intended, it had the effect of making New Year's more of a holiday. Harold and I were delighted with the placemats and especially since they happened to be that fortunate color of green. We plan to decorate the interior of our new house with two shades of green, some touches of wine color and a neutral color for the base tone. So, your choice fits in beautifully. They will also fit in well with our informal way of life.

You scored a hit, literally, with the rattle. Let me explain. We unwrapped it for Tommy. Then Harold placed the rattle in his hand, folded his fingers over it and stood by to watch the reaction. For a long time, there was none except that of his parents who thought he looked so cute with it in his hand. Then he raised up his hand and bonged himself on the head. His finer senses, like those displayed in playing with a rattle, have yet to be cultivated. I guess we'll be waiting a bit longer before we can all fully appreciate its benefits, but I'll thank you for it now anyway.

I can assure you that the other gift is timely and has been used almost constantly since its arrival. I've never before seen lap pads like these. But I am here to recommend them to anyone who'll listen. Holding the baby is much nicer with them. Since they came, we've ignored the former quilted ones. These are so much more sanitary, lighter and easier to care for. I truly mean it. Just ask Harold. He's the final authority around here. In his longwinded way of saying this, he said - and I quote - "These are really O.K."

I hear of you folks once in a while from Mother. We're eager to hear more details about your trip back East and to bore you with the details of our adventures. So, we'll really have to have a good gabfest or two when we finally do get Outside.

Loved by your sister,
Harriet

Hope, Alaska
January 16, 1954

Dear Mother,

Our house is surely going slowly. Harold just hasn't had any time to work on it. When he does get a day off, it's a short day, and he spends half of it shoveling snow in and around the roofless building so that he can begin to work. Now he has decided to work only forty hours at the mill and to get it in five days if possible. This will give him more solid time to work upon the hill building our new house. Poor Harold! How he chafes to get at it. You can easily imagine. You know him.

In spite of the slow progress, I've begun to arrange my stuff for moving up to the new house. To others, it may seem that there isn't much up there to indicate that I have to hurry, but I have great faith. Besides, starting early gives me the option to work at my project a little bit at a time. Furthermore, I want to do it right. My plan is this. Since we'll be fixing up the inside of the house while we are living there, we need to minimize clutter. Therefore, I'm sorting carefully to pack away what we won't need for our simple existence and keep out only what is necessary. The boxes of stuff-to-store we'll put in our new attic out of the way of everyday life and that crucial finishing work.

Harold and Ross are in Portage today hoping to get the last pieces of the planer out. I'll surely be glad when they get it here on our own soil because the whole affair seems so dragged out. In the first place, they had a hard time finding the owner of the planer and making arrangements to buy it. Then when they first went to move it, they decided to wait for the ground to completely freeze because of all that spongy muskeg around the planer's present location. That way they could drive right down to it with the truck to take it out.

This old planer was found at an abandoned mill that was located up a small stream opening onto Turnagain Arm. At the time the mill was built it could be reached at high tide by boats for hauling away the lumber. Then geography changed with the little bay being silted in which precipitated the arrival of our ubiquitous muskeg. Ironically when they put in the new road to Anchorage, it went over that stream about a hundred yards from the old mill site. The fellows reasoned that with a deep freeze, they could drive from the highway right over the muskeg to the site. Unfortunately, that kind of freeze didn't come as soon as we'd hoped and now they are afraid that the snow will be too deep if they wait much longer.

The solution to this dilemma is to take the planer apart at the site and pack the sections out by sledding them down the frozen stream to where the truck is parked just off the highway. There they use a "come-along," a strange name for a little winch, to get the parts onto the truck the two biggest pieces were the side plates, which Ross estimated to weigh almost a thousand pounds apiece. With any luck, today should mark the end of this important but torturous project.

Who said there wasn't a market for eggs here in Hope? We keep finding people who are interested in eggs. Mr. Rucker asked Harold the other day if he could have a couple of dozens a week. Harold said that likely we wouldn't have the eggs, but that Alma would. Alma didn't want to have to deliver up on the hill so guess what? We bought nine hens from her. Guess we'll go into this in a big way. No, actually we think we could sell around 10 dozen a week. That's no fortune, but it is a nice supply of spending money - especially when I get to do the spending. Ha!

I had an interesting experience this afternoon, especially considering that it is well into deep winter in Alaska. There was a salesman for the Encyclopedia Britannica. Can you imagine trying to sell Encyclopedias in Hope at this time of year? It really stretches my imagination. This time of the year, people are just trying to meet grocery bills and keep warm, let alone thinking of anything to improve their culture and intellect. If it sounds desperate, then you are in the perfect frame of mind to hear this story.

When I answered the knock at the door, the salesman explained that he wanted to show me his wares. I warned him that I wouldn't buy, but he started in any way. I was intrigued by his technique. One of the study courses that came with the set was on baby care and motherhood. There I sat with my little baby in my arms, and he didn't once mention this course. I just happened to notice it on the folder lying in front of me. I thought that he was missing a good bet. After all, he should know that would be one of my chief interests right now.

He did give a good case for buying the books and you know I would be a sucker for something like that when I could stand pat against a lot of more frivolous things. I do want my family to have access to the world of knowledge through books. Anyway, in spite of missing the opportunity of pointing out the childcare course, he built up a marvelous case proving beyond the shadow of a doubt that these books would be valuable. Then he showed me how cheaply I could buy them on the installment plan. Since we had used that particular encyclopedia in my classroom in Mullinville, I am familiar with it. Thinking of my egg money, I was starting to be tempted.

However, just at that moment, his boss barged in. I guess my salesman was just starting his training and needed a supervisor along. Anyway, this supervisor came breezing into the house and plunked himself down on my laundry hamper without waiting for me to ask him to be seated. Then of all things, he reached into his pocket and pulled out a candy bar on which he proceeded to munch noisily.

Now, Mother, you have raised me to be open minded and understanding about other peoples' actions. But his rude, uncouth behavior offended me, especially when he proceeded to treat me like an uneducated person. Here he was, this know-it-all supervisor, trying to sell me a beautiful set of books designed to appeal to my intelligence, all the while insulting my intelligence. He even tried to shame me, saying that if I didn't buy, I would be neglecting the intellectual rearing of my weeks old baby by depriving him of the potential in their books.

The salesmen concluded their interview with the inevitable question, which is supposed to crumble all my resistance. " Is it just money that keeps you from taking advantage of this opportunity?" I looked them right in the eye and answered, "Yes, it's just money. I'd be very tickled to accept them as a gift, but the money I don't have. Don't you consider that a good enough reason?"

Then they made some comment about that "large, fancy car" that we had sitting out in front of our house. Implying, I suppose, that anyone with a car like that could surely afford the measly eight hundred dollars required for a set of encyclopedias with five correspondence courses and six magazines thrown in free. I don't know what got into me but thinking of all the problems that our car possessed, I suggested that perhaps they would be interested in accepting the car in exchange for the set of encyclopedias. Their startled response didn't include an affirmative answer. Soon they were walking meekly out the door and climbing into their "miserable" brand new 1954 Lincoln.

Mother, when is the college spring vacation? Maybe we can visit you then if you don't have other plans. Now mind, I'm not saying I'll come for your spring vacation, Mother. I am just wondering when it is. Boy, I'm not going to commit myself anymore. Except for this one thing. I'm coming out and bringing this little character with me. You'll get to see your crazy Alaskans yet. Take care of yourself. Tommy sends his love.

Love,
Your Alaskan Daughter, Harriet

P.S. I found a candy bar wrapper on my table a minute ago. To quote a trite phrase: "The nerve of some people!!"

Hope, Alaska
January 22, 1954

Dear Mother,

I was actually dreading your letter last week. I was worried about your reaction to our having to postpone our trip out to see you yet again. But you are a wonder and are so gracious in your acceptance of our variable plans. How I regret having told you that we would be out in February. Then the very next week we have to turn around and call it all off. Harold was so remorseful that he said I could go ahead and go out in February anyway, but I'm betting that if I did, he wouldn't get out at all. That wouldn't do. So, you seem to be handling this even better than we are. I know you are disappointed too. Maybe after the delays and disappointments, we'll all enjoy it just that much more.

Now for the egg report - I told Harold the other day, "We might as well be buying eggs or keeping just one or two hens, the way we are rationing ourselves." You see, the inevitable cold snap has set in, and our egg production is down slightly. Since we think it is only

temporary, we want to hang on to our customers. The logical place to cut down is in our own consumption. I hope that things warm up soon because I'd like to get back to our previous consumption levels since that is the primary reason, we took on chickens in the first place.

This morning Tommy was gurgling and talking to himself in his basket. "Listen," Harold said.

"Oh! Phooey. He didn't say 'Daddy'" I retorted.

"Well, if it didn't sound like that to you, what made you mention it? I didn't." Harold replied with a clever smile spreading across his smug face. Caught in his trap, I was.

I suppose that he is just trying to make up for his terrible failure to teach Tommy to play peek-a-boo. I think I told you about that a couple of weeks ago. I'll say this for Harold. He hasn't given up. It's the old coaching instinct, I suppose. He tries for a few minutes each morning and a few minutes each evening. Tommy just stares solemnly back at his crazy father. Undaunted by disappointments with peek-a-boo, Harold has worked out a new game that has instantly become Tommy's favorite. It is called "kick-o." That is when Harold holds him up in his arms so that Tommy's feet are against Harold's stomach. Then if Tommy pushes a little with his feet, Harold sails him right up in the air. Harold then waits and waits until Tommy pushes again. Up he goes. They both laugh happily. Probably will give the infant a false impression of how strong his legs are. Oh well!

You'll probably be horribly shocked by our parenting system when we come to visit you. I feed Tommy when he's hungry; pick him up when he screams, and go under the assumption that when he cries, something is wrong. We may raise a very spoiled child, but to date, he's been very sweet and well behaved. Our theory is that if we care for his needs when he does cry, he'll not come to associating crying with anything other than getting his needs met. Complicated? Well, we'll see.

Again, we have some real winter weather. It was thirty-two below one morning. The last two days I've worn and enjoyed long underwear. We could keep the house warm enough to get along without it, but it's just easier this way. This little house really wasn't meant to be a winter dwelling. The walls even frost over on the coldest days and steam and drip on most of the others, but we can keep plenty warm by staying in the kitchen area with the cook stove fired up.

We keep Tommy's basket out in the kitchen and have no trouble keeping him comfortable. Next year we'll be in a well-insulated house that is easier to heat. I'm glad that it will be so because I can imagine how hard it would be to keep a little toddler in one spot. Right now, I have the baby basket on the oven door. In the open position, the door makes a nice warm spot for the basket on these cold days. I keep a thermometer in his basket, so I am sure of having the right temperature. Dr. Hall told us that babies don't need really warm temperatures. In the upper sixties would be fine, he said. While Tommy is cozy in his basket, I wear layers of clothing, and I also am cozy.

Really, we haven't minded the cold spell all that much. With the excellent skidding conditions, the fellows have gotten a lot of work done, and our stockpile of logs for next summer is growing nicely. It hasn't gotten cold enough yet to keep them in. I don't know that it ever will. There are those around town who think that Ross and Harold are absolutely insane to keep going to work each day in this weather. It is an absurdly difficult process for them to eke out any work at all on these short cold days.

Harold goes over in the early morning dark so that they can start the routine for getting the truck running. They start by igniting a pan of gas under the engine. This sounds dangerous, but just the fumes in the low walls of the pan burn. Thus, a shallow pool of gas lasts for some time. This warms the grease and bearings throughout the engine. The next step is to heat the radiator fluid, which was drained from the engine the night before until it reaches a warm liquid state. Then it is poured back into the radiator. When the engine first starts running, Ross plays a torch across the front of the radiator so that the flame is sucked through the radiator core. When they get the truck out to the woods, the whole engine area has to be covered with heavy blanketing and the truck is started at intervals during the day to keep the engine from seizing up.

Once in the woods, the men now need to get the dozer started. Its garage is a trench dug deep in the bank of a hill. A tarp piled high with fine brush covers the dozer. If it snowed during the night, there would have been sufficient insulation to make getting the diesel engine started an easy process. But with extremely low temperatures, if there is not adequate snow to provide insulation, getting the Cat started can be a time-consuming process. It has a little gas-powered starting engine that always kicks right off. This starting engine then engages the main engine to warm it up and get it going. One time this process took so long that Ross used all of the gas in the starting engine's tank and about half of the next tank-full before the main engine started. Harold helps get the dozer uncovered and then while Ross gets it going, he gets started sawing trees. Wrestling that big chainsaw around is a strenuous activity, which helps keep him warm. In fact, he has to shed some layers of clothing as he works but hastily puts them back on when the heavy work stops.

At the end of the day, when they shut down in the woods, much of the process I just described has to be reversed in preparation for the next morning including draining the truck radiator and engine block. It is a good day when they get in four or more hours of actual logging.

I, of course, stay inside next to a nice warm stove all day long. But I'm not without some tribulation of my own. I guess I've been having my hands in water too much. They are surely getting sore. I've been cutting down on my "wet" work as much as possible, but that always means more work for Harold. Last summer Erma Ann got herself some rubber gloves. She was kidded about them a great deal, but she faithfully wore them to protect her fingernails. Well, it looks like I'm going to have to do the same thing, although not for beauty reasons, just to keep my hands from hurting.

Last Sunday they had a real skating party on the flat. I guess Mrs. Mitchell and even Doc were there. Doc was showing them all how it was done in the "old country." I would like to have seen it. Really, he is an amazing person. He shuffles around the store at his own deliberate pace almost as if his feet hurt. Then at the community dances when Alma cranks up one of her lively polkas on the accordion, he suddenly becomes light on his feet and really quite graceful. Harold says that the same was true when he was skimming along with the kids at the skate Sunday.

It sounds like Tommy is dropping off to sleep, so I'll turn him over and tuck him in, then creep into bed myself. Goodnight!

Love,
Your Alaskan Daughter, Harriet

Hope, Alaska
January 29, 1954

Dear Roomies

Nothing makes me so conscious of the rapid passing of time as does the lamp lighting hour. After that long summer of almost perpetual daylight, the need for a lamp at bedtime was strange. Gradually, insidiously, the darkness moved in. Before long we were using a lamp for supper preparations, then late afternoon work, then finally I was likely to wake up from my early afternoon nap to find myself in darkness. Thus, as I needed the lamp earlier and earlier, I was aware that winter was setting in. But all of a sudden that is over. Winter has been on the way out for exactly a month now. Well, not winter but darkness. Already I have noticed a dramatic difference. I didn't light the lamp today until four o'clock, and a month ago I was doing it as early as 2:30. I was planning to be stoic and noble about the long winters and short days, but if this is any sample, and I suppose it is, the situation isn't all that bad.

The middle of the night is dark, dark here. For a while, we left a lamp lighted so that tending the baby at night would be easier. But the Aladdin lamp would frequently "run up." That means that the flame would blaze up from the wick and smoke up the glass chimney globe. When it does this, the odor is quite unpleasant. So now I crawl sleepily out of bed as I grope around for the flashlight so that I can locate the matches, light the lamp, and stagger to Tommy's side while listening to him bawling the whole time lustily. When I get there, I often gaze down at his face with truly mixed feelings, for now, he's smiling happily. Maybe he is smiling impishly at my awkwardness in getting to his side. But he commands, and I obey.

I just reread the above paragraph and need to add something. In the middle of the winter nights it is dark, dark inside the house, but when you look out the window, you can clearly discern buildings, the paths, and the car by the gate. Walking outdoors at night without a light is often done. I suppose the moon on the snow has something to do with it. There is really quite an enchantment to the long winter nights in Alaska.

In spite of the nocturnal beauty, I'm glad to be finally noticing the longer days. It sure seemed to take a while for the change to become apparent. Perhaps, I don't have the true Alaskan instinct like Mrs. De France, for instance. She is a very interesting woman who lives nearby with a rather odd family. She told me the other day that she notices the change in daylight the very first day. Truly, I do find some of her statements astounding. They make me question my own perceptions. I was in her home one day when she was taking loaves of bread out of the oven. She lifted each one to her ears and listened for a few seconds. Then she put one on the counter and another back into the oven. She explained to me that she could tell when the bread was done by listening to it.

As far as disciplining her family and her house-keeping habits, I think it would be very charitable to say that she was relaxed. She walks around her house barefoot even in winter. But, at the same time, in conversations with her, I have been astounded at how well read she is. She quotes Shakespeare and Plato as a matter of course. Conversations with her are stimulating -- when we aren't discussing daylight and bread testing.

Well, we are in the poultry business in a big way. Harold had asked Alma, my sister-in-law, to order us a bunch of little chicks to be here when we arrived. I have told you about the dressed chickens we sold last summer. The main reason for the chickens, however, was for their egg production. Harold declared that the boat-delivered eggs, which are standard fare around here, just don't appeal to him. He mentions how they flatten out all over the plate when cooked. Anyway, by fall we had culled our pullets down to just over twenty. We hadn't realized how productive those birds could be.

Another thing we hadn't realized was how many people around here would really like to have fresh eggs if someone else saw to it that they were produced. Suddenly I had a thriving business. Most people would come by the house to buy the eggs or Harold might take them around after work. But occasionally I had delivered eggs on nice mornings when the few hours of daylight produced cheerful sunshine.

It was just such a delivery, last December, that got Tommy and me into an incident that still scares and embarrasses me. It surprises me that I'm telling you about this. I certainly didn't want Harold to tell anyone around here. And I have no intention of ever mentioning it in a letter to either mother. But evidently, I need to tell someone, so I'll go on.

I had dressed Tommy warmly and put on his little cap and his thumbless mittens. I'd tucked him into the baby basket and surrounded him with blankets. I then fastened the baby basket securely to the sled to take off for my egg delivery. One stop was the Carters, who live up on the hill near the home site where we are building. We went up the hill to Carter's place. Marge paid me for the eggs and invited me in. But unbundling Tommy was too much work, so she and I just talked briefly at her door, and I headed back home.

Going up the hill with the sled behind me had been an easy task. But going down the hill was another matter. I was less secure of my footing, and the sled kept running up against my legs. Progress was very slow. By the time Tommy and I had reached the gentler slope, I was impatient with the fact that this whole project was using up so much of my good morning. I had a bright idea. I would let the sled go ahead of me. I held onto the rope and eased the sled down the road in front. Soon, however, its tugging was making my footing on the slick and snow-covered road even less sure. So, I decided to let the sled go down on its own. I could move down briskly to catch up with it when it reached the bottom.

I hadn't counted on how fast that little vehicle with its precious cargo would accelerate. Faster and faster it went down the hill. I watched it with horror. As the sled reached the bottom, the road took a turn, which caused the top-heavy sled to flop over and spill Tommy out into the snow. I can't describe the emotions of those moments as I hurried down that slope to where Tommy was lying, flailing his arms and crying angrily. He was still angry when I picked him up. I think he was still angry with his careless mother when we finally got back to our little house where I crawled under the bed covers and held my little son close.

Tommy and I no longer worry about a repeat of that unfortunate incident since the invention of the "sleggy." This is a combination of a sled and buggy that Harold designed and built for me as a Christmas present. It is a complete delight because I have the baby in front of me when I go on walks, I have complete control of the speed of the vehicle, and it serves to actually steady my footing.

This has been a year of adventures in several directions. Many delightful new experiences have enriched our months here. Having Tommy, as you know, has changed our perspective on many things. There have been some disappointments also. Many aspects of the milling project have not gone according to our optimistic plans. But in other ways, like the purchase of equipment, we are way ahead of projections.

We have been learning a great deal about the ancient and time-honored system of barter. Of course, by far the biggest deal was the planer for the mill that I told you about. But this summer we also acquired a welder in exchange for lumber. At the time we had lumber but no cash. Harold received an excellent set of traps in exchange for some hauling. And I am faith-fully paying for my used washing machine at the rate of two-dozen eggs a week. That machine only represents a promise for the future. Right now, we are living in one little room of our house - with the bed, the huge rocking chair, Tommy's stuff and everything else we need for daily existence. There is just no room to get a gas-powered washing machine in here as well. But we are counting on the washing machine to be a wonderful addition to our life when we get into our new home up on the hill. In the meantime, Harold does much of the work in getting Tommy's stuff clean. The bigger items we take over to Alma's and borrow her machine and her space to use it in.

Another reason for relegating the luxury of a washing machine to the future is the water situation. Harold gets our water from a nearby old-fashioned hand-dug well with protective sides around the top to keep people or animals from falling in. With Resurrection Creek so close, the water table is near the surface so that it is only a few feet down to fresh water. From the top of the protective enclosure to the water is only 8-10 feet down. Last summer he drew the water by lowering a bucket on a hand-held rope and flicking the bucket so that it would fill and then be brought back up with the rope. He soon got quite skilled at the flicking technique. Bringing in the buckets of water required to fulfill a normal day's needs could be done rather quickly.

With the onset of winter, the water-getting process has continued to present new challenges. At first, there was only a skim of ice was over the water. Dropping the rope-attached bucket with a thump was enough to break it. As the ice got thicker, a large stone did the trick. Harold has begun to worry that he might be filling up the well with these large stones. He's starting to wonder if he will have a stone-removing project next summer.

Recently the extreme cold has frozen the surface of the water well so thick that he has had to climb down into the well and chop a hole large enough that the normal procedure for drawing the water can be accomplished. So, believe me, I have respect for water. I have learned all sorts of techniques to make that water serve me multiple times. For example, water used to rinse dishes is fine for the baby's bath. Then that bath water works well for house cleaning or to be put in the diaper pail to soak diapers. Right now, we are careful to keep the tea-kettle filled with hot water in case that is needed for an exit out our front door since it has a tendency to freeze shut.

You asked about our trip Outside. I was sorry that we had to put it off and not go out at Christmas time, but obstacles just kept coming up. And I confess that I was less courageous about traveling with Tommy after he came than I was in planning the whole thing ahead of time. It now seems wise to make that trip Outside during the very worst weather for logging. In other words, the spring thaw. So that long-awaited trip is most likely in late March or during April.

Here is a story that may interest you. Yesterday I was delivering eggs to some of our customers. One of them, a middle-aged bachelor, speaks English with a heavy Scandinavian accent. So, I quite often nod and answer and then stop to figure out what he said. But this time I was floored. I had handed him his eggs, and he had handed me the money. Then, bless his heart, he said, "Would you like to see my toilet? " I was sure that this was what he said. He smiled in a kind, fatherly way and the first thing I knew I was walking into his house. So, I walked through his very neatly kept front room and kitchen, and sure enough, there was the beginning of his bathroom. He has been constructing it during his spare time and is very proud of it. Well, he might be, too, for there are only about four of that kind of "inside plumbing" in Hope. He didn't have it completed by any means, but the beginnings were nice, and he'll have a "picture perfect" bathroom when he gets through. He's an interesting fellow, Pete Thornsen.

Harold has helped organize a local youth fellowship. The time that our pastor can allot to Hope doesn't allow for any work with the young people. So, while a few faithful attend church on Friday night, Harold has started having the Young People's meeting on Sunday night. Since he started, he has had wonderful attendance. What an ideal set-up to be working with kids in a community that has such limited activities. He nearly always has 100% of the potential. Even so, he is not dealing with a crowd. I'm glad to see it working out so well because people here, as so many places, have the feeling that young people are interested only in playing during church youth activities. This group has recreation, to be sure, but Harold has been handing them out some pretty stiff courses of applied religion, and they are eating it up. Guess some of them have never been challenged that way before; they find it fascinating. At least I often overhear fragments of discussion during the week that are direct carry-overs from the last week's topic. Most of these kids don't have the background and the adult support that they need for their spiritual lives. I have never before lived in a place that existed so independently of the church.

We also have some interesting social life in spite of our remote location. Once every two weeks, the village throws a big shindig starting with a potluck supper. Don't think of the big church dinner spreads in your part of the country. These potlucks are often a little on the skimpy side because they aptly reflect the seasons and the current financial status of the individuals in the village. Sometimes the pickings are so lean that I have to be sure to take a hearty "main dish" so that poor Harold won't have to subsist on beans. Other times the table is really laden with wild game dishes prepared with interesting variety. Following the supper, the town hall is turned into a theater with Doc's generator-powered projector spilling out a movie.

At the end of the affair comes the dancing. This is enjoyed by all ages and fueled by Alma's energy on her accordion. She is really enthusiastic, and her music is much loved by young and old alike. The dances are particularly lively when there are some young soldier lads here from Anchorage. But the stepping lively is certainly not limited to the young. I may have mentioned in the letter about Doc how much he enjoys dancing the polka. Alma sets up the rhythm to the evening with her music. She also sets the tone. If there is excessive drinking or unseemly behavior, she simply stops playing. The entire Hope community is well aware and respectful of this musical caveat.

I am continuing to enjoy these round-robin letters so much as they make their way around to those of us with so many memories in common. Sometimes it seems to fly with great speed around its circuit and other times it only plods. Nevertheless, it is a very special day when it arrives with its messages from each of you. Harold and I enjoy reading about the activities in each of your homes and the adventures that your little ones get into. So, until the moment when I can enjoy sitting down and visiting about our life here in Alaska, "Viva the Round Robin!"

Love,
Harriet

CHAPTER 9

February 1954: The Pinch of Winter

*D*ear Karen,
 Your questions about the letters in January have led me down some really interesting paths as I tried to discover information that will help me give you a better answer. I feel like there is a little cloud of irony over my head as I cast around the Internet to find out little details about life in 1954. Certainly, we never imagined an information resource like the World Wide Web when we sat out that winter in the backwoods of Alaska. Nevertheless, it has been helpful to me in fleshing out answers to the questions you pose. What are lap pads? What is a cobbler's apron? And what is Pablum?

First are the lap pads. Long before the "absolutely leak-proof disposable diapers" that I see advertised on TV, we used non-leak-proof diapers. By the time I was launched into motherhood we did have the plastic panty that went over the absorbent cloth diaper. But still, there were occasional leaks. Therefore, we frequently used lap pads when holding a baby or when changing diapers. Those lap pads were usually quilted for absorbency. The lap pads that Clarke and Jean sent were lightweight rubber pads with some sort of fabric fused onto them. They worked very well and were much appreciated.

Recently I received a mail-order catalog that had cobbler smocks for sale. So, the concept still exists. I checked the Internet. Yes, there are many sources of information on "vintage cobbler's aprons" there as well. A cobbler's apron is a garment that covers a person's front and back much like a sleeveless shirt. I'm sure that it derived its name from the large and very handy pockets across the bottom of the front which imitated the pockets that a cobbler would have had for nails and other items needed in the construction or repair of shoes.

Your question about Pablum led me down really interesting paths. When I went on the Internet and gave my search engine the word Pablum, a myriad of sites flashed back at me. I was intrigued by a site, which said that Pablum was the Word of the Day for Friday, December 19, 2003.

Pablum | PAB-luhm |, noun.

Something (as in writing or speech) that is trite, insipid, or simplistic.

Only after several examples of this trite, insipid, or simplistic writing did they write that our use of the term "Pablum" comes from Pablum, a trademark used for a bland, soft cereal for infants. Well, there you have it. As used for Tommy and in my letters, Pablum was a bland, soft cereal for infants.

However, Karen, I can't resist giving you more information about Pablum. I remember as a child on the African mission field having Pablum as one of our choices for breakfast. We all ate it, the whole family. It was our breakfast cereal. We added sugar and milk to the precooked flakes and enjoyed it.

Pablum was first marketed in 1931. Three Canadian doctors had collaborated in developing a very important food product for children. Pablum (from the Latin word pabulum, meaning food) had the necessary minerals and five of the six known vitamins that growing children need. The Mead Johnson Company in the United States agreed to sell the new product. And it sold well. For a period of twenty-five years, royalties from Pablum sales reverted to the Toronto Pediatric Foundation for research. Thus, you will note that in 1954 when we bought Pablum in Doc's general store in Hope and brought it home to our new little son, royalties were still helping to fund Canadian research.

Don't you find it interesting, Karen, to speculate how that word Pablum evolved from being a well-respected baby food to meaning something that is "dumbed" down? Even the Thesaurus entry is "Cereal, Drivel."

Well, let's move on to February 1954.

From the perspective of so many years I now realize how precarious some of our existence was; how much like early pioneers we lived. As this next batch of letters will reveal, February and early March were weeks of concentrating on pure survival. Having enough water in the buckets and having the needed firewood on hand were major concerns. In my March fifth letter, I mention Tommy's being sick and recovering nicely. But now I wonder how we would have handled it had he, or one of us experienced a medical emergency when the roads were impassable! What if that attic fire I describe in another letter had flamed out of control? As I remember it, we were warm and comfortable in the small part of the non-insulated cottage to which we had retreated in spite of the record cold temperatures in 1954. But reading those letters again reminds me that extreme cold was often a menacing presence lurking just outside the door.

The next group of letters you will be reading, tells of the most trying parts of our experience in Alaska, both physically and emotionally. Those deep winter days in Hope teetered on balance between the promise of spring, as the days lengthened, and the awareness that winter still had a very firm grip. It was hard to deal with the realization that winter's grip would continue for weeks and weeks. There would be the days of false warming trends, then the return to bitter cold. Yet, ever there was the beauty of snow scenes unsurpassed, the resilience of a community united against the elements, and the "centering" of life in our little cottage.

Love,
Grandma

Hope, Alaska
February 9, 1954

Dear Mother,

What a peaceful world this is! It's snowing great big fuzzy flakes, quietly giving the world a face-lift. Looking from my window, I can't help thinking that it looks like a big sheet of white corduroy. And to add to the sense of serenity, there is the silence that comes when Tommy drops off to sleep. He sings and coos to himself for sometimes an hour trying to win the battle against sleep; when he succumbs to it, all is quiet.

Yesterday we had one of those slick, slick days. Whenever it warms up in this country, the roads get bad. Isn't that crazy? But Harold found an old pair of creepers over by the planer. Creepers are spiked metal affairs that strap on over your boots for ice walking. The ones he found are still a little big, but he strapped them on my feet yesterday, and I walked to the store over the ice. They are wonderful. I could relax and not slip a bit. That removes all the tension from taking a walk. But because it's snowing now --big beautiful balls of white --yesterday's slick roads will disappear.

Thanks for telling us when your spring vacation was. Harold and I have reached another decision. We intend to make this one stick. He just can't leave the work for any extended length of time until the breakup. So, I'm coming outside with only your grandson to take care of me. We'll get to York sometime during the last part of the week of March 14 or the early part of the week of March 21. At any rate, Harold wants me to be there in time to settle in for your vacation so that we can really utilize it. Since the time of spring thaw is indefinite, we aren't sure when Harold will join me. It won't likely come before the first of April, so we are planning on a couple of weeks apart for sure.

I don't think I'll fly all the way. I would like to fly as far as Denver so that I can cut down on the train time, but I may have to come by train from Seattle. I'll surely let you know by telegram in plenty of time to meet me. We can't set a specific date because so much depends on weather conditions.

As to "headquarters," we plan to stay at your place. Believe me, if you could see the one little room to which we have retreated, you'd realize that your place is ample, yea verily, it is spacious. Of course, we want to spend quite a bit of time with Evelyn and Bob and with Clarke and Jean. But we just as well do it when you can be with us don't you think?

I'm glad that it's all settled about the trip. I wish Harold could be coming along; that's the only drawback. But I know he would be worrying about the work time he was missing. All I have to say is that he is certainly working hard at this mill-establishment project. If it doesn't succeed, I don't want him to have any regrets about having done anything halfway.

We are indeed beginning to feel the "pinch of winter." It has been talked about so much that I had dreaded it. I did not know what to expect, but the universal agreement about the trials of this time of year convinced me that something significant was going to happen. I've tried to analyze my observations and here's what I think it is. At the same time that weather confines people to close quarters most families are running short on the cash they saved for the winter. Everything is getting tight and strained so that a severe form of cabin fever sets in.

One important effect of this is that Doc's store has given out so much credit that some people will have to work for a month or so at cutting ties and then turn everything over to him. I guess some families have terrific store bills there. This, in turn, cuts down his capital so he can't order much stuff ahead and raises the price on the stuff he does have. So, we all feel it from that angle. Also, fewer boats are coming in now, and some things are hard to get.

Even though we are probably in better shape than most, we haven't completely escaped the trials of the season. We are out of the moose meat and have to resort to mostly chickens, canned meat and expensive hamburger bought when the fellows make that rare trip to town or when Bill Brattain, the mailman, brings a special order for us. Doc's regular shipment hadn't come in until this week. So, for the last week or so we've been rationed on several necessities. It gives you a kind of frantic feeling knowing that there are some things that you can't get. But Doc has been wonderful to us. Let me give you a couple of examples.

Consider flashlight batteries, which are so vital to our existence. There were none in Seward and none in Moose Pass. I must have a flashlight for getting up with the baby at night. Well, Doc saved some for me even after he was telling others that he was out. Of course, lots of families have six or seven flashlights they use, and the children use light lavishly. You can bet we are hoarding ours carefully during the night. We use the flashlight just until we can light a lamp. But I did appreciate his consideration, and I'd like to think that no one else really suffered.

Then there was a shortage of canned milk. Millers, for example, normally use cases of it, but found themselves cut down to a few cans now and then. Harold suddenly found himself drinking tea instead of hot chocolate for lunch. Finally came the day when Harold returned home with the rumor that Doc was completely out of milk. Harold was considering the possibility of needing to make that seventy-five-mile trip to Seward where canned milk could still be purchased. While he watched the baby, I rushed down to the store and told Doc what I had heard. He stood there for a very long minute in silence with his hands on his hips looking at me. Then he said in his deep, richly accented voice. "I saff some for da babee. What you tink?" He glared at me in righteous indignation for even suspecting that he wasn't taking care of his village people. My relief was so great that his grumpy response brought only a smile of happiness and a gushing of grateful thanks from me as I accepted those cans that he had stashed away for Tommy. And actually, Mother, I don't want you to start worrying about such events in the life of your pioneer daughter. Harold could have made that trip to Seward. But it does make an interesting story, doesn't it?

Since Ross was gone yesterday, Harold took that day off and worked on our house on the hill. I guess he's really coming along on it. He's putting up the sheathing around the outside now. That is the kind of work that really shows and goes fast. We may be in there by the end of February. I hope so because I'd hate to have to pay another month's rent.

Harold's walk up to the site from our place usually takes ten or fifteen minutes. Even when the road is slick from thawing and freezing his calk logging boots give a grip, which allows him to move right along. If it has snowed, he has to shovel everything off. Then it takes quite a while before he can get started on the actual building. The days are short but rapidly getting longer. Now I'll tell you something interesting about how he comes down the hill at the end of the day. He rides on a sled. That's right. My little-boy husband rides a sled home. In the morning he drags the sled up and sometimes uses it to haul things he may need for that day's work. Coming home, he gets on the sled and goes whooping down the hill and over the low, single lane, side-less wooden bridge that spans the creek and almost into our front yard. This sets up a scary story that happened a few days ago. My breath catches when I think of it.

The water in Resurrection Creek has been continually freezing, but the stream keeps running. The ice has built up so that it fills the creek bed with ice several feet thick. The water is racing down an open channel in the ice, but just before it gets to the bridge, it disappears into a tunnel through the thick ice.

He has always assured me that he would ditch the sled mighty fast if he saw that he was going too fast to make that sharp turn onto the bridge over Resurrection Creek. Well, yesterday he made it onto the bridge safely enough, but his angle was wrong. He went flying off the bridge and landed on the ice. He rolled off and headed for the bank as fast as he could, while the sled skidded on. It went much farther and stopped back-ward with the rear end of the sled a few inches over the open water that was cascading into the tunnel. Harold crawled out and retrieved the sled. Although he assured me that he was in no personal danger and that his only concern was losing the sled, Harold did admit that the thought of being sucked into the tunnel was indeed a "chill thrill." Harold handles himself well, and I suppose he could have rescued himself if he had landed in the water. But you can't always account for the numbing shock of the sudden cold or being struck on the head or something. Anyway, he came home and began second-guessing how he should have handled the sled to prevent the episode.

No sooner than we get past Harold's little scrape with dan-ger and our community is facing a real concern about Gran-nie Clark. She had another heart attack. She hasn't been at all well. In fact, they took her to Seward to the hospital yester-day or the day before. When she gets back, if she is able, I'm going to interview her about her life. I think she could tell me some very interesting things about early days in Hope. I kind of hate to ask her, because I might not ever get it written up, but I don't want to miss the chance. Besides, I really think she would enjoy talking about it.

I will always cherish the memories of the afternoons that I spent with Grannie Clark last summer. We worked with two kinds of yarn at that time: my yarns, with which she was teaching me to knit, and her yarns, tales of Alaskan early days.

I suppose I better wind this up and get going on the other stuff I need to do today. Tonight, I'm going to take a dessert to the potluck supper. I'm going to open that quart of rhu-barb, which Mom W. canned when she was here last summer. I plan to fix a rhubarb crisp. It is baked rhubarb with a crumbly mixture on top. Actually, I use the recipe for the topping that we used to use for Sunday dessert at home. Harold isn't crazy about rhubarb anyway, and this is a good way to use it and still have a fairly inexpensive dish. I suppose I really should take something made out of hamburger now that we had some brought up from Seward, but any recipe that I have would require so much meat that it would deplete our supply rapidly. By taking rhubarb crisp tonight, Harold and I can make our hamburger stretch for quite a while. So I think I'll just be selfish. After all, it is the "pinch of winter."

Guess that's the letter for this week.

Love,
Your Alaskan daughter, Harriet

Hope, Alaska
February 12, 1954

Dear Mother,

Those giggly sounds are the kids from the school next door. They are having a Valentine party. It can't be above 15 degrees right now and likely less than that, but they have the windows open. Hence, it's easy to hear the joyous sounds that drift out from the classroom.

Linda has been eating over here this week again. You remember she did that for a while last fall before the baby was born. She got into a scuffle in the schoolroom last week and broke the curtain rod. So, Mrs. Blair told her she couldn't eat in the schoolroom for a while. Mrs. Blair irks me so. I don't doubt in the least that Linda did that and probably other things. She can be a naughty child at times. But Mrs. Blair has no business complaining when she doesn't stay around to supervise. She goes upstairs to her apartment the whole noon hour and leaves the children to their own devices. What can she expect? I've had some very nice groups of children to work with, but I know better than to leave them alone too long during free periods.

If Mrs. Blair stays here for ten years, as is her present plan, I'm not going to be here. I refuse to have Tommy go to school with her. She is a big, swearing, smoking, and foul-minded woman. I understand she tells stories in the classroom which shouldn't be told at all. She has taken several days off and just dismissed school. No fewer than six former teachers are living in the community, but she never bothers to get a substitute, and the children won't be making up those days.

Now that I'm started on the subject, I might as well tell all, "meow! meow!" She's selfish! She stood at the Community Thanksgiving dinner and whined because they wouldn't start the meal until everyone got there. I'll admit that it's irritating for people to be late, but it's even more annoying for someone to make a fuss about it as she did. She made such a scene, by the way, that they did go ahead and start. There were some hurt feelings over that, I fear.

But don't let me stop here. I have truly come to believe that teaching is merely a sideline with Mrs. Blair. Her chief occupation has been to marry old bachelors. She has been married four times, and by coincidence, each of the three times she was widowed she was left a nice amount of money. She doesn't even have to marry them, it seems, to have a good inheritance. Recently, her boyfriend in Anchorage committed suicide and left her as the heir to his estate. One of the things he left her was a beautiful trailer house. It was in this trailer house that he had put a gun to his mouth and pulled the trigger. Mrs. Blair told Alma that, " ... he got blood all over the sofa. You'd think he would have gone out into the woods to do it."

Then a few days after he died, she came over to buy lumber from the mill for a coffin. Rough lumber, since the planer is not yet working. It seems that the funeral directors in Anchorage didn't want her to try to bury him until after the spring thaw, but she felt they just wanted to charge her extra for keeping the body in cold storage until then. And, as she explained, the cost would come out of the estate. So, a wooden box made of rough lumber and a hasty burial was her solution.

Let's see, any good qualities. Mrs. Blair is very frank, and you never feel that she is two-faced because she says what she thinks. The little kids love her and revere her; the older ones are a little more skeptical. Ah! The paper I've wasted on her. As I look back over this tirade, I'm a little disturbed by the strength of my own feelings. Maybe I have just a touch of "cabin fever." But it is all true and well, suffice it to say, I'm not overly fond of her. I suppose I should explain a little about the situation that keeps her here. The territorial government assigns teachers to Hope, and the local citizens have no choice in the matter. Several mothers are put out with Mrs. Blair, but nothing will be done about it. Once before, the town had an unsatisfactory teacher, and some of the parents appealed the case to have him ousted. It just happened that he was popular with several of the non-parent citizens. I guess it split the community-wide open and gave Hope the reputation of being a place that was hard on teachers. Everybody wants to leave that reputation behind, so that is why nothing will be done now.

It is well past time for a quick and necessary change of subject. The Beutedahls made a day trip out here last weekend. They are getting excited about spring planting and the like. They brought us a little sack of oranges and apples. I thanked them for it and then the next morning I gave them a dozen eggs. "Pay her for them," Mr. Beutedahl insisted. I was embarrassed. I explained that they were a gift. "Oh, then we'll bring you something from Anchorage when we come," she insisted. It kind of irks me when people always try to balance up gifts. Actually, that was what we were doing, but I hope I didn't make it that obvious. It's blessed to give, but it is also blessed to be able to receive graciously. See, I haven't forgotten all that you taught me.

Grannie is back from the hospital now. I haven't been down to see her yet because I thought she'd have too many callers anyway. Alma said she stopped in for a minute yesterday and there were four people there. I do hope they don't give her a setback; stopping in is fine because she loves callers, but people sometimes don't use judgment. I'm going to wait until she's feeling a little stronger and then gently lead her into an "interview" because I love to hear about the old days and she just relaxes into the pleasant task of reminiscing.

By the way, Mother, you really don't need to worry about our food situation. We are doing just fine. For instance, we are having goat soup for supper. The wild goat soup we made last fall is really wonderful. We may be prejudiced, but we haven't tasted any better. It is a thick stew filled with many vegetables and chunks of meat. We haven't many jars of it left but are allowing ourselves to indulge in a meal of goat soup every once in a while.

The jams are holding out nicely, and we are enjoying immensely the pies made of the canned fruit. And do you smell the fresh bread? I just took it out of the oven. The project of making bread is getting easier all the time. It has become just a routine that I fit into my schedule.

Furthermore, we have community meals, which always add some variety to our diet and give us an excuse to get out of the house to be with other people. There are other opportunities for food and fellowship as well. Wednesday night we went over to Alma's for supper. She had gotten back a new set of her stereo pictures and had some of Tommy. They were very good. It had been some time since I had been over to Millers, so I really enjoyed the visit. After supper, while Ross, Harold, Lewie and Erma played a game of Rook, Alma and I decided on what kind of seeds and how many of each kind I should order for our planting. We want to develop a garden on our own land, but we may not be able to take the ground away from all that brush and those stumps in time for this year. We don't want to miss those fresh vegetables that summer can bring. So, we'll plant a garden elsewhere and then work at getting our own garden spot on the hill ready for the following summer.

So, you see, Mother, even as we are stretching out the last of our stock of this year's food we are already into the cycle of planning for next season. We are really in pretty good shape, considering that this is our first year here in Alaska. Doc continues to do his part to make sure that we have what we need. The chickens provide a regular supply of eggs if they know what's good for them. If they fail in that task, they will feed us in other ways. All in all, I think we're doing fine in the food department.

Besides, spring is on the way. I don't have to light lamps until almost 4:30 now. The days are really getting longer fast. Truly this is a beautiful country, beautiful and interesting. Because of the deep snow up in the higher areas the moose are coming down to enjoy browsing in the lower areas where things are more open. One can see any number of them most anytime that you venture away from the main street of town.

Love,
Your Alaskan daughter, Harriet

Hope, Alaska
February 27, 1954

Dear Evelyn,

I certainly was not prepared for the beauty of winters here. Even on those short days, it didn't really get dark. The moonlight on the snow made it plenty light enough to walk around outdoors and gave a muted glow to buildings and a variety of objects around. Then the absence of wind allows the snow to lie where it falls. Trees are delicately etched. Each little twig has its miniature burden of snow. The weeds along the road become patterns in white and even the lowly fence posts and fence wire have a claim to beauty as they flaunt their tall caps of white.

Oh, Evelyn, I have written so many letters Outside extolling the beauty of this Alaskan winter. And every word of that is true. What may be false is what I haven't written. There are scary things about winter here. I want to tell you an incident that you must promise not to tell Mother. You know how she worries about me, and she doesn't need another worry right now. I must tell somebody, and since you are my understanding little sister, you are selected. I'm just going to write it here in this letter, and then we won't have to say a word about it when I come out. If you can't promise to keep this to yourself, stop reading right now and put this letter into the wastebasket.

As I am sure Mother has told you from our letters to her, we have had a record cold February. I listen daily to the weather conditions as broadcast from Anchorage and am grateful that we are snug here. I am grateful that Harold can load up the wood box each morning and that he can break the greatly thickened ice at the outside well where he dips the bucket for water to fill up the boiler on the stove and the water for us to use. I am grateful, oh so grateful, for the radio that keeps me company, brings in the outside world, and fills my morning with news and music and our evenings with shared radio programs. We never miss the Six Shooter, for example. We really like Jimmy Stewart's interpretation of the good-hearted footloose cowboy. We also listen to Gunsmoke and some of the quiz shows. And, like everyone in Hope - all over the territory for that matter - we try never to miss the Mukluk Telegraph.

With that background of true gratitude for our life here, I will tell you of the incident that I mentioned. I was getting supper for us a couple of days ago. Working at the cook stove, I happened to glance up. The stovepipe goes up through a hole cut in the ceiling on its way to the roof. When I glanced up there, I saw little flames of fire starting to crawl around that stovepipe. Instant panic. Instant prayer. It was way too cold for me to be able to bundle the baby up enough to be safe outside, while I took him and went for help. There was no way I would leave him in this house while I went for help alone. And, of course, there was no way to phone for help. I thought about firing three shots into the air. I have been told that this is generally understood as a call for help. There was a gun in the house, but I didn't think there were any men close enough to respond in time anyway.

I knew with a kind of calm certainty that I had to put that fire out myself. The entrance to the attic was a small square hole in the ceiling over the counter. A small sheet of plywood covered the hole. I hurriedly placed a chair on the counter. I then placed the bucket of water on the counter beside the chair. Another chair helped me get up onto the counter with the bucket and chair. I crawled up on the chair sitting on the counter and pushed the plywood cover back. It was loose and slid away nicely. I then reached down for the bucket of water and was able to get it up through the hole and set it on the floor of the attic. I shoved it back so that I could try to get up there with it. I don't remember just how I did it, but I managed to crawl up through that small square hole into the attic. I hurried carefully across the attic to the fire. I had to walk on two-by-four ceiling joists across the attic floor, or I might have stepped through the ceiling. The potential damage to the ceiling didn't frighten me as much as having my leg caught some way. The fire definitely had been spreading by the time I got there. Yet putting it out was fairly simple. A few well-aimed splashes sufficed. I didn't even have to use all the precious water in the bucket.

There I was standing on the ceiling joists in our attic holding a half a bucket of water frantically studying every inch of the area around the stovepipe to make sure that the fire was really out. At last, I sagged with relief, but I was so drained by the adrenalin rush, which had served me so well up to this point, that I found the getting down out of the attic difficult. I realized that if I put the partially filled bucket down on the chair, I wouldn't have a place to step down. The bucket seemed too heavy to lift over the edge of the access the way I had when I got up. Finally, I left the bucket, in the attic and crawled down without it. I went over to the basket where Tommy had been sleeping through all this. I took him out of the basket and sitting in that big rocker I held him still sleeping and mixed tears of terror and relief with prayers of thanksgiving.

When Harold came home after work, I tearfully told of my experience and said that I had left the bucket in the attic. He said he would be glad to get it down. But he, himself, had a little difficulty with that assignment. He was simply incredulous that I had been able to manage the process. So was I. Well, there you have it. A true story of great crisis averted in the Alaskan wilderness; a story I wish was about somebody else, but I feel better having told it to you. Remember, you promised not to tell Mother. I'll be seeing you soon to make sure. Oh, it won't be long now! I am both excited and disappointed about the trip Outside. I am disappointed that Harold can't make the trip out with me. Without him, it will be a much harder trip and much less fun. Still, we both think that this is the way to go. So, it won't be too long before you see me, not to mention that new nephew of yours.

Greet Bob and remind him that he's going to have to learn to act like a staid uncle now instead of a typical college student.

Love,
Harriet

Hope, Alaska
February 27, 1954

Dear Mom Walker,

Well, we're back from Seward. Did you miss us? I guess you may need a little more to go on than that before you can say. A couple of weeks ago Harold received a letter from Donald Dalberg who is the basketball coach at the high school in Seward. The letter was an invitation to referee two basketball games last weekend. You remember that Harold did a little refereeing in Seward at the time Tommy was born. Well, he must have impressed Coach Dalberg because the letter was very complimentary about your son's abilities and offered ten dollars a game, plus expenses, for the refereeing job. We decided it was an opportunity that we just couldn't pass up. So, we made the necessary arrangements and headed for Seward last weekend.

I'm still a little ashamed about the attitude I had starting this adventure. The trouble is that some things about being a referee's wife are almost worse than being a coach's wife. I was a little uneasy the whole time about Harold's being so unbiased that he will even foul out the son of our gracious hosts. Gene Boe is a very good ballplayer and the beloved star around Seward. But sometimes he is too aggressive.

It wasn't very long though before I was able to develop a more positive attitude. Being with the Boe family was wonderful. We do have a feeling of such gratitude toward them for their help at the time of Tommy's birth. Harold felt that his refereeing was a small way of returning our gratitude to the Boes. As he pointed out, Gene Boe should be allowed to use his considerable talent in a game that is controlled by proper officiating. Besides, this Seward, Alaska, the team will be flying out to have an exchange game with the high school team in Seward, Nebraska. Can you conceive of anything like that? I find it hard to imagine. But that means that each game of the season here is doubly important because of that trip.

Well, Seward lost its second game, but it was a very thrilling, tightly matched, a contest decided in overtime. Of course, some of the people who were praising Harold so loudly after Seward won the first night were strangely silent after the second game. But Harold felt that they weren't very rough on him. One of the nicest things about the trip was that we got to stay two days in the Boe's nice warm house. It was such a refreshing break from our life in Hope. This is going to be the coldest February on record I think. We've had weeks now of subzero, and I do mean "sub" zero weather. Funny thing about it is that so many natives are complaining about the weather and really, it's the sort of thing that I had expected.

What I hadn't expected was what a terrifically difficult job it would be to live in our little non-winterized house. When the natural moisture of air inside the house comes in contact with the frigid walls, they ice over. Sometimes we can't get the front door completely shut without chipping off the ice that constantly forms on the sill. We've moved all our operations into the kitchen. You remember our tiny kitchen area. Try to imagine us all living in that part of our little house. Yes, sometimes it does take a bit of juggling. Of course, we still sleep in the living room. Often the pile of comforters has frozen to the wall on one side. But we can crawl in from the other side, of course, and it doesn't take too long to get cozy and warm. But Tommy sleeps and lives in his basket. We keep a thermometer hanging in the basket at the foot end. That determines whether we place the basket on the table or on the open oven door.

One thing we have not had to worry too much about is refrigeration, although it has been a moving target. First, we used the back bedroom for a root cellar and refrigerator. When that area started freezing, we closed it off and moved operations into the middle room. Finally, in spite of the lamp that we kept lit for warmth, things started freezing in there too. So, we moved operations into our living room, so the middle room is the refrigerator now. Needless to say, the warmth, both physical and hospitable, of the Boe's house in Seward was a welcome change, as was the freedom of movement.

When we got back from Seward Sunday evening, we found the house all frozen up as we had expected. We'd planned for this and even taken all of our canned goods and vegetables down to the Speckings so they wouldn't freeze. But we had forgotten the possibility of needing hot water right away for Tommy's bottle. So, when we went down to Speckings to pick up our food, they let us warm up his bottle. They surely are swell neighbors. I do wish that you could have met them. We enjoy them so much. They are most like us of anyone living here in Hope. You'll just have to come up soon and get to know them.

As a thank you for their help we later took a chicken dinner over to share with the Speckings. Harold wants me to tell you about his experience of picking the chicken for that event. He selected what he hoped was an unproductive chicken and decapitated it. Then he carried a pail of boiling water outside and began the process of picking feathers. He said that he dipped the chicken in the water, but when he reached for the steaming wet feathers, they were frozen stiff. He got only a couple of dips out of the water before it was uselessly cold. But, surprisingly enough, the chicken got picked clean and my job of cutting it apart and cooking it was simple by comparison. The Speckings seemed very appreciative of the meal, and we were able to express our thankfulness for their help while we were in Seward.

Even though we consider the outing to Seward a general success, it has had its consequences. The hens have gone on a sit-down strike. What I mean is that our egg production has been way down. We're still getting plenty for us and a few to sell but not the quantity we were getting. So, we've started to cull the flock. We've killed about four hens so far. We've learned that hens have to be pampered during the cold weather to keep production up. We had been taking them warm water several times each day and keeping the eggs gathered, etc., but when we made that trip to Seward, they received only the minimum of care. We now know what it takes to get hens to produce well and what will cause them to stop. However much we might miss the egg money we used to get, fresh chicken is a welcome addition to our diet.

After so much writing about basketball in Seward, I know that you will be surprised to have me combine the words "Hope" and "basketball" in the same sentence. But Harold has run into an intriguing situation. The kids have gotten together and asked him to coach them in a little basketball. You remember from last summer that there are only a few high school kids around here, so he includes everyone from the sixth grade on up. They now have the grand sum of a dozen players. They have fixed the inside of the community hall so that it is basketball proof by putting up removable window guards and making new takedown tables. I know you remember what a little cracker box that community hall is, but the young folks don't seem to be aware of that as a problem.

His experience with basketball here at Hope confirms a theory that Harold has had about coaching. He believes that the foundation of being an accomplished athlete is the ability to handle one's body well. The kids here have had no basketball training whatsoever, but they were fortunate to have a good tumbling instructor about four years ago. So even before the basketball goals went up, these kids and Harold started working on the fundamentals of movement and ball handling. It is unbelievable how quickly they mastered some things that in three years of coaching Harold had not been able to teach kids in a formal basketball program. Of course, a lot of it is just plain old try. Perhaps it is that they have the advantage of being so naive as not to understand that young men and women of their ages ought to be bored with almost anything that some adult is trying to teach them.

Speaking of developing athletes, Tommy is getting to where he turns quite far to one side. I think he would be able to turn completely over if he had room. There isn't room for much experimentation in his basket. But he's going to have to stay there as long as the weather remains so cold. If he keeps growing like he is now and the weather doesn't break soon, this might become a problem. He's getting really big to lug around. Last night Tommy was trying a little crying to get attention. He kept watching us to see our reaction. Sometimes he'd even forget that he was supposed to be crying and would coo a while until he remembered. He's too smart for us.

I was going to write this letter to you yesterday afternoon but your granddaughter, Linda, came over and spent the afternoon. You can just bet I didn't get any writing done with her here. They get out of school at 2:30 on Fridays. Actually, the little folks get out every day at that time. What with having to walk across the flat with Linda in the morning and then coming to get her early in the afternoon this time of year, Alma has a very short day. That's why she sometimes lets Linda stay here to visit before she comes to get her.

This cold weather has really meant a lot of extra work for, Lewie. Hauling water has become quite a chore in the cold since he has to go all the way to Bear Creek for it, you know. He also manages the wood supply, and the Millers burn an immense amount of wood, of course, with the greenhouse stove going all the time. And when he finishes with hauling water and wood, there is the extra attention the goats, chickens, geese, and rabbits need in the frigid conditions. I'm afraid he's found it a bit difficult to squeeze his schoolwork in. But on the whole, both he and Erma Ann are getting along nicely with their studies, I believe.

As you know, they are taking a Territory approved high school correspondence course, which happens to be put out by the University of Nebraska. This allows them a lot of flexibility with when they do their schoolwork. This flexibility really helps now with the huge load of chores cold weather has brought for Lewie. I'm amazed that there seems to be almost no limit to the courses that can be taken this way. For example, Erma is taking a clothing course, and Lewie is taking a course on gasoline engines. Then, of course, they have their history and English courses. The work is sent into the U. for grading and comments. Then if it fails to meet the mark, they have to do it over. Your two grandchildren have done very well with their work. Some of the local kids haven't fared so well. There are five taking the course all told. One is a freshman; two are sophomores, and then there are our two juniors. They work on it at home and take their tests under supervision. Erma Ann and Lewie like to work by blocks. I mean, they will concentrate for a while on one subject only; then they work a few days on another, instead of dividing it up into periods each day. It seems to be working out quite well for them.

Harold and Ross have made a lot of progress this week in getting the planer set up. Harold is excited about the prospects of getting it to work right away. However, this cold weather has absolutely halted progress on the building of our house on the hill. So, it doesn't look like we'll be able to move in by the end of February as we'd hoped. Especially since the end of February is tomorrow. Sometimes Harold feels very discouraged because everything goes so much slower than he plans. But it's been hard to account for all the variables like the cold, cold weather of deep winter in Alaska.

It is only two weeks now until I leave for the States - two or three, that is. I am still hazy about the rest of my trip. As you know, I'm going to Mother's place in York first, and then I'll wait until Harold joins me. Next, we'll visit siblings and friends around York and nearby locations in Kansas. Finally, we'll go down to spend a more extended time with you there at the mission in New Mexico. I'm really looking forward to seeing you again and filling you in on all the news from our little place here in Alaska.

Love,
Harriet

Hope, Alaska
March 5, 1954

Dear Mother,

I suppose you have noticed that I have a new typewriter ribbon. It's pretty classy. Guess you can read these letters easily enough, eh? When I ordered this ribbon, I couldn't decipher from the catalog description of ribbons, which one I should order. After a little more study, I noticed that they did have my typewriter described perfectly. Or one just like it, that is.

So, I acted like a real ignorant fellow and asked for a ribbon to fit the typewriter and used the catalog number of the latter. It got me to thinking. I'll bet they do get some really rip-snorting orders. Some of the things ordered by backwoods Alaskans would surely make an interesting story. We got a letter from them telling us that we were among their best customers. We have ordered a lot of things this year, it seems, but best customers? Really!

We had heard that we would likely get most of our snow in March and it seems likely to be so. In fact, I think that we have already equaled the record for the rest of the year and the month is still very young. The first day of March it began to snow, big fat squishy drops of snow and it didn't stop for hours. Since then we have had snow off and on all week. Therefore, we have a lovely big covering of snow all over the landscape. The trees are exquisite. I don't know if I have ever seen anything as beautiful as this country when it is all covered with snow.

Right along with the snow has come a sudden surge upward of the mercury. Of course, that would have to be true before it could snow like this. So this has been a lovely week in all. We are enjoying the warm spell. I now use both the kitchen and the main room of my house. It's a luxury. I had hugged the stove so closely for so long that I had almost forgotten what it is to move around. The temperature reaches almost to thawing most of the time now, and therefore it is plenty warm enough to bring out the Alaskan flies.

In spite of the warmer weather, I haven't had any walks, because I'm just a little leery about taking the baby out until he's completely well. You see, Tommy has been sickish this week. He came down with quite a cold last Saturday night. I sat up with him until early in the morning when Harold took over. Poor little guy, he was so sick and couldn't understand it at all. But now, even though he still has a runny nose, he's feeling chipper and lively again. We're glad to have our little old boy back with us again.

He was enough better that I did risk taking him down to the Post Office today. We can purchase money orders, buy stamps, etc. on Friday. We are really supposed to mail our letters then, too, but Mrs. Mitchell is very nice about taking them on Saturday. So, I suppose that fact lurking in my subconscious and my natural tendency to procrastinate account for the weekly rush just before Saturday. As I started to say, I had Tommy at the Post Office with me. Lying in his basket, he was the center of much attention from the folks in Hope who were also utilizing the Friday afternoon post office hours. One of those was Doc. You would have to know him, Mother, to realize how ridiculous it was to see this old character leaning over the basket making faces and absurd sounds to amuse Tommy. And he was successful. Tommy's face just lit up with a smile. Wise child. And who wouldn't laugh at Doc's antics? I couldn't help thinking of how Clarke always said it was more amusing to watch a person trying to entertain a baby than it was to watch the baby.

Tommy is growing like a weed. He is now over twenty-six inches long and weighs fifteen and a fourth pounds. He is learning new things right along too. He notices and plays with a rattle. We have tied one on a string, which hangs into his basket. He beats it with his fist and stares at it. It's a small thing, but thrilling, nevertheless. What a delight watching his young personality unfold. His other two latest adventures are the discovery of his hands and turning over. He looks so cute as he gazes in awe at his hands and makes them meet, etc. Harold thought it was very ornery of me when I played a little trick on him. Tommy was holding two of my fingers, one with each hand. I just made a little transfer, and he was holding one of his own fingers with the other hand. He really didn't know what to make of it. He didn't know what to do and how to let go. Then there is this matter of his turning over. He works and works, strains and strains to get turned over on his stomach. Then as soon as he succeeds, he's very unhappy and wants back on his back. I put him back and away he goes, trying to turn over again. What's the future in that?

Harold stayed with Tommy tonight while I went to church. Mrs. Elliot was there again with Freddy and the baby. Poor woman! She surely has her hands full with both of them. Five-year-old Freddy hasn't the slightest inclination to behave, you know. The littlest Elliot is much smaller than Tommy even though she had a three-pound head start at birth. But she is a sweet baby and was all dolled up in a little white dress. I'd forgotten how dainty and feminine some baby clothes are. But, of course, when you are looking for darling, consider how Tommy looks in his little he-man clothes.

I've been wearing the rubber gloves this week. It really has helped my red, chapped hands to clear up. For a while, I thought my soap was too strong and used only ivory soap, but that didn't help either. It's just the water, I guess. But washing baby clothes, dishes, and all the other little things that require wet hands just demanded too much from them. Anyway, they are healing fast, and I'm getting so that I don't mind the gloves too much.

Keith Specking loaned Harold a pair of skis. He's filled with joy. Right now, he's sitting beside me trying to read Time magazine and wax his skis at the same time. I think he's successful. He will use them to cross the tide flats each morning on the way to work. I'm glad that he has them. He was instrumental in seeing that Lewie got a pair for Christmas. And he couldn't keep the desire out of his eyes. I would surely like to get him a pair, but that is out of the question financially. So, this will work nicely.

The more we think about it, the more Harold wants me to fly the whole way on my trip. Tommy is so heavy and such a squirmer that Harold is eager for me to make the trip as quickly as possible. It will cost quite a bit more, of course, but maybe it will be worth it. We'll see. It would just mean that much less for me to spend after I get there, but I can do a lot of shopping on a little amount of money.

It certainly won't be long now until I see you. Much as I hate to be gone from Harold, I shall enjoy the visit, I know. This is probably the last letter you will get from me before I get there. We will, however, be letting you know more specifics of the trip by telegram as we find them out ourselves.

Love,
Your Alaskan Daughter, Harriet

CHAPTER 10

March and April 1954:
Going Outside

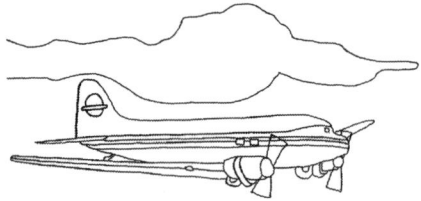

D ear Karen,
    I can see that the last group of letters elicited more than
    the usual number of questions. We'll start with your ques-
tion about the slowing down of the number of freighters coming
into Seward during the winter. Yes, fewer boats were coming into
Seward during February. It's true that Seward was an all-year ice-
free shipping port, but commerce just seemed to bog down at that
time of year. That, of course, affected the supplies available for dis-
tribution throughout the Territory.

Yes, "sheathing" is kind of an odd term. It means the material
that is put directly over the outside on the framed skeleton of a
building. The sheathing that Harold used for the house he was
building on the hill was 1" thick boards, which he nailed on the
studs at 45-degree angle for extra strength. He then covered them
with building paper and put on wide rough-cut 1" boards horizon-
tally and overlapped them to give a drop-siding effect.

I suppose that it does seem silly to have the windows open in
the school building during the coldest time of the Alaskan winter.
Here's why it was such a common occurrence. It was not unusual
to control inside temperature by opening windows when a heating
stove was over-producing. Mrs. Blair had the boys stoke the fire,

and saving fuel was not a priority. So, overheating was not uncommon, and open windows were the result.

Your question about "stereo pictures" is also pertinent now that I think about it. I haven't seen many of those around lately. Alma had a special camera that simultaneously took two slightly different views of every picture. Tiny slides from this camera were mounted in a circular frame so that the picture pairs are mounted beside each other. When seen through a device called a "View-Master," the picture was three-dimensional. It is the same kind of effect as a 3-D movie but for color photographic slides.

Your e-mail showed your understanding of my panic about the attic fire. Even after all these years, your positive, supportive response makes me feel good. Thank you. Yes, I'll see if I can explain how the fire got started. It started in the sawdust that had blown into the asbestos-lined box that was to insulate the stovepipe from anything flammable. While there was no insulation in the walls, there was sawdust put in between the ceiling joists as cheap ceiling insulation. Openings allowed air circulation in the space above the ceiling and wind had blown sawdust against the stovepipe. It was this sawdust that caught fire and spread flame to the wood around the insulation box. And I'll ever be grateful that I happened to look up at just the time when the little flames were just starting.

What does it mean to "cull the flock"? Yes, that might be a phrase with which you are unfamiliar. That meant weeding out the chickens that were not actually producing eggs. Harold had earlier used the time-honored method of feeling for the laying spread back between the chicken's legs. Those failing that test were invariably heavy with fat and less active than the layers. He reasoned that when he went out to feed the hens, the last ones off the roost were the lazy nonproducing hens. Thus, he started choosing the last one as the one to butcher. That method of culling proved infallible since we never discovered any eggs in those we butchered.

You asked about Grandpa's skiing across the flat starting in February. How had he been getting through the snow before that? He had a path that he kept tramped down as each new snowfall came. Rain late in January changed the path into an icy ridge with its edges eroding away. It was difficult to walk on this even wearing his logging boots. Apart from the path, the snow was too deep. With the skis, he could pick any trail he chose across the flat to the shop and mill site.

Now let's turn to this next group of letters I've attached to this message. Right away, you'll understand why I had second thoughts about including these very personal letters with the other letters, which tell the story in a more general way. What finally tipped the balance is my own awareness in re-reading these letters that they reveal a turning point in our thinking about living in Alaska. Without these letters, some of the things you read later will not make sense. So I've included them.

Until the Alaskan experience, our married lives had been built on a two-career course. We had talked about family and planned for it. But when we actually had that new little person living with us, we began to feel differently about what it meant to be a family. This new way of thinking affected us profoundly, and we began to re-align our priorities, as you will see in this batch of letters.

Love,
Grandma

Hope, Alaska
March 12, 1954

My Darling Harriet,
By now you should be in York and well settled in with your mother. To overcome the intervening miles that separate us, I must once more take recourse to my emissary, the pen. Since we are attuned so finely to each other, and the way my thoughts are reaching out to you, I cannot but feel that what you read on this page will merely be an echo of a more sublime conversation already transpired. Still, I must try to capture these thoughts in this mundane medium as a thin, but vital, nourishment to our relationship while parted. Otherwise, I

fear, we risk descending from that plane of love so cherished by us, young romanticists. Best we cling to the lifeline provided by the written word and so embrace each other over a distance.

Let me start at our parting. I was very proud of you, little mother, as you set off so bravely on your journey from Anchorage. You never saw my last wave of goodbye. I know that, at this point in our relationship, it is appropriate that we achieve the neat parting we did. But how difficult it is to prepare oneself for the agony of loneliness, while in the consoling company of the one who will soon be desperately missed. Perhaps there is something to be said for long wrenching farewells.

After leaving the airport, I could not stand to go to our hotel room. So, I went to see the movie "Hondo." Unfavorable reviews seemingly failed to keep people away from the box office. There was a waiting line in the street long before I got my ticket. The reviewers must be content with submitting only a minority report because I joined the crowds in enjoying the picture - even alone. As I went back to the hotel, I dreaded going to the room where our happy little family had spent the day. I was soon dozing off while watching television. I did finally go to bed. Knowing me, you'll not be surprised that I was soon in the midst of pleasant dreams. If insomnia is the true sign of the lonely, I'll always be a flop. Nevertheless, when I am conscious, your absence is constantly in my thoughts.

The next morning, I packed and checked out about 7:20 AM. The hotel bill came to $7.20, which I think you'll agree was a pretty good deal. The cash we had brought held out fine. Even after a bus ticket, breakfast, a tax book, stamps for a letter to Willard, and candy bars, I still arrived home with seven cents. Actually, even if I'd been stripped after paying the hotel bill, I still could have made it home in fine shape. I had my lunch in a sack and could have gotten a couple of meals out of it. I also had the checkbook.

In the bus station, I met Frank Walunga who does that ivory

carving like we saw at McMullens. You remember that Wa-lunga was the one who pushed me back to third place the last time I competed in the Seward 4th of July race. He was on his way to Seward from his native St. Lawrence Island. After our conversation, I'm hoping we can visit St. Lawrence someday. It sounds wonderful. He made the trip on the bus more pleasant.

I got off the bus at the Hope stop, Mile 58, and I pulled on my warm clothes. I ate my lunch and started down "Moose Alley." Those critters were everywhere. I saw over forty just walking less than two miles to where I met Ross in the truck.

From there we went to Portage to pick up a circular saw blade for the mill. Some jerk had stolen that good blade we found just lying around at the old mill site where we salvaged the planer. I had wanted to take it when we got the planer and then check with Berg, the owner, to see if it was all right to keep it. You remember, Ross thought that this might not be ethical. Perhaps he was right. But when we made the first payment on the planer and mentioned the good mill saw blade to Berg, he couldn't understand why we hadn't followed my inclination. No one need ever fear being cheated by Ross Miller. Now that we have the right to keep the saw blade, it's gone. Tisk! Tisk!

Well, the rest of the week has moved along. After the first cold night, it warmed up considerably. I've not even needed to keep the fire going during the night. Consequently, there are still clothes hanging around. I surely don't want to put them away the least bit damp. You might be interested to know that I still have quite a little room left in the dish stacking area. Ha!

You are truly missed, my dear. Sometimes I feel like I'm just spinning my wheels without you and Tommy around to create our home life. Last night at church the Eliot baby suddenly let out a little baby sound, and it made my heart do the dumbest flip-flops. I'm used to there being just one infant in the world. I'm trusting that you are having an awfully good time, Honey, because believing that is what makes your absence bearable.

Love you, Love our child,
Harold

P.S. Here is a work progress report. We have the ice put up except for packing it in sawdust. All logs that were on the long rollway have been sawed into lumber.

York, Nebraska
March 12, 1954

Dearest Harold,

We arrived here in York with no mishaps ... unless you count the two times, I dumped the contents of the typewriter case. I wish I had listened to you. I thought I was so clever packing the things that I needed for the flight into the portable typewriter case. I should have checked with someone to see if I could borrow a little suitcase. Twice on the trip when I had Tommy in one arm and was carrying my purse and the case in the other arm, the latch flew open and baby things spilled all over. I was so embarrassed. But each time some compassionate fellow traveler helped me collect myself and get on with the trip.

Tommy is the hit of the campus, of course, and I can see that I am going to have to make a real effort to keep him from being handled too much. You see, Mrs. Bias's mother died, so jack-of-all-trades, Mother, is matron of the dorm until Monday. So, we are living here in the matron's apartment, which seems to be everyone's apartment. The college students wander in and out freely. One girl even picked Tommy up out of his crib. But I'll just have to see that it doesn't happen anymore. I can do it! I've been an austere and firm college newspaper editor, you know.

The Christian Emphasis team from the East has been here on the campus yesterday and today. I have enjoyed that contact with a more vigorous expression of Christianity than we have been experiencing in recent months. It is really exciting! It reminds me of the days when I was on the national executive committee of our denominational Youth Fellowship. The team leaders even remembered my past work with that illustrious group and were very cordial to this retired executive committee secretary.

The weather has been warm, but windy. It's raining a little right now, and there is snow in the Northwestern part of the state. Things still look fine for travel this weekend when we plan to visit Clarke and Jean. In the meantime, we have visited a lot of friends around here. Guess what! Ruth and Norman have a baby boy. I have always been happy for people with new babies. But now, I really know more the depth of joy that a new little son can bring.

I am feeling fine, even though I am still overly tired. I really appreciate some of the luxuries. Bathtubs are a good example. I miss you, Darling, and long to share this all with you. A pen is so inadequate; more so is this cold clicking typewriter ...

Love,
Harriet

P.S. Here's what egg money is left. Sure, I know I don't have to send it, but please make pleasant use.

Hope, Alaska
March 19, 1954

Hi honey,
Harriet, I am counting on hearing from you in the morning. I know that you have written. The slow postal service to this remote region has stretched my wait for a letter from you to nearly two weeks. I sometimes wonder if your letter has reached Anchorage or is sitting on a siding in Moose Pass. But tomorrow, it will arrive I'm sure. I told Ross that I was sorry, but no work until after mail - after all we haven't even been

married five years. Loving ya'! If I wait to read your letter before I write, I will miss the mail, and you'll be waiting two weeks to get my letter. So, I will write in blind faith drawing on our deeper connectedness to provide continuity.

How did things go this week? Oh, I've managed. I've started my old clipboard scheduling routine, and I like it. Naturally, I have more tasks listed than time to do them but have been checking some things off. This dang house is the worst. I've swept it well at least several times. I have mopped right in front of the stove, but whoopee! Yes, your mopping used to do a lot of good even if it didn't stay looking "freshly mopped" The dishes are all done. The clothes all put away. The only real problem is that I didn't understand about the diapers in the kettle. Surely, I should have known there were more diapers inside the kettle than what was draped over the top. Anyway, I didn't catch on until Wednesday night ... sorry. I'm doing everything I can to save them. I put them through yet another process Thursday morning, which included boiling them. I hung them outside by the log house to dry and air out. I'm still not guaranteeing that I've saved them, but I'm hopeful.

Monday, we went to Anchorage and got the logging trailer along with four extra tires and tubes. This will really help our hauling capacity, but I spent all of Tuesday fixing tires.

We got out a batch of house logs worth about $204. That money will certainly be welcome. Now we are also free to refill the rollway for more lumber production. As you know, that puts us out in the woods again logging. The deep snow makes it rough on the "faller," me, natch! The snow is about four feet deep where we're after the house-logs. That McCullough chainsaw is sure "fun" to wrestle around in that stuff, and then digging down around the tree to make the cut is more "sport." There is something to be said for summer logging. Ha!

Overall, we are starting to get things in pretty good shape, Darling. The mill is set to run more efficiently than it ever has before. We have a large stockpile of logs from our winter's logging. The problem is that we are out of cash and have no pending orders for our lumber. I'm considering trying to persuade Ross to let me go to Anchorage and drum up some business. It would only take a few solid orders for our business to take off. With the arrival of spring, the area is going to be just crying out for building materials. It feels like our dream is almost within reach.

The last letter from Willard was enthusiastic as well. He really understands the potential of this mill. His suggestions have been extremely helpful. I keep thinking that when Willard comes, he will be able to help Ross see things more our way. If the mill could start to reach its potential, then we would be freer to get on with the next stage of our life. I could go to school and get that law degree. Then we would be set for the life of public service in the political arena that we are envisioning for our future. At this moment it feels almost within our grasp. And yet I'm troubled as I think about it.

Every day I watch Ross putter around the mill deciding what to do next without the stress of a high-pressure operation. He already has his dream. It's a beautiful little mill operation perfectly designed to meet the custom lumber needs of neighbors and friends in the local area. As the area builds up in the coming years, there will probably be enough local business to keep things operating at our present level. That means enough income to keep a family or two afloat. Sometimes I wonder if our big plans are the best thing for everyone concerned.

All I know is that I truly miss you and Tommy. I need to talk through this dilemma. It's funny; six months ago, our dream seemed more important than anything else in the world. Now all I can think about is wanting to be a family together. Can so much have changed in so little time?

Harriet put away those thoughts of the earthbound, work-a-day world and join me in my nightly reverie. Share with me these wonderful, sad-sweet moments of yearning and knowing that, even though we are apart, you really are mine.

We were in no need of the awakening that temporary separation can bring, but oh how strongly soul-shaking it is to let my thoughts reach for you. Lately, the thought of last year's top tune keeps running, softly spoken, through my conscious being:

"Go you with God, my Darling. Go you with God, my Love. Go until it finally brings ... "

Kiss Tommy for me and let his laughing eyes speak to his mother for me.

Love,
Harold

York, Nebraska
March 19, 1954

Darling Harold,

I found the first few days here very, very depressing. I longed to turn around and go right back to Alaska so that I could weep in your arms. I somehow managed to keep from letting Mother know my feelings. That turned out to be wise because I wouldn't have wanted to add to the stress she was already under. I hope that you didn't pick up too much of my negative feelings from the letter I sent you, but I suspect that you did. Anyway, now I can write this letter with a clearer head, I hope.

As I told you, Mother was in the dormitory when I came. There was, in addition to her regular work, the long hours of dormitory work, the necessity to play hostess to the four members of the mission team sent from headquarters, the need to play nurse to Mary Lou-taking meals, cleaning her room, etc. and then the frustrating attempt to visit with me. She was so tired! I hated it that I had come at that particular time although there would have been no way for either of us to have known in advance.

Then there was the final straw --Tommy. I couldn't relax

my guard a minute, but someone would be handling him. He was so sweet and so good that they all wanted him. I was sorry at times that he didn't fuss more because then he might have been less appealing. Saturday, at Mother's insistence I accompanied Evelyn on a couple of extensive shopping sprees. Mother kept Tommy while we shopped downtown in the morning and in Lincoln in the evening.

That night we got back from Lincoln, and I found that Mother had had a really hard day. Tommy had been fussy, so she had been forced to let him be handled by the kids. That night he was so nervous and jumpy that I was heartsick. He just couldn't seem to get calmed down enough to go to sleep. Boy, I hated myself then.

He's all over it now and is back to being a well-adjusted baby. You can just bet his mama won't let that happen again. I think I can understand now why some babies are so nervous. I've learned a lesson. A baby can take a lot of playing and passing around, but he still needs rest and privacy like anyone else.

We are now living over in her apartment in Oliver House. At first, Mother was awed by Tommy and too busy to pay much attention to him. As time has gone on, she's enjoying him more and more. Gradually, she has wanted to do all kinds of things for him. He's been the perfect child. Each day she gets to be more and more like a grandmother. She's so proud of him. It's really fun to watch.

Would you believe it, the weather hasn't been good enough to take our little Alaskan baby out much since I've been here. We've had rain, snow, and hail in that short while and always that Nebraska wind. That has been what has bothered Tommy the most. The first night I was carrying him back from Evelyn's house, and he gasped and wouldn't breathe. I shook him to get him to breathe, and it happened again. Boy did my heart jump about. He just couldn't get used to the wind. Now I muffle him up horribly and fight with him the whole way. But I'd rather have him struggling than to have him not breathing.

I have had those medical check-ups that you wanted me to

get. I found out that I could have a rather extensive checkup here at the clinic. That is easier and probably less expensive than going to a large medical institution as we had talked about. Dr. Jim Bell said that I had an extremely low basal metabolism, but that it wasn't dangerous. He gave me some little pills and a generous diet to follow. I do feel better and have a much better outlook on life with considerably more pep. So that's what counts, in the long run, I guess.

For the dental work, I decided to go to our college friend, Dr. Tom Robson. I realized afresh how long it had been since we graduated from college because there was a classmate with the official title of "Dr." It was a funny feeling having good old Tom peering into my mouth. Tom and Ruth seem pretty happy with their set-up. York is a little overcrowded with dentists, however, but they like the city and have decided to try and make a go of it here.

I don't know what my medical and dental bills will be. I'll let you know as soon as I get a good estimate. Had X-rays on my teeth. That hasn't been done for several years. I hate the fact that it hurts to spend money this way. Someday we'll just spend money on such things as a matter of routine-like buying groceries. Won't we?

I've been doing a lot of thinking about us. I am almost convinced that we should try very hard to go on to graduate school next year. I wonder if there isn't some way to make that possible? Sure, I would love to have another glorious, easy year at Hope just being a housewife. I know that it would be easier, more economical and comfortable next year in our new house.

However, I am convinced that you have an unusual dedication to serving society. I am willing to do all I can to help you. Perhaps I could teach for a year to get us started. You would have a lot of time at home with your studies, and we could have a baby sitter in the mornings. Tommy will be old enough and nine months of part-time care won't ruin us. We could still go back to Alaska again for a wonderful summer and income from the mill to make ends meet.

I love you so, Harold. I wish you were here so I could talk to you. Darling, I'm as convinced as you that we could go to law school in style if we waited a while. But I'm no longer convinced that's the right thing to do. I have thought that we were undecided about our future place in life, but having talked tooth-ers, I am convinced that we do have a clear-cut pattern to follow. I believe that pattern directs us to a path of public service. Actually, going to grad school will only be a short time apart from our life in Alaska. It is there that we want to build our gracious home and live a full, rich life. Maybe if we try to do our schooling too elaborately, we'll be spreading ourselves too thin. I'm saying it poorly. I'm running out of space, I'm frustrated because you aren't here to react. But I want you to know that I love you and will keep trying to be the kind of wife you need.

Love,
Harriet

P.S. Since it takes so long for mail to go back and forth, we are going to have to be making decisions about your trip. If you want to revisit our college on this site, it will have to be now. On the other hand, with a new student body, the college that we knew would be mostly the faculty. I wish we could finish this trip together. But if you decide not to come, I will accept it.

Hope, Alaska
March 27, 1954

My Darling Harriet,
In all this great world of confusion, there is for me one stable source of order. That source is comprehensively embodied in a single thought of you, Harriet. This is not a mere conjugation of words, but deeply heartfelt. If these words

bring you joy, that is only right. Should they make a patient smile, forge its way across those lips I so love to caress - a smile for your "little boy" husband, that is better yet. Beyond that, I want you to realize that everything I wish to accomplish in this drastically needy world, to satisfy my soul's longing for fulfillment, is perfectly parallel to what I already have in our love together. To me, a true life of service takes its cue from a relationship such as ours. It seems more than a trifle odd that I should feel compelled to tell you these things now in writing. Surely, we have come to perfectly understand these things in mutual knowledge during our time together. And if we haven't, could the pen possibly pierce those unplumbed chambers of the heart?

Today your letter came. It was so nice and thick. You can, without trying very hard, imagine how I trembled with anticipation opening it. This week's letter was wonderful. Even the struggles you enumerate are handled in strong and intelligent ways. You are noticing by now that I've decided to wait until after reading your most recent letter to write mine. I will send this letter with Specking to catch the mail in Anchorage. This will shorten the lag in our communication, which seems important in light of all the vital issues you raise in this most recent letter.

I am very proud of you for going through the check-ups at the doctor and the dentist. If you aren't satisfied with the clinic's work, please move on to a bigger institution for a more thorough going over. Did they check your thyroid? My wishes for you in this are all in the prayer stage.

I've made up my mind to take the car to Anchorage and either sell it or trade it in. That car has served its purpose and also had some fun booting us. If I decide to trade it in for another car, I can assure you we will get something that is cheaper to operate. If I am able to come Outside to the States, then I'll have to sell rather than a trade-in.

About whether I am coming Outside to York or not: please stand by for two weeks. That decision really hinges on the work situation at the mill. Ross and I have been doing very well. I was really beginning to think that my trip Outside was going to be possible. Then today we received a beautiful order for 25,000 board feet of heavy rough stuff. The order is from a druggist in Palmer who is building a recreation center on the Seward Highway down by Summit Lake. He's coming down next week to talk terms with us. If he says he is in a hurry for it, then I'll have to stay here to meet our obligations with that order. I'm sorry to keep you hanging like this, darling, but you know that this is a very crucial time for our mill venture. Another factor is that if we're shooting hard to go back to school next fall then I probably ought to stay "put." We will need every financial benefit I can get us to make it possible. I suppose if we just waited to see what summer brings and waited for a later term then I could get Outside with you yet this spring.

This brings us to the question of going on to school next year. That certainly seems like an important idea to consider carefully. You make some interesting points, Harriet. Time to think with family and friends certainly can alter one's perspective. Even being here alone in my work-a-day world has brought new reflection on what our future might be. Your thoughts about going Outside to school next year are not far away from my growing concern about the venture here at the mill. Maybe there is a way to slow down the development of our business and speed up our preparation for public service. You're right in thinking that it would involve sacrifice and I do so admire your willingness to make a concession. It seems impossible to work through this responsibly without talking face to face. That is something I want to do desperately!

Well, I'd best close for tonight... The days have been lonely. The nights are quite lonely as well. All filled with thought; Lonely of lovely you.

Love,
Harold

York, Nebraska
March 31, 1954

Darling Harold,

Just got the bonus letter from you ... by that I mean the one that you had mailed in Anchorage. Your letters are so thrilling! I am humbled when I think of my prosaic ones. You are the writer. I am the recorder of events.

I'll wait here in York until I know for sure that you are or aren't coming out. But remember, it will be two weeks of visiting after that to see all the people I have contacted. Besides, I'm getting awfully eager to be with you. If I don't hear to the contrary, I'll continue my plans for leaving here April 10.

I have received replies from everyone to whom I wrote about the trip. This way Tommy and I will be met at one place and then taken to the next. We won't have to use public transportation until the trip from Mullinville to New Mexico. That should help some with the cost and result in pleasant experiences. It's not the easiest thing to travel by bus or train with a baby and all the stuff required.

I was interested in your decision about the trading of our car. I feel that it was the wise thing to do. We will likely take a loss on it in anything that we decide to do, and I do feel that we'll be happier rid of it. It will at least give us a change of problem.

I had another thought about coming Outside to go to school next year. I am beginning to think that we've been putting too much emphasis on selecting the right school. Wherever we go, the knowledge will be presented, and you'll get it. The only important thing is that it be respectable and accredited. This is especially true if you choose Alaska as your field of operations. Alaskans don't seem very impressed with big-name schools. Clearly, a law degree is something you need, but it is the means, not the end.

There is something that I've started to worry about if we plan to go to school next year. What about our house? Will we lose it if we come out this winter to go to school? How do the rules for an Alaskan homesite work in these circumstances? I just don't know how leaving so soon after staking claim would affect ownership. Even if we do have to lose it, I still feel that getting on with your education is more important.

Tommy is such a darling baby. He is really no problem to care for and is so popular with all. I am convinced now that he isn't being spoiled by all this attention, although it keeps me on guard to watch for signs and such.

He rolls over in an instant and does seem to be near to crawling. I have my fingers crossed that he doesn't start that until I get him home because then I'm sure I'd have something to worry about. He can raise himself up on his hands. His arms get completely straight, and he holds his head high. But if you speak to him, he gets so excited that his elbows bend, and he goes down with a flop. So far, his chin has maintained its shape. He's lying on the floor right now looking up at me with interest. He has that pleasant half smile and inquisitive look on his face. He's so lovable. I wish that you could be with him - that WE could be with him.

I attended prayer meeting Monday night. I couldn't help being aware in an overwhelming way of the dedication of people like these professors who have committed their lives to teaching in a Christian college. You can picture, I know, the Nolls, Wielders, and Morgans. Just being around them is almost a religious experience in itself. We must do something to make religion more tangible in our home. Or maybe it is more personal and just an uneasy feeling in my own life. I mean, I pray that in our home religion would never be a cause or a crusade but instead would be core to our living.

I've been having a lovely time with Mother. It's been so wonderful to have time to visit and catch up on the news with her. Mother had a tea in my honor yesterday. It was quite nice, and I did appreciate it. Also, we've been doing a lot of sewing.

You'll be impressed with my new wardrobe when you see it, I'm sure.

Since the college is having a longer spring break this year, Bob is driving a carload of kids out to California. So, Mother and I are moving over to Evelyn's house to stay during spring break. It will be fun to have that as our base for visiting.

Mother and I are taking the early bus to Lincoln on Saturday. We'll spend Saturday and Sunday with Clarke and Jean. Evelyn and Bob will come over for us Sunday and spend some time there.

I see so many two-toned green Buicks. I never thought I had any feelings other than occasional hatred toward our car, but I do have a funny, excited feeling when I see these cars. My subconscious wishing you'd drive up, I guess.

Guess who dropped in on us last Saturday!! Your kid brother and wife drove up from Esbon, Kansas to see us. I was surprised. But it was good to see Cecil and Becky again. They ate dinner here and then went back around 3:00. They seem to be getting along nicely but certainly, aren't sold on staying where they are living now.

I went to the first show I've seen since I've been here. It was a zany show about "The Long Long Trailer" produced by and starring "I Love Lucy" Ball and her husband. I'm glad that I wasn't viewing a dramatic and serious love story because even this absurd and ridiculous one made me long for you with an intensity that is startling.

I don't know if you'll get this letter yet this week ... I know it's too much to hope ... but I'll send it anyway. Bother the typewriter; it's so cold and impersonal! The pen is slow but more intimate. How wonderful and rich is our love! What a fine result such love brings to our lives. When I think of the years of rich fellowship ahead of us, I am filled with a delicious sense of contentment.

How nice it is to hear from you so soon. Wish this letter could reach you equally soon. Yet our love is not limited to physical transportation; but is as steady as a heartbeat, as swift as a sigh.

Love,
Harriet

~~~~

Hope, Alaska
April 4, 1954

My Darling Harriet,

It's late Sunday night, so I've missed the mail in Hope again this week. But again, I have the advantage of responding directly to your most recent letter. I will still be able to get this to you promptly from Anchorage, but that leads us to the bad news. This week we got out most of the house-log order, but then the truck broke down. I pulled the engine yesterday afternoon; sure enough, we have a broken crankshaft. It won't be too expensive but will cost us at least three days' work in addition to the dollars. Ugh! I've got to go to Anchorage early tomorrow to get a new crankshaft. Hope I can get the Buick started.

Best we stop fooling around and get down to cases. I've had enough vacation -- the fact is you can't get back soon enough to suit me. I'm not going to try to come Outside. There is too much to do here. We just can't really afford the time and the cost of my travel. So please, Honey, what say you wind it all up and get back to your ever-lovin'?

If you need money, let me know by return mail, and I'll wire it to you. Gosh, I'd certainly like to be meeting you in Anchorage in a couple of weeks if you can see your way clear to part with civilization that quickly. Let me know your exact itinerary - and remember our emergency address is: Anchorage, General delivery if you should need to telegraph because of a delay or something.

Wish you could see our little house now. All the rafters are up. I need to get the truck fixed to haul some more sheathing. Lue Stainbrook raves about how "cute" it is-wouldn't you know? Very soon I'm going to start "camping out" up there. Of course, I'll wait until you get back to move up there for good. However, living up there now will give me a little more time each day to get things ready. Harriet, I think we will be able to start moving the minute you return.

Tonight, I had the best service with the young people that I've ever had. Took a little time to prepare it and then gave the story from the Lord's Supper up through Judas's hanging. They stuck to every word and continued to draw me out some time after I intended to quit. It was undeniably a thrill.

Though I write only to you, I think of those around you. You never can tell me enough about Tommy. The pictures came in the mail last week. There are three of the most precious ones of our son.

To answer your last letter and your kind words are so kind regarding my ability to express myself via the pen. But you underrate your own abilities, Harriet. Frankly, I cloud up with loving emotion each time I read your letters. I know that you don't write for that effect, but the clarity and sincerity of your prose has a deep emotional impact on me. It's truly a good feeling, I assure you. You write to say that I should be a writer. No, my Darling, I should be a lover-your lover- and these written words are only bridging girders to help span the distance that physically separates us.

Kiss and hug our young 'un for me.

Love ya' mucho,
Harold

York, Nebraska
April 9, 1954

Darling Harold,
Mother just came over with the most recent letter from

you. The college office had called to say that it had come in. I was so excited, but I couldn't leave Tommy to go get it. Mother bless her heart, left work for a few minutes to bring it over.

It is another thrilling love letter. Darling, again proving my side of the debate that you should be a writer. However, I am glad at this time for you to concentrate your writing talents on me. I love you so much. You write truly beautiful letters. No one is around now as I write to you, so I am letting my eyes water unashamedly.

How wonderful it is to hear from you, even though the news about the truck is sad. I can certainly understand your need to stay in Alaska, but I am disappointed. Yet you needn't worry. Tommy and I will finish our journey and get back to you as quickly as we can.

I have finally laid plans for the rest of my stay on this side of the world. I have decided that I had better stay here through most of Mother's vacation, even though this year the college has extended it so that it is a week longer than I had thought it would be. I am enjoying the time, but I never feel quite complete without you here.

I've asked Cecil and Becky to meet me in Bellville on the night of the tenth of April and to take me on to Clayton the next day. I've also asked Tom and Lois to drive me to Dodge City from Clayton where I'll be met and taken to Mullinville. I'll spend a couple of days in Mullinville and be there over Easter. Finally, I will head down to New Mexico for some time with the other grandmother, your Mom.

I'll be in Alaska on the 25th of April. I get a little quivery when I think how close I'm cutting corners. But I just can't wait any longer to see you. This is my plan. I'll leave New Mexico in time to get in on some early morning flight, then as soon as I get to Alaska, I'll get in touch with the hotels to see if you have a room reserved. I will try the Anchorage Hotel first. Then, if there is no reservation in the Walker name, I'll take a room and wait. I'll remember about General Delivery in

Anchorage if I need to send you a telegram with last minute changes in plans. It will be so wonderful to be together again!

Saturday morning Mother, Tommy, and I went over to Lincoln on the bus. With Mother baby-sitting, Jean and I went shopping in the afternoon. What a thrill those beautiful, big department stores provided. I found myself entranced by just the artistic displays in the windows and throughout the store. All that and I haven't even mentioned the merchandise yet. I about went berserk. I can see the advantage to living out as remotely as we do. There are a lot of things that you never realize you ought to "have" when they're not placed enticingly before you.

Clarke and Jean are quite the couple. They seem happy in their life, too. I am satisfied that Jean is the perfect wife for Clarke. We played a new game in the evening. It's called "Scrabble." This game is sweeping the country, I understand. That's easy to believe because it's really fascinating. It is a word game, which is a cross between anagrams and crossword puzzles. The challenge it offers really grows on you. I am tossing over in my mind the purchase of a set for us. I think we two might have some fun with it. If only we had the time.

Since Clarke and Jean were in the choir, I sat by myself at the church on Sunday. Mother had thought it best to stay home with the baby. I've more or less let her decide when we take him out and when we leave him at home. Evelyn and Bob drove over for the noon meal and then brought us home to York.

Again, I must try to express some very important and powerful thoughts to you via a typewriter. And, as usual, I can't see your face and note your reaction to know what to say further. I'm not exactly a "yes" woman, but how you often react tempers how I feel.

You know how you've always said that you would just wait for things to open up. And so far, we haven't gone wrong. Well, it could just be that just such a thing has opened up for us, and again, it may be just a series of coincidences.

I've become more and more aware of a feeling that maybe we shouldn't beat our heads against technical walls to get you into a specific law school. In the first place, even though a degree from York College may not carry the prestige to pave the way into a top law school, I am so glad for the four rich years we had here. The opportunity to meet each other, our friends, and our memories, are far more valuable in the long run. In the second place, a democratic and skeptical society such as you plan to serve in Alaska would be little impressed by a big name school. In fact, Nebraska's governor is a Harvard man, but Clarke says that he keeps that fact concealed for fear it would hurt him among the local people. And in the third place, you are an able person and will profit from any legal diet that is set before you.

What am I getting at? Well, when I was in Lincoln last weekend visiting Clarke, the idea was born that we might serve as Youth Directors in the big Trinity Methodist Church. They have a budget allowance of four thousand dollars for a full-time person and have been dramatically unsuccessful in acquiring one. Clarke and Jean have been filling in that capacity for one hundred dollars a month and are begging for freedom. The pastor has been conducting a frantic search for someone to fill that position. He has another young couple on the string right now but is worried that they want a Sunday only job. This job needs someone fulltime. The pastor was interested in us and excited by the prospect.

Don't get excited. I didn't commit us by any means. I told them frankly that Nebraska certainly wasn't one of the places that we had considered in our choice of law schools. Additionally, there is the problem that we wouldn't be available for all twelve months since we need summers in Alaska. However, Clarke and Jean are saying that they would be willing to fill in while we were gone. I suppose we couldn't expect full pay because we wouldn't be really full time. However, I think that with the two of us splitting the work we would be more than full time while we were here. Clarke is sure we could get a living out of it -- say around two hundred and fifty dollars a month or so. I don't know what we would need to live on and pay school expenses, but that isn't a sum to be sniffed at.

Our duties would be this basically. We wouldn't sponsor any Youth Fellowship directly but would work through three other young couples that do. We would coordinate their activities, direct the total program, order worship, visual education, and recreational materials, and help plan the few activities each year, which include all groups. In addition to that would be committee meetings, sponsor meetings, and a certain amount of calling. Clarke and Jean have had a few good ideas but haven't really done a terrific amount of work, and yet the whole young people's work has progressed very satisfactorily under their leadership. Let's brag a minute. We are well rounded. We have a church background. I've had experience with National Youth Fellowship work on an executive level. You're tops with recreation. We've had music and drama. I think we could do a very good job.

To complete the picture - we would be in a very advantageous position to equip our house at the very minimum cost to us. Evelyn will be leaving, and we can have the furniture at Mother's that she has and could likely buy a few pieces also for a song. We can get one bedroom set from Clarke that used to be mother's because as Jean puts it, she would be glad for me to force her to buy a new set.

Now do I want to do it? No, not if you don't want to do it, but, yes, if together we see it as an opening of the way for us to go ahead. I've been thinking about it all since Sunday, and it hasn't really cooled down in possibilities. Of course, we'll have to wait until we can talk about it together before any kind of decision can be made. I thought I would just lay it out in this letter for you to think about.

I'm beginning to get that old queasy feeling about desperately needing to be with you. I love you. Let's never get separated this long again. Shall we not?

I smile at some of my married friends who wonder, like

Patty, how I can stand to be away from you. She assures me that she certainly can't be away from Mike like this. Many say things like that. Still, I think that they aren't as close when they are together as we are apart.

Tommy has been so good. I've heard it remarked over and over again that he is "the best baby I ever saw." He's growing and developing rapidly. He is trying desperately to crawl. Most predictions are that he'll be doing it before he gets to Alaska. I rather hope not, because he is so easy to handle this way. I just put him on a section of the floor, and he stays there gaily kicking and squirming. Then, too, he stays cleaner. He is so changed that you likely won't recognize him. His little tooth juts up proudly, but so far, its sparkle is a solitary one.

His little hands are sweet and busy playing with anything in reach. He was lying on the floor by me the other day and amused himself with my dress skirt. Often, though, he just looks in amazement at his hands.

He has taken to making all sorts of noises. He makes crowing, choking, coughing, and gurgling noises. He has a very endearing way of smiling bashfully and ducking his head when you talk and smile with him. I love him so much. And I love you so much. With two men like that, I am the luckiest gal around.

I am having a nice time. I truly am. But right in the middle of a laugh, I might stop because of a little pain in my heart that I'm not laughing with you. I agree with you that this little separation wasn't necessary to prove our feelings to each other. Sometimes I want to pack right up and rush home to your arms. But I won't. I'll go on visiting here, visiting in Mullinville and along the way, visiting your mom, and then, in what seems like ages from now, I'll be with you again.

Love,
Harriet

Hope, Alaska
April 18, 1954

Darling Harriet,

In just a week we'll be together again. Then I can swear off this pen and settle down to lovin' you as you should be loved. I'm worried that this letter will not catch you until you are again with me, but I must write anyway. Never would I have believed how much I could miss you. My love affair with Alaska precedes our relationship. Yet this short time we have lived together in this country has changed me. I can't love it any longer without you here with me. Alaska and I eagerly await your return.

Spring is drowsily luxurious in its waking, and I so anticipate sharing it with you. There is much to tell - I am aware of many things that are completely new to me. No other counterpart to me can hear what I have to sound against you - let us "corn" by saying: as a vibrating string I'm unheard because you are the rest of the instrument.

Friday night the church was actually crowded. The kids did well on their instruments, but Rev. Elliot jerked the rug out from under them by refusing to let their special be accompaniment for the congregation. Consequently, they played only one verse of each hymn and were tight and self-conscious - their singing was hardly a whisper. Nevertheless, worship was well attended, and the congregation was most appreciative of the kids' contribution.

Honey, I surely hope you are ready to help me catch up after you get here. Of course, we will need to allow time for you to rest. I didn't do so badly on my work until last week. Then that truck went "plunk," and it ruined many of our plans. I ended up spending three days in and around Anchorage getting parts. This constituted a significant loss of time and money. My house building was set back at least a week, not to mention all the other little things that I'd been trying to click off. I even had to just leave the Buick out on the road because we couldn't get it started, although now we've had it towed in from mile 73 and got it running again. I had to bum a ride from Jim Carter one day and rode along with Keith Specking the other two days to get the truck business done in Anchorage. All totaled, the truck was out of operation for nine days. Rats! Oh, well, I've still got my health, and financially we are better off than we've been for a long time. If too many bad breaks don't hit, we should make out pretty well. But you, my love, I very much need. I even tried fixing some dessert to take the drabness out of my lunches. I really didn't accomplish very much except to just make you more wanted around here.

One of the byproducts of the whole affair with the truck was that Keith Specking introduced me to a part of the Alaskan public that I have not been able to meet yet. Since I was using him as transportation to Anchorage to scrounge truck parts, I had to travel along his sales route with him. Keith thought it was a great opportunity for me to get to know a sampling of my constituency if I were to run for an elective office. I talked to a lot of people that I would not ordinarily have met. Many of the conversations focused on politics. Harriet, the truth is I came home completely disillusioned about my prospects of adequately representing these people. I am very disappointed because it is apparent that many Alaskans differ significantly from me on important issues. I guess no matter how much I love this country, I'm a Midwesterner at heart. I have some serious doubts now about my being able to represent Alaskans in the way I had thought.

That plays into the decision about law school next fall, I suppose. I haven't had enough time to think about it yet and really need you here to talk to anyway. I suppose you're right about the school's prestige, but I do want to be successful and need to take every factor into consideration. Maybe as you say, we should consider the school at Lincoln.

The youth director job does sound like an interesting opportunity. We'll have to look into that more. Still, I feel completely incapable of making any kind of important decisions like this without the opportunity to talk to you face to face. Sounds like you may not get much of a chance to rest when you get back because we will have a perpetual gabfest.

The exciting news is that in spite of delays I think I will have the new house almost livable when you get back. I've been staying up here the last couple of nights, and it has really spurred me on. Just a little more work this week and I will have it all closed in. We just as well start moving in right away, and then we can finish things off right while we are living here. Even with construction not quite finished it will be a lot more comfortable than the Beutedahl place was during the winter. So, if that entices you to come home more quickly, that is just what I had in mind. Love Ya!

The calendar and I make daily steps with you. Thanks so much for the words that bring our little Tommy home. Goodnight, and let my wife know that I still love her,

Harold

CHAPTER 11

May 1954: A New House

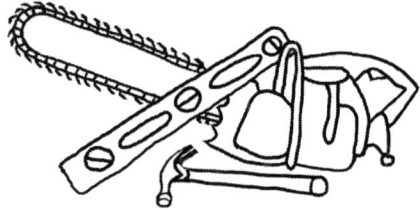

D*ear Karen,*
 I am glad that you asked about Frank Walunga. You are right. The Fourth of July race he and Harold were in was the same race that Harold chose not to enter the year we lived in Alaska. Frank was an indigenous Alaskan native from St. Lawrence, way up north. He was a skilled ivory carver who could carry his trade wherever he went. This was fortunate because at the time we were there, his wife needed to be in the tuberculosis sanitarium in Seward.

Frank Walunga and Ralph Hatch were the regular first and second place finishers in the Fourth of July race up Marathon Mountain near Seward. Ralph was also a Native American who lived in Seward. These two trained regularly on the mountain. Harold didn't get to train there and was fortunate these times to beat out all the rest of the entries and take third place. During the times he was entered in the races, Harold became friends with both men. In fact, Harold was invited to dinner at the Hatch home the night after your father was born.

I smiled at the question about the 25,000 board feet of "heavy rough stuff" that the Palmer druggist ordered. If you think of it in the context of mill operation, the "heavy rough stuff" makes sense. Actually, it was rough sawed, unplaned building logs for which the druggist was in a great hurry. Most of the order was for logs sawed on two opposite sides to be fit together in the building construction. One of the interesting things about this particular order was that the logs could be made any width from 6" to 10" depending on the cut that would make the best-looking building logs. The builders would take it from there, matching out log widths so that each tier of logs would be balanced. The lodge that resulted from that order became a landmark at Summit Lake along the Seward highway.

This next group of letters I scanned for you will tell about our new house on the hill. When Tommy and I returned from Outside, I was surprised and delighted with all that Harold had managed to accomplish toward completing that house. It was still unfinished in many areas, but I could see that the moving-in date was just around the corner. During the previous weeks, my mind and my correspondence with Harold had been so centered on the possibility of a major shift in our plans that I really gave little thought to what Harold was achieving in Alaska as day after day he labored on the house. The very day we arrived back in Hope, Tommy and I had a tour of the inside of the house. I could see where the kitchen worktable would be and where we would put the bed. Harold would be constructing a sort of playpen in one corner. The dreams we had shared came tumbling into reality.

The next afternoon Harold again took me up the hill to view the house. Before going into the house, we were standing there absorbing the beautiful panoramic view of the inlet when Jim Carter sauntered over in a neighborly way to see my reaction. Karen, you would have been interested in hearing what Jim had to tell about the construction. He said that Harold's approach to building was both appalling and awe-inspiring.

Before Jim got involved, Harold had built a sturdy 18' X 26' "box" on a timber and mudsill foundation. Harold had started working on his own, but when Jim offered his help, Harold was quick to take advantage of his experience with construction. Jim persuaded Harold to jack up the unroofed house and replace the mudsill logs with concrete piers. Jim marveled out loud that Harold had done all the sawing with his chain saw including squirreling around on the structure as it went up without the benefit of ladder or scaffolding. While admiring Harold's artistry and accuracy with his chain saw, Jim had insisted on using his own miter saw for the final trim work. He also had brought down his ladder and helped construct scaffolding before he and Harold finished the upper part of the house.

Jim described all those building stages with a sort of pride in Harold. However, by then I knew that it had come at a cost to Harold's physical wellbeing. In all this "squirreling" around Harold had seriously injured his knee. He assured me that the worst was behind him, but he had needed medical treatment to recover. Even after the doctor's corrective treatment, Harold was still limping some. As I realized the severity of his injury, I sadly imagined him coming home in pain each night to a cold cottage with no warm meal awaiting him.

But now Harold was holding Tommy as I stood there surveying our new home. Jim was watching my face to see my reaction to this house on the hill in its perfect setting. He had no inkling of the change of plans that seemed to be evolving in our thinking. On the Outside, I was very enthusiastic over what had been accomplished and pouring forth ideas for decorating the interior. At the same time, I was wondering how we could let go of this long-cherished dream to launch out in a completely different direction.

I tell you, Karen, in the years since that day, I have occasionally wondered how different our lives might have been had we followed the form of our Alaskan dream instead of its purpose. The beauty of the country, the simplicity of the lifestyle, the challenge of building our own home on the Alaskan frontier had an allure that was really gripping. But measured against the original purpose of our Alaskan dream, these things had begun to seem a frivolous detour. Our original purpose had been to free ourselves financially and equip us for a life that was family-centered and dedicated to service. More and more, life in Alaska was standing in the way of reaching that purpose. Even as I stood there looking at the house Harold had built, I knew we'd have to choose between Alaska and the purpose we had envisioned for our lives. I knew that we would *choose to go. Nevertheless, for a short time, we found much joy in making this first house we had ever owned into a true home for our little family of three.*

Love,
Grandma

Hope, Alaska
May 9, 1954

Dear Mother,

Today is Mother's Day!! This is a new kind of Mother's Day for me because this time I've crossed the line and am a mother myself. It is a stirring feeling. But I feel even more keenly how thankful I am for the wonderful mother you've been to us. I can honestly say that I am going to try to pattern my own mother-hood after yours. Your generous, loving attitude, your enthusiasm for our interests, created the wonderful environment we grew up in. You have a zest for new things. You understood the little needs we had as children, like getting out of the car to sample a school playground in the middle of a long day of driving. In your frank respect and love for Daddy and your Christian life itself, you have set an example worthy of emulation.

I have a Mother's Day present for you. The decision has been made! We will be coming Outside this winter so that Harold can go to law school. He is planning to apply for admission to the school in Lincoln. For now, we are hoping that the Youth Director job in Lincoln that we talked about when we were visiting Clarke and Jean will work out. But even if it doesn't, we still plan to come anyway and make something work. It will be wonderful to be closer to you next winter and to have mail service that doesn't involve a two-week turnaround. We will miss Alaska, but we know this is the right thing to do for getting on with our lives.

My Mother's Day present is where I'm writing this letter. I am writing this letter to you from our new house! It is simply wonderful, Mother! Although the interior is unfinished, it is clean and new and very much ours. We already feel at home here and love it. Harold's guns are hanging on one wall and look very much in place in a frontier-like fashion. I'm going to get some drapes around the closet and some over the picture window. Before long, it will really look swell, we think.

I shall attempt to describe it to you. I'm not very good with directions, but maybe you'll get a general idea. The corner where I am sitting looks out over the Turnagain Arm of Cook Inlet and across it to some beautiful snowcapped mountains. A little to the left is Porcupine Creek. To utilize this wonderful view, we have two huge picture windows, one on each side of the corner. They are each six feet wide by about three and a half tall. So, we can certainly see the view. Then at the opposite end of the house where Harold has built my kitchen counter, are three smaller windows. They are set high in the wall so that I won't be bothered with glare, but I can look up and see the road above our house and how it winds down the hill to where we live. I can also see the mountains across that way too.

So we have a million dollar view even though what we live in is just a "shack." Our house is eighteen feet by twenty-six feet on the inside dimensions. Now that we are all moved in, I'm able to say for certain that we have the most room we've ever had. I didn't realize it before, but we have as much room as the Millers have in their living quarters. No wonder we seem to have such ample space. Then, as soon as we get the stairway built, we may move our bedroom upstairs. The house is a story and a half, and we figure there will be room upstairs for two small bedrooms. The space under the eaves will be utilized for storage. After all, a bedroom doesn't need to be so large, and these will have plenty of room for closets and bed and a small dresser of some kind.

I don't suppose we'll do much about finishing the interior

this summer since we don't plan to spend the winter here. Rather, we'll spend the nice days this summer working on other kinds of improvements around the place like a chicken house, a summer garden, and clearing out the underbrush. This is a piece of virgin land, and we want to plan carefully how we tame it.

Tommy is enjoying himself right now, making a variety of sounds. He makes such queer ones that at times I'm afraid he'll ruin his voice apparatus. But he does enjoy it so. His latest achievement is to patty-cake, and his instructor was his father. He and Harold sure do make some pictures. Harold is sitting outside the bars of Tommy's crib, and Tommy is sitting inside the bars. The two of them are grinning and patty-caking like mad. In fact, Tommy is so proud of his accomplishment along that line that he sometimes starts patty-caking the minute he sees his father, looking around eagerly for the abundant approval that this talent brings. Just yesterday, however, Harold decided to start teaching him to wave "bye-bye." After all, as he explained it to me, we can't have Tommy just patty caking his way through life.

The bars of his ample crib-bound Tommy's world. The cabin floor is a little too cold yet for him, so he has to spend his life inside the crib. Fortunately, it is a big oversized crib made of metal typical of the twenty's era. Harold remembers sleeping in that crib and poking his fingers into the holes that are part of the decoration in the two metal end panels. Since then it has been the bed that greeted each of the Miller kids. Now it furnishes our son with his primary context for life.

Right now, Harold has gone to Youth Fellowship. He has moved the regular meeting around to Sunday morning. That way he can work in a worship service very much like a regular church service. He used Easter, about four weeks ago, as the starting point for this change. Before sunrise, the Hope youth met with Harold down on the beach of Turnagain Arm for the observance of Easter. They had a short, chilly service as the sun appeared over the mountains up the Arm to the East. The beach was littered with broken pieces of the glacier that had been shed into Cook Inlet and carried by the incoming tide up to land on our beach. Some of these little icebergs were as big as a small building and using one of them as a shelter from the sea breeze, the youth cooked their Easter breakfast. In the early dawn light, these hunks of ice had appeared as ghostly gray shapes in a haphazard array along the high-water tide line. Their color was due to having been rolled around in murky glacial-silt water. As the sun rose, they took on a pale rosy hue. The large iceberg chunks made an excellent setting for hiding and chase games after the breakfast and before the next tide came in.

Harold still meets with the kids twice a week for recreation, in addition to Sunday morning. Their latest project is getting a volleyball set and starting to learn that sport. I am sure that the work Harold has done with them this winter has been very worthwhile.

I thought that Harold and I were confiding every thought and every activity while we were apart. But other than reading only that his sore knee was slowing him down, I had no concept of what he went through. This all happened because he had to crawl around so much building our house. He had what is called carpenter's knee, which means that he had fluid buildup under the kneecap. He even went to a doctor who extracted the fluid with a "huge needle." I didn't know any of this until I returned.

He did practically all the work on the house with a chain saw, and he squirreled around the house even putting up the ceiling joists and the rafters without a ladder. Now he has been gradually getting back to normal as is attested to by our living here now. But it has been slow. Work that should ordinarily take only a couple of days has taken the full week.

But perhaps it is best this way. If he had been working at the mill, he would keep going no matter what. That's the way he is. But during this downtime, he's taken more time to rest. I think I could safely say he's well now. He'll be going back to work at the mill tomorrow. Spring break-up is over, and Ross is back from his trip to Kansas to see his mother.

But, oh, it is still painful to think of the evenings Harold would come back from work to our little cottage while I was on the Outside, no light in the window, no heat in the stove, no warm meal waiting. His feelings about those hard days have come out only gradually. But even though it is way behind us now, when I think of that period when I was visiting you, living in comfort, being invited out to bounteous meals while here in Alaska Harold was dealing with such trials alone, I get a clutching feeling in my heart

I'm sorry that Mother's Day slipped up on me without my thinking in time to send something to you, but I'm sure you'll understand. Besides, maybe it's better to get out the memories of our wonderful time together and look them over. They are worth infinitely more than any purchased thing.

Love,
Your Alaskan daughter, Harriet

P.S. Am sending this letter to Anchorage with Marge Carter so it will still get to you on time.

Hope, Alaska
May 14, 1954

Dear Mom Walker,
We're pretty well settled in our new house. In the last letter, I sent you. I think you noticed that Harold had some real problems with his knee. Now it's getting much better. It has been slow and irksome, but healing is nearly completed. He started working up here the first part of last week. Each day he did as much as he could and was sad because he couldn't do more. When we resigned ourselves to taking it easy and doing just what each day could handle, we at least felt better, even though we got no more done. So, we moved up in sections.

Taking a load up in the morning, we would work up here for a while and then maybe go back after a load in the afternoon. Harold had quite a bit of finishing up to do, so while we ate our first meal up here a week ago Thursday afternoon, we didn't spend the first night up here until Friday night. Our final load came up early this week and then everything was out of the little cottage in Hope. We finished up by midweek by giving our former home a really good cleaning. Now we're out for good.

We still have one corner for "organized mess." That's where we have box piles that will go either into the root cellar or into the upstairs. We still get to the upstairs by way of a rather tricky ladder, so Harold does all the carrying in that direction. Therefore, each evening he takes a couple of boxes up. The pile is shrinking at a nice pace. The root cellar felt the effect of his efforts last night. He almost completed the stairway down there. Most folks around here have ladders to get down to their cellars, but he didn't want me carrying things down a ladder, so we're going to have a nice firm stairway. He still has shelves to put up before it's completed.

One night this week he tore around and built a very pretty little switchback path down to the creek. After rationing water so carefully through last winter, I now have an abundance. You see, I actually enjoy going down that path to bring water back. It may get to be an odious task someday. But I enjoy it now. When I finally got Harold to understand that I intended to go after water myself, he built a yoke for me so that I could carry two buckets at a time. It makes one think of Dutch girls seen in old National Geographic magazines. No wonder those Dutch girls use yokes. The task is much easier. Balance is natural, weight is distributed, and movement is easy.

We don't have our chickens moved up here on the hill yet. Harold needs to wait until he can have a morning to finish up in the chicken house. It isn't quite active enough a job for him to do it and successfully fight mosquitoes in the evenings. But he finds plenty to do. He just tears around. It seems funny that he is finally turning his energy to his own place.

Speaking of mosquitoes, you should see me now. You would think that I had been afflicted by the plague for sure. And it's entirely my own fault. Harold and I worked very hard getting this place mosquito proof. We chinked around the windows and doors. We thought we were all set. Then one bright afternoon last week I thought it was such a pretty day that I'd open the door and let the brightness in. That night we were all but carried away. I'll bet there were hundreds of those little guys, and they all headed right for me. Fortunately, we had the mosquito net over Tommy's bed, but the rest of us had to suffer. Harold doesn't swell up as I do, so he carries no battle scars. However, I am surely an awful sight. The next time that I get the urge to let in some bright sunshine, I'll remember how the mosquitoes long for the cool interior of a dark corner to lurk during the daylight hours so that they'll have plenty of energy to ruin me in my sleep.

The following night's sleep, however, was pure bliss. Harold invested in some kind of spray, which he eagerly rushed around using. He watched with fascination as his prey staggered or flew lopsidedly and then finally dropped into grotesque forms of death. He counted forty some dead on just one windowsill. Every time I start doubting that there could have been so many mosquitoes in here, I just look in the mirror.

Tommy is beginning to show signs of not wanting to stop playing. As you know, he's always enjoyed being played with, but always seemed content to be put back and left alone. Well, yesterday he didn't want back in his bed after his stint on the floor, and again last night he had to fuss a little to let us know that his dignity was ruffled by not being consulted on time to terminate his fun time with his daddy.

He still experiments with sounds, producing all varieties from the musical to the blood-curdling and throat splitting kinds. He doesn't recognize words yet but is highly amused if you mimic the sounds that he makes.

I am delighted with the little red wagon that Harold bought

me. Now I can continue my walks with Tommy. A regular stroller isn't sturdy enough for the roads in this country, and of course, now that the snow is gone, the sleggy is worthless. The little wagon will serve us in other ways as well. It's handy for wood and other little chores.

I guess school is over in Hope. How can I tell? Mrs. Blair has been having them come half days for weeks now. The older boys spend their time building doghouses and that sort of thing. I don't think they've pretended to have school for about a month. Final tests have even been over. Don't see how she can do it legally. Of course, she spins them a long line about not taking any vacations and all that bunk. But they took as many vacations this year as we took in Mullinville, and I felt rushed to get all my subjects done by the end of the year. And as it was, I never got all the little projects that I had in mind executed. It may be sour grapes, but I can't believe a really good teacher would have so much time left over. She's just covering the material. I guess today was the last official day of school. Goodness knows when the last day actually was.

Alma and I both got nice letters from Elsie last week. I wish that we could get over to see her. It's a shame to live so close and yet to be so tied down. Maybe she can come down to Hope for a week as she did last summer. I'm going to suggest it. I know it's not the same as visiting with Dave, though. Our car is still its untrustworthy self. It might make it to Wasilla, and it might not. Harold planned to sell it or to trade it before I got back. But he wasn't offered anything that he could even consider. He says that it was just ridiculous. We expected to take quite a loss on the car. It's older, and it's in poor shape, but we can't afford to give it away. We're still stuck with it, therefore, and wondering what to do. Our latest idea is to try to get it fixed up and ship it outside for our use this winter. We'll see.

Oops! Have reached almost to the end of the sheet of paper. Well, guess that's all for now. I'll write again soon.

Love,

Harriet

Hope, Alaska
May 21, 1954

Dear Mother,

Well, I did the interior decorating for our house yesterday. You'll be interested in the fabrics I used. I decided to see what I could do with material on hand and then order only what I absolutely had to. As it turned out, I'll not need to do any ordering, which is good, because the temporary nature of our present situation makes spending money on interior decoration too much of an extravagance. I made drapes for over the picture windows with the blue, tan and black monk's cloth we had from when our family lived in Coffeyville. I believe it was in Clarke's room at first and then in mine for a while. I have the feeling that we got it while we were in Africa. Can that be true? Anyway, I used three panels draped across the windows and one panel we'll use to cover the headboard of the bed.

I used the rose-colored denim, also from high school days in Coffeyville, for skirts around the worktable of my kitchen. There was enough to make matching drapes above the kitchen windows. An extra bed sheet will cover the closet the same way we did in Mullinville. Someday I hope to get away from the use of so many drapes, but in the meantime, they do make the place much more livable.

I almost have my kitchen area all arranged to my satisfaction. I still need a couple of shelves for Tommy's things before everything is complete. Harold brought in a board cut from a tree that had a burl on it. It was sawed two inches thick and is 78 inches on its long side and about 30 inches on the shorter side. It is interestingly shaped -- sort of a lopsided triangle with the very intriguing grain of the burl around the edge and the pattern in the surface. We have fastened it to the wall under one of our picture windows as a breakfast nook counter.

It's still a little green, but when it cures out, we'll sand and varnish it. It has drawn so many comments in the short time that we've had it up. We're thinking we'd like to fill our home with unique features like that.

One unique feature in the kitchen area is that Servel kerosene refrigerator that Harold brought up on the truck a couple of summers ago. It is very impressive standing there. It dominates the kitchen. Hardly anyone in town has one. Am I proud! Only one thing is wrong. It doesn't work. Somehow on the trip up over the Alkan, the poor refrigerator was internally injured. The only thing that can make it work would be a completely new set of innards. In the meantime, it is wonderful for storage. It keeps things nice and clean. Harold admits that it still gives him a bit of a jolt to open the refrigerator and to see the freezing compartment full of spice jars.

Completing my set of kitchen appliances is a beautiful little Monarch cooking stove. It is compact and efficient with a full-sized firebox and an ample oven. Probably the most interesting thing about the cooking stove is how it came to our house. You remember that I wrote you some time ago about how Harold and Ross were working for an interesting fellow named Nash getting out some hydraulic mining pipe he was salvaging. Well, that job led to us getting our cook stove.

Gold was the enticement that brought many people into Alaska. In the gold rush days, before there was a road into Hope, access was by water. The little town of Hope is located where Resurrection Creek empties into Turnagain Arm, but it was not the main gold camp. That was further up the arm at Sunrise where, for a very short time, that town boomed to a population larger than its contemporaries, Seward or Anchorage. Although Hope was a good location for a town, the major gold strike was at Sunrise on up the arm. When the gold field played out there, Sunrise became a ghost town, but the little village of Hope survived. Even when the glory days were over, there was still a little mining activity up Palmer Creek. The gold for our wedding rings had come from there, but no real paying proposition based upon gold mining has existed since the original rush. However, there was one gold mining enterprise that remained until very recently. Its financial soundness depended upon a local "gold fever" promoter, who is none other than our friend Mr. Nash.

Nash had several claims up Palmer creek, but he did not mine gold for profit. Rather, he used the gold he found to promote "gold fever" on the Outside. His real mining was done among the citizens of the West Coast states. The raw nuggets he carried and his stories of the chance to make a big strike enticed men to grubstake his summer operations in the hope of sharing his anticipated riches. For some years, the money from his promotions supported Nash and the families of men who helped him work the claims. These men worked honestly enough with no expectation of actually getting more than enough gold to fuel the next year's promotion. While Nash paid the men a reasonable wage, the biggest incentive to work for him was the "grub" part of the grubstake. No expense was spared in seeing that the best food obtainable was available for the cook of the camp to put out mouth-watering meals. To make sure that the meal quality was top level, Nash himself did the cooking. That being the case, it was not surprising that the stove he used was the best he could find for his purposes, the very stove that is now a salient feature in our kitchen.

After the grubstake scam had run its course, Nash was on to a new enterprise. He had acquired the rights to the mining water pipe for some abandoned placer mines, and that was how we got involved with him. He hired Ross and Harold to log some pipe out, and in addition to a cash payment, he gave Ross the rights to whatever could be salvaged from that old cook cabin up on Palmer Creek. The original access had been by trail up the creek grade, but now the quickest way to get there was by a road, which ran by about one-eighth of a mile above the cabin. A trail down to the cabin had to be improved before Ross and Harold could get a sturdy sled down it to the cabin. The men made several trips down to that cabin and labored up with the salvage. The two heaviest loads were that stove and a massive anvil that was on a big stump beside the cabin. The anvil was the real reason that Ross had made the deal. He had seen it there a couple of years earlier when he was moose hunting and was much taken with the possibility of getting it to his shop. The stove originally was just put into the Miller's garden shed where it stayed until it found a home in our new house on Porcupine Creek. Now, how many people have a cook stove with a history like that?

I fixed some raspberry Bavarian for tonight. Harold really likes it. To chill the Jell-O, I set it on a step into the root cellar. But it wasn't really cool enough to chill the canned milk for whipping. So I dug down into the sawdust around the house, and sure enough, there was some snow. It didn't take long for the can, buried in snow, to come to the right temperature. Sawdust works as wonderful insulation, which is why it was piled up around the house. This insulation business works both ways. It certainly keeps the snow from melting as well as it holds the warmer temperatures inside the house.

Tommy is making great progress in his crawling but hasn't mastered it yet. His father is urging him daily, and his mother is being very passive about it. I point out that then my chasing begins, but Harold assures me that my load will be lightened in that Tommy will be able to pull his own feet out from between the crib bars where he often wedges them. The bed is a little too springy, so he has to save his crawling practice for the times when he is on a firmer foundation. He does get up on his hands and knees and rock and rock before collapsing ungracefully on his stomach. He still persists in thinking that he'll make progress by traveling on his toes. When a toy is placed a little ahead of him on the floor, he rears up into a beautiful and difficult push-up, balancing himself on his hands and the tips of his toes. I could never do that, but I can crawl, and I don't drool. Anyway, he remains poised in that odd position for a few seconds before landing on his well-padded stomach a few inches farther from the toy than he was before. He continues this backward progress until he is quite a way from his goal. It all works out in the end because when he gets far enough away, he just turns around and decides that that's just where he wanted to be in the first place.

Right now, I am disciplining Tommy. He has developed a clever little habit of savoring his food by blowing bubbles with it. In the first place, he gets only half of what is aimed in his direction. In the second place, his small personal volcano tends to make me look like I've been hit by a plague, green or yellow, depending on the food. So tonight we decided not to continue feeding him if he starts in with the bubble blowing. We plan to wait a while longer until he was really hungry on the premise that then he would gobble it all down hungrily. We are waiting. He is neither getting hungry or seeming the least bit bothered by our cruelty. On the contrary, he is cooing happily to himself. We are beginning to wonder who is disciplining whom.

It's getting to the place that we hardly need any light at night now at all. Boy, we've been having some glorious spring days. Spring is here for sure. All ice is gone, and the water is running freely in the creek. Of course, it's still too wet and a mite cold at night to get the gardens in, but Alma has been having lettuce from her greenhouse for some time now.

Jeepers, I hope we have a letter from Clarke in tomorrow's mail. It's not unreasonable for them to wait in answering since we waited too long to let them know. But of course, we are eager to settle matters now that we are determined to move in that direction. I do hope that the Lincoln deal goes through because I feel that it would be a great way for us to go.

I guess that's all for tonight.

I love you,
Your Alaskan Daughter, Harriet

Hope, Alaska

Harriet Walker

May 25, 1954

Dear Clarke and Jean,

We received your letter on Saturday. Certainly, we are disappointed that the plans fell through but, as you pointed out, we knew all along that the other couple had already been asked. Lest you feel that you were personally responsible for jarring our lives, I want to assure you that in changing our line of thinking, you did us a real favor. Even with this minor setback, we feel that some of our hazy ideas are beginning to jell into a course of action.

Before the opportunity for the Youth Director position, we really hadn't given the idea of going to school in the Midwest much thought. Now, however, Lincoln seems to be the wise choice for several reasons. We have found out that Harold's credits will be accepted without question. The opportunity to work with a group of people in a familiar section of the country is another reason. The more we think about it, the more we like the idea of locating in Lincoln. We see it as a highly desirable place to live with its large "small town" environment. Then, as you pointed out, there would be the advantage of your working there the year around to give a sort of permanency to the whole thing.

Perhaps, in the long run, our not getting the church youth director position this fall will prove to be a good thing. It has started us thinking through the contingencies necessary to move us into the next stage of our lives. A key issue is securing ownership of the property we are living on. We are required to live on this site for five years as a condition for owning it. So we are trying to factor that into our planning.

Recently we were tempted by an offer from a school in Seward for Harold to take a teaching and coaching position. We've firmly decided not to take it because it would have been just a stall- a good one financially - but a stall, nevertheless. We don't have time in our lives to get everything done that we want to do and certainly not the time to "stall." Getting Harold back to law school has to be our number one priority.

One plan is to live here through this fall and focus on getting all the loose ends tied up. If sawmill production is good, then we should be set to come Outside by the second semester to enroll in law school at Lincoln. We trust it wouldn't be too serious a handicap to start mid-year.

On the other hand, if by mid-August it looks like the mill's production won't be sufficient to clear up our present deficits, see us through the winter, and allow enough to put us through the semester of school, then we'll be looking for teaching positions. At the moment we are thinking that these would need to be in or around Lincoln so that we are positioned to get Harold going on his schooling as quickly as possible. We certainly prefer the first plan but will do what we must get on with our lives.

You may know we are now living in our new house. I am sometimes amazed to realize that it is ours and built completely by Harold with a little advice and help from a neighbor. We have a very lovely location. There have been several little pleasures that even I didn't anticipate. For example, I know now the feeling of agelessness that watching the constant movement of the ocean can give you. I've heard the violent pounding of the surf and the gentle lapping of the ebbing tide. We also are enjoying the coming of the Alaskan summer as viewed from our huge picture windows.

It is hard to imagine how much the tide in Turnagain Arm affects the backdrop of life here in Hope until you actually experience it. It is really a very dramatic scene right out our front window. When the tide is in, we are on the shore of a great sea, but when it is out, we are perched on the edge of a great plain of mud. In fact, there is a story around Hope that helps to understand what an amazing effect the tides have on this little corner of the world. Harold's nephew, Lewie, really gets a kick out of this one.

One late afternoon some stateside tourists drove down onto the tide flat beach with their camping trailer and set up camp. They parked with their car pointing up the gentle slope. A couple of local men strolled down to where they were preparing a meal and told them that at high tide the water would reach the area where they were camping. This conversation took place during low tide, and the only water was in the channel over against the mountains some six miles away. The campers could hardly see the distant water. Perhaps they thought the locals liked to play jokes like this on tourists and decided not to be gullible. For whatever reason, they remained where they were.

During the night high tide came in, moved up past where they were camped, and then receded again. Imagine the surprise of the tourists upon awakening the next morning to discover their camper cocked at an angle to the car, and their trash can was gone. The perpetrator of this disturbance was again in its channel almost out of sight. The tourists stormed into our town full of accusations about the local teenagers "pranking" them. But faced with the consistently confident response of local adults, the tourists finally left town convinced that they had been very fortunate victims of their own foolishness in challenging one of the world's most amazing tidal phenomena.

Tommy is changing daily and a constant delight. He's so much more aware of people. Right now, he's on his tummy on the floor watching the typewriter with fascination. Whenever I stop and watch him or speak to him, he starts cooing and wiggling with happiness. He already reacts to music. When we sing to him, he responds by kicking his feet and with other happy signs. But one of his new tricks is to observe us closely. Then the minute you look at him, he starts to groan and whine. If you then walk toward him as if to pick him up, his whines turn into coos of pleasure. Oh, we'll have to watch this one.

Well, it is probably past time to give Tommy his lunch so I shall stop. Thanks for all you've done on our behalf and for your faith in us.

Love,
Harriet

~⊃✕⊂~

Hope, Alaska
May 29, 1954

Dear Mother,

Harold finished making the chicken house and has moved our hens up here from their former home. They are producing much better again now that I can water and feed them in the middle of the day. Before long we should have our production rate right back at the fabulous mark it has been most of the time. Harold is going to make a little chicken house this week-end. By little chicken house, I don't mean to imply that the house will be little. Because actually, the little chicken house will be bigger than the house the big chickens are in. You see, we are planning to get more little chickens than we have big chickens and so in spite of the relative size between the big and little chickens, the little chicken house will have to be the bigger. Then, too, the little chickens will doubtless grow, and some of them will lose their heads. You know how it goes.

We had Jim Carter down for supper the other night. His wife had to take a job in Anchorage to lay ahead some cash. They feel that they had a rather rugged winter. Jim also took a job and is doing roadwork near Hope. Anyway, they have been very good to us. When I was gone Outside, Harold had invited Jim down a couple of times. In many ways, the Carters have done more for us than anyone else around here besides the Millers. In the first place, they told us about this home site and encouraged us to get it. Then Jim told his cousin about our mill when the cousin was planning some building. Jim's cousin's enthusiasm over our lumber and his spreading the word to his friends has resulted in some of our biggest lumber sales. Jim also has helped Harold build this house. Of course, we're going to pay him for his labor. But the labor is minor compared to the value of his teaching Harold about construction which we got at no extra charge. So, all in all, we are very grateful to them. Marge will be home this weekend, and we're planning to get together to make ice cream.

Well, as you know, the mail had some rather disappointing news for us. Clarke's letter came with the news that the potential youth director job is closed out. But I'm sure we'll work something out. We are undecided just what course we will take from here. We may just wait and see if we can make enough this summer and fall to come out for the second semester. Or we may accept a teaching position. Harold won't have any trouble getting a teaching job even as late as August, I bet. He just may not have his pick. I know Clarke feels bad about having to convey this news. But he mustn't. We knew about the possibility of the deal's falling through, and at any rate, it has opened up a new line of thought to us. So, it may all be the best in the end.

Given the strong possibility that we'll be Outside this winter, we're changing our goals for the summer. We won't put in as extensive a garden as otherwise and raise only what will give us fresh stuff this summer. Rather than rushing around to finish and winterize the interior of the house, we'll concentrate on the grounds and outbuildings. This is plenty nice for summer residence as it is.

Tomorrow night we are going to do a big washing again. The washing machine is sitting out in the yard on its wooden platform, ready and anticipating it regular task. I'm going to have the able assistance of Harold D. Walker as an engineer in the project. We've really been hitting our washing hard. We washed twice this last week. We had gotten so far behind. But now that we have our own machine, we' re working at catching up. When we do, we'll try to keep up. You remember that we traded eggs for this machine. Harold found a gas engine to put on it to get it working. You know, there are so many things around a place that don't look a bit dirty when you're doing the washing by hand. But suddenly you realize how dirty they are when washing becomes a little easier. We're doing rugs, work clothes, gunnysacks, and about anything else we can wash. Of course, I did have to keep Tommy's washing up right along, but how nice it will be to be able to have all my washing done in such a flash. The washing machine is an old rattletrap affair, but I love it!!!

Tommy's latest trick is refusing to bend. The other morning, I had to give him a bath standing up. Well, I guess I always stand up, but usually he sits down. This time we both stood up because he just wouldn't sit down. He gets as rigid as a little length of two by four lumber and stays that way. He doesn't pull himself up, and he doesn't try to stand, but he sure does have strength in those legs. I've solved the problem about trying to get him to sit when I place him on the floor. I just lay him down on his stomach or his back. He can't foil me with his unbending attitude.

The other morning Harold grubbed out a tree stump, which was cluttering up our front yard. He tied a chain around it and pulled it out with the heavy truck. He tugged and tugged and then pretty soon he was driving up the road with that thing bobbing along behind, its roots waving and clawing the air like so many spider legs. It was quite grotesque, I thought.

We had Bill Brattain, who delivers the mail, bring us up some fresh meat this week. He brought us the five dollars' worth we asked for and charged us one dollar service charge for bringing it. He brought the meat in last night, so we haven't had a chance to try it yet. It looks good, but it is very expensive. Six dollars' worth won't go very far, but how we shall enjoy it while it lasts. Even if it does cost more, we're going to have fresh meat this summer some way. Of that, I am resolved.

The other night Vern Stall took a boatload of people passed here in his little motorboat. We could see the boat from our window, but we didn't realize how many people there were in the boat until these people started to walk back by our path. It seems that Vern broke a shear pin of his propeller and didn't have another one with him. Since the tide was going out, he couldn't row back against the current, so he guided the boat into a cove, and they walked the mile and a half or so back to town. He had fifteen people in that boat, just imagine, and that includes Mrs. Blair! Well, I suppose the four little kids in the group helped with figuring space and weight, but they were really excited about the adventure.

Just a few minutes ago Carl Clark went steaming out of the arm for his summer's fishing. We got a couple of snapshots of it. Should be pretty interesting. These fishermen used to have it really made. In a short summer, they used to make enough to last them the entire year. But now things are a little tighter. Still, they can't get used to the idea of working for more than three months. Other people must.

Mrs. Mitchell, who runs the Post Office, has offered us the loan of her high chair. When she asked me if I had one, I said I didn't, so she told us we could use hers. Her husband, a great joker, looked horrified and asked where he was going to sit now. Actually, they surely haven't used it for some time, because her youngest child is now in the seventh grade. But then babies aren't too common around here. We'll be glad to use it because I'm sure it will come in handy.

We are all feeling well. Harold is hardly even aware of the pain in his knee. So, I think his cure will be complete. I hope all is well with you and that you aren't too rushed with closing activities at the college. Give our best to Bob and Evelyn. Let us know your plans as they work out, and we'll do likewise.

Love,
Harriet

CHAPTER 12

Summer 1954: Goodbye Alaska

*D*ear Karen,

    Well, we are winding down. These are the last of the letters I'm going to send. Since the due date for your project is coming so soon, Harold and I have decided to pick and choose among the letters from the rest of the time we were in Alaska. Most of the summer of 1954 was spent getting ready to leave and preparing for our new life. I think a few selected letters from this period will round out the story just fine.

    What a wonderful project this has been! Harold and I have truly enjoyed reliving our Alaskan adventure. Sharing the letters and stories with you has really enhanced the experience. I have so appreciated your reaction to them, and your questions have demonstrated how many changes the fifty intervening years have brought to our culture.

    You asked me to explain more about the ice right by the house, which I used to cool the canned milk. This ice was accidentally "put up" by Harold in the process of building the house. When he came up during winter to work on it, after a new snowfall and before there was a roof, the new snow would be piled on the floor of the house. Before he could start to work, he had to scoop all that snow off the floor. Over time this process formed a great pile of snow. Also, all his sawing created a lot of sawdust. When he swept that up and scooped it onto the pile of snow, he accidentally created ice storage that did not completely melt until mid-June.

Even more interesting than the accidental ice storage was the intentional venture that produced tons of ice for our use during the warmer months. In the summer of '54, our icehouse was a leap toward modern living, even though it was a generation behind times in the States. With it, we had ice handy all summer long for freezing ice cream and cooling our home-built iceboxes. Let me clarify what I mean by "icehouse." At that time there was not any actual building structure to cover the ice storage facility. Ross used the dozer to dig a deep trench into a side hill. Then they laid down a floor of new-milled sawdust in the bottom to stack the cakes of ice on. When all the ice was in place, the men covered the ice with a deep layer of sawdust filling in the trench.

The ice blocks themselves were made of crystal-clear water, but we did not use them to cool our drinks. Those clear blocks of ice had been harvested from a beaver pond, and a few blocks contained bright beaver-chewed twigs frozen into the ice. The men delighted in saving those trophies for someone's later discovery when the ice was used. Ross was especially pleased with himself for finding the beaver pond used to get the ice. It was fed by a good spring and close enough to a road so that he could easily make an access way with the dozer right to the side of the dam. From there they could efficiently load up the blocks of ice onto the truck for hauling to the icehouse.

At first, the men were afraid that the ice would be too thick for the chain saw to reach all the way through to the water. They started sawing straight down through the ice and pulled no water up with the buzzing chain. However, when they finished the fourth side of the first block, it dropped four inches straight down onto another layer of ice. Evidently, after freezing almost two feet thick, the water level had dropped, and a new shelf of ice was formed. This created ideal conditions for ice harvesting. The men cut the blocks from the upper level of ice without danger of getting wet while using the lower level as a work platform. In this way, a full supply of ice for three families was stored away with relative ease.

Harold wants me to clear up one potential misconception before you get into this last set of letters. He's worried that when you read about preparations for the hunting trip, you may be a bit perplexed about the amount of ammunition that he was preparing since you had always heard that he was pretty much a one-shot game harvester. Karen, the truth is that there is no way to completely understand what men do when they are preparing for a hunting trip. But Harold's point about the amount of ammunition is valid. Jim Carter, his hunting partner, did not miss on his two animals. Harold wasted only one shot finding the needed elevation on a difficult long range, downhill shot at the Dall sheep ram he got. His caribou fell on one squeeze of the trigger.

There is one other thing that I want to carefully point out as we approach the final stage of this story. In reading back over these letters, I'm very worried that you might get the impression that Harold was miserable in his frustrations with Ross. Nothing could be farther from the truth. There is no denying that there were frustrations, but they were minor compared to the joy that he took in working with Ross. This is especially true about their work in the woods. I don't remember him ever having anything but praise for Ross in the process of the logging operation. I clearly remember Harold telling about Ross's patience in showing him how to fell trees in a way that made for more efficient skidding.

The real issue causing frustration was almost completely internal for Harold and me. Our high regard for Ross was in conflict with our dream for the mill. We wanted a mill business that would grow fast and become valuable so that we could sell it to create a comfortable financial base for the life of public service we had envisioned. Ross wanted a slow growing, stable family business that would provide work and income for the indefinite future. Both dreams could not become realities because they each required radically different approaches to the work. This issue never became an open point of contention between Harold and Ross. As we figured out what the options were, we worked our way through to a resolution that we have not regretted. Yes, many times we have missed Alaska's beauty and the wonderful little community of Hope, but we have had great joy in the life to which our choices led. Additionally, we have maintained a good relationship with the Millers, while Harold and Ross have always had a special friendship.

Well, here it is then, the final installment in this project. Thank you so much for asking us to be involved. We have just loved revisiting this wonderful year of our lives with you. Let us know how your grade turns out.

Love,
Your Alaskan Grandmother, Harriet

Hope, Alaska
June 12, 1954

Dear Mother,

Well, Harold won the discussion about whether or not our new chickens are big enough to eat. He won it by killing and plucking a chicken. When I have a chicken naked of feathers and minus a head lying on my kitchen table, I don't argue. It weighed two pounds dressed and was delicious.

We ordered an ice cream freezer. Harold is just mad about ice cream, and it is a good nutritious dessert as well as being fun to prepare. We've had it with the Carters several times lately. You remember that Jim Carter and Harold went together to put up ice this winter. It is in a hole dug on our property and covered in sawdust. They have plenty put up for all that both families can use. But we may want to have ice cream sometime in a group that does not include them, so we feel that it would be a good idea to have our own freezer.

Harold has taken an interest in the neighbor boy. Stevie Stainbrook is about fourteen years old and very behind scholastically. I think he's in the seventh-grade next year. He just doesn't apply himself. He is intensely interested in mechanical things but needs more background in academic subjects to be successful. His parents aren't in agreement on how to deal with him, and the end result is that he has little desire to get ahead and is no help around his home place. So, Harold is supporting him in the idea that he can build a shop. Stevie has always wanted one, but now that Harold has set out to help him, the dream is more likely to come true. Here is the plan to make Steve's dream become a reality. He is to come to our place and work by the hour at little daily tasks that Harold lays out for him. He will take his pay in lumber. Harold has helped him plan his little building and encouraged him to use number three lumber for the construction. Number three lumber is very inexpensive because it is technically culled out of standard orders but is plenty strong to use for the shop. He has been over here a couple of evenings planning and dreaming with Harold, and every day he comes over and checks in with me for the job of the day. So far we've kept him on mostly simple chores to test him out. He's worked right along and seems very eager. As he proves more responsible, we'll give him more constructive tasks like laying the floor of the chicken house and building a chicken fence. He's a likable kid, and I hope this all proves beneficial to his personality.

We just got back from church. Harold held Tommy all the time and issued the verdict on the way home that he was worn out. I don't think I could handle this character now if I were to make a trip like I made a few months ago. He's big as a horse and wiggles constantly.

I cut Tommy's hair yesterday. I'm not bragging, you understand, just sadly stating the truth. In defense of my abilities, I feel that I had all the odds against me. I sat on the floor with my legs straight out in front of me. I put Tommy on the floor between them in the vain hope that some of his wigglings could be curbed. Every time I took a snip I found myself gazing not at the rear of his head but at the front. He was truly curious about what was going on behind. I was pretty proud of the results until I started feathering. I stopped after one attempt. I should have stopped before one attempt. But if it is combed right, it doesn't look so bad. He looks like a hick from the sticks, to be sure, but a respectable hick at that.

Tommy gets to a sitting position frequently now. In fact, you might say he sits about half of his waking hours. He looks so cute sitting on his bottom with his legs straight out in front and his back stiff as a ram-rod. Right now, he is systematically tearing up his bed. How one little guy can wreak such havoc with a bed, I don't know. But he does it again and again. Last week I took him downtown as usual in his little red wagon, and he proceeded to crawl right out onto the ground. So now his daddy and I realize that a seat must be constructed so that he can ride sitting up.

We bought a new chain saw last week. Harold has been hankering for one a long time. He feels heartsick when he thinks of the hours that they wasted trying to get the old one started. Ross always figured they could tinker around and patch it up some more. Well, when we finally got a little cash, we bought one of our own. Harold has already set a record this week in the amount of timber sawed in the woods. He says that it is great the way it will take right off. I wouldn't be surprised if Ross may come to think that the mill should buy it. That would suit us okay because we could still have the use of it in our place. Either way, I'm glad that he got it. It will be worth it in wear and tear on emotions if nothing else.

It's too bad the chainsaw is not the only example of struggle with equipment problems at the mill. There is a lot of time wasted because of breakdowns, which they just cobble up to wait for another breakdown. Harold has resigned himself to the idea that there will always be that sort of trouble because Ross is just that way. He's very good at cobbling, but Harold wishes they would just do it right in the first place. The problem is, Ross refuses to borrow money. Harold admires him for that principle but believes that there are times when it is very counterproductive for the mill.

It's times like this that we realize how Harold and Ross differ in their basic philosophy. For instance, Harold has pushed for laying out an entire week's work in advance and then following the plan. But often by the second or third day, Ross instigates a change of course. Sometimes the mill will be shut down for two hours while Ross and a potential customer draw up building plans resulting in the need for lumber in two dozen custom cut lengths, widths, and thickness.

Harold believes that turning out such a specialized order greatly slows down the mill's output. His idea would be to cut each log according to the maximum it can produce and then stockpiling the various dimensions in an organized fashion. This would allow customers to select what they need from already produced lumber. Ross, however, enjoys the challenge of cutting for a specific job and he likes to accommodate people.

There are other ways that the philosophical difference between these two men shows up. Harold wanted to organize the shop with a specific place where each tool was to reside. Ross vetoed that idea with the unimpeachable reasoning that it was less waste of effort just to pick up a tool from where it was last used. Nevertheless, I am proud of Harold that this difference has not affected their relationship or their work. He shares his frustrations with just me. And then, of course, I pass them on to you. However, with the change of direction in our life, Harold has given up some of the ideas he'd had about the mill. Now he's finding it easier to put up with these frustrations. I imagine Ross finds him easier to get along with, too.

Harold set up my classy washing machine out under the trees. It is sitting on a solid, level wooden platform he built there to support it. Each Monday night we wash the clothes. This is the procedure. All day long I heat a huge tub of water on the stove in preparation. When Harold gets home, he eats supper and begins to move the water from the stove to the machine and rinse tub. He also carries up some buckets of cold water from the creek. Then he starts the little gasoline engine.

In the meantime, I've sorted my clothes and have taken a tubful out to wash. It all works very well, and I'm thrilled to have it. Once in a while, a few leaves flutter down into the rinse tub, but I just pick them out. It's a small price to pay for doing that job in such a beautiful setting.

We are rapidly approaching the longest day of the year. Harold says he doesn't notice the difference in length so much living right here as when he came up from the states for the summer. By the way, we have lived here about a year now. As we were living our way through the year, it seemed that our accomplishments came at a painfully slow rate. But now, looking back on it, it does seem that we have gotten quite a bit done. The longer I live here and see how slowly some of these locals get things done the more impressive our accomplishments seem to me.

That's all for this time.

Love,
Your Alaskan Daughter, Harriet

Hope, Alaska
June 24, 1954

Dear Mother,

My goodness, summer is really flying by. It will soon be the Fourth of July. Around here that is as important as Christmas. It sort of marks the beginning of the last half of the year.

Harold is not going to run in the Seward Marathon Mountain race again this year. You remember that he ran in three 4th of July races before last summer and took third place each time. I think he wants to capture first place. He was so near before. I don't think he is in proper condition, because he hasn't had any time to run like he did before the other races. I think he would try it anyway because he was planning on competing until he found out that the Fourth was on Sunday. Then he said he wouldn't run. "I'll never run a race on Sunday, if for no other reason than out of respect for my parents." So, I guess unless they run the race on another day he'll not be competing. Anyway, I don't want him to run because I don't think he stands much chance with the knee trouble he had this spring. Besides, I would rather he would use his energy other ways. If he were in top shape, it would be different. He's terribly strong in the back and arms; actually, he never has been stronger. But that isn't where you run a race. I must be a failure as a cook because he still is very light, only around 160 pounds.

Harold is going to be surprised tonight when he comes home to find out that we have fried chicken for supper. I know he thinks I can't capture one of those beasts. But I did. Captured him; decapitated him; stripped him; eviscerated him; and dismembered him. Yes! Our chickens are really good sized, and we have been enjoying them so much.

We are still doing very well on our egg production.

We found that our hens have been hiding their nests out in the brush. Therefore, we have to hunt down nests every once in a while. But that's a small matter. The younger chickens are so cute. They come rushing in from everywhere when I appear on the scene with the feed. We are enjoying our little "farm" immensely, but it has its challenges.

We had a chicken hawk tormenting us the other morning. We were still in bed, but Harold rushed out and shot at it with a rifle. Even though he missed the hawk, he forced it to drop its load, and we rescued the little chicken unharmed. We'll just have to get that hawk. Funny, but I can remember so well the chicken hawks when we lived on the mission field in Africa. We used to run out and yell at them. It's one of my clearest childhood memories.

Another chicken related problem is George Adney's dog. Saturday morning, we found a dead chicken. We had no idea what had caused its death. Then that afternoon I heard a horrid noise up the chicken way and rushed out of the house just in time to see the dog take off with a chicken in its mouth.

I wasn't sure whose dog it was. There were some cars parked up at the turn around above our place because they are beginning work on the Methodist camp. I asked Rev. Elliott if any of the workers had dogs, but he was quite sure they didn't. I then checked with Stainbrooks, but as soon as I saw their dog, I knew it wasn't the one. So, I trudged on down the road to George's, and there was that dog with the chicken. The chicken died on the way home, so I stopped at Stainbrooks and got its head off instantly. We had to throw away a good deal of it but still had enough for a meal. Today again that dog was chasing chickens. The trouble doesn't stop with the fryers, but he gets the layers upset too. George isn't the least perturbed about it. Guess we'll have to scare him once with a shotgun ... the dog, that is.

Now that I've mentioned it, I might as well explain that the Methodists have begun a major construction project planned for this summer in our neck of the woods. They are building a Bible camp further down Turnagain Arm a little way from us. Right now, there is no one living between our house and the site of the new Bible camp. In the future, new home sites will probably open up between us, but right now we are next-door neighbors with the campers. The location for the new camp is lovely, and I think it will come to be a real blessing when it is finished.

The new Bible camp is being constructed almost entirely by volunteer labor. Most of the workers last weekend were young adults like soldiers and young married couples. There were some college kids too. Several of our Hope young people joined in as well. One of the nicest things for us was that they conducted a worship service last Sunday morning. We attended and really did enjoy it. The singing was good and the message fine. It was very pleasant to be once more in a formal church service on a Sunday morning.

This week eight young people from the States arrived to stay up here for six weeks helping to build the new camp. They are college-aged and very attractive. We are looking forward to church for the next few weeks. I know we will especially enjoy the singing. We will likely have the workers over for ice cream shortly. Should be good to be back with college kids for some conversations.

Actually, we have done quite a bit of entertaining since we moved into our house up here on the hill. Our first event was when we had the Carters down for a meal. They furnished the dessert in the form of ingredients and the freezer for ice cream. We helped with the labor.

A while back Harold invited a group of five soldiers who had camped up the hill from us down for breakfast. He had formed quite an attachment to them and thought they would appreciate a home-cooked meal. We had omelets and biscuits. They came in carrying their boxes of "C" rations as a hostess gift. Later, when we went through them, we found about a dozen cans of meat meals, some fruit, coffee, sugar, cookies, crackers, and jam. We actually feel that we came out ahead on that deal, even though that wasn't what we had in mind when we invited them.

We had a lovely group of young people up for Sunday dinner a couple of weeks ago. Alma and Ross had taken Linda with them for a trip to Wasilla to visit Elsie and Dave. Since they left Erma Ann and Lewie home for the day, we decided to have them over for salmon steaks. George Windle was up from Seward that weekend, so he was included as was Laura Stainbrook. Rumor has it that George and Laura are very serious about each other and what I have observed would certainly bear this out. For the meal, we used a table made out of saw horses and rough lumber planks, which worked very well. If not terribly elegant, it certainly was a stable table

We had the Boes out for lunch last Sunday noon. They had houseguests and decided to drive out from Seward to show off our beautiful countryside. Augustine Boe's aunt was with them. The aunt actually came over from Alsace Lorraine many years ago and was instrumental in bringing Augustine to the United States. What a dear soul, but almost impossible to understand. Compared to her, Augustine speaks completely unaccented English. Augustine's niece was along as well. Her fiancé is stationed in Anchorage. So, there were seven of them counting the fiancé. That made a meal for nine. It all worked out. We had plenty of room on the sawhorse table.

Tuesday night we had Grannie Clark up for supper. Gee, I actually believe that she had stage fright. She has a constant stream of callers from morning until night over whom she reigns like a queen, but I suppose getting her out of her environment makes her a little ill at ease. We all got along nicely. After supper, we looked at pictures and then Harold, and I sang some songs for her. Grannie likes to hear us sing, which is good-hearted if poor in judgment.

So that's the list of folks that we have entertained so far in our new home. It's pretty impressive don't you think?

Stevie Stainbrook is coming right along with the shop he's building. He works with Harold every evening on clearing around the place and checks in with me each morning to see if there are any chores that I need help with. I usually don't want anything, but I do try to figure out something for him to do. For some reason or the other, Harold still wants him to stop in. Of course, on washdays he runs the machine for me, so now I don't have to wash at night. That is a real blessing. His family is so tickled about his little "house." His sister, Coleen, has made a flowerbed in front of it and his mother is already mentally buying curtains, etc. I do hope that this project helps Stevie.

Tommy is now able to pull himself up to standing position. Poor child! All the interesting things are just out of reach. For a while, they were just across the floor from him, and he couldn't crawl to them. He just flopped around futilely. Now that he can crawl they have moved up higher, and he must struggle and struggle to stand up. The other day he worked so long and so hard and then lost his balance just as he managed to achieve a standing position. He cried more, I dare say because he was irked than because he was hurt.

Oh-oh, there go those little noises that indicate Tommy is

waking. The clock says it's time to get on with the other business of the day so I'll wind this up.

Love,
Your Alaskan Daughter, Harriet

Hope, Alaska
July 16, 1954

Dear Roomies,

According to my records, it had been a while since the packet of letters in our round robin passed my way. I know that it takes a while to get all the way to Alaska and back on to the next person, but I don't think we can attribute all the delay to Alaska this time. I was overjoyed to get the fat envelope containing all of your letters last Saturday. So, I am determined to speed the packet on its way as soon as possible by sending my installment out in return mail! Of course, that still gives me a week to get the letter written. Nevertheless, I hope my example will encourage the rest of you to keep our circular communication moving at a steadier clip.

The real reason for my mild anxiety about the pokiness of our little round robin is that I have some news that I want to tell you before you hear it from other sources. Harold and I have decided that we will be spending next school year Outside so that Harold can start his law degree. We will probably be living in or near Lincoln since the University of Nebraska is where he is applying. As much as we have loved the adventure of getting a mill started, we have learned that it is not really the type of thing we find fulfilling long term. We really want to be working with people. This may sound like a retreat after all the drama of our grand Alaska plans. But if it is, we are both convinced that we are retreating to a life that will allow us the most opportunity for making our existence worthwhile.

We have been moving toward this decision by slow incremental steps for many weeks. It started when I was Outside visiting during March and April. We became intrigued with an opportunity to become youth directors in a large church in Lincoln. Even though that deal fell through, it got us to thinking about our lives in a new way. There have been several experiences that have pushed us into this new mode of thinking. For instance, Harold has been working with the Hope youth since last fall and has found it extremely rewarding. Then this summer we've had another little taste of youth work. The Methodists have had a work camp going on here for several weeks. We have so enjoyed those college young people as an addition to our worship services and in casual contact. Let me back up and explain for you a little bit more about the situation behind this camp.

The Methodist Church has decided to construct a summer Bible camp facility very close to where we are living. The site is across Porcupine Creek and down a path from us toward a promontory called Dog Nose, which was one of the visible landmarks around here. Because this has been going on so close to us, these college campers have truly become more and more a part of our lives. They are a swell bunch of kids and, of course, Harold is in the height of his glory when he can do things with them and for them.

For example, we hosted a meal for them this week. We made a table of sawhorses and planks from the mill and served cafeteria style right down on the beach below our house. We featured our fried chicken, and I had just piles of food which really went in a hurry. I began to get in a panic about not having enough until Mrs. Knight, their sponsor, assured me that she always worried about the same thing and she had been cooking for them for six weeks. I had mentally rationed the food, and it should have been ample for everyone with some left over. As it turns out, there was indeed plenty.

Mrs. Knight is a lovely woman. Her husband is superintendent of the church conference in northwestern Oregon. At one time he was superintendent of the Alaskan conference. He also was responsible for building the church at Hope and had served in Moose Pass. Their son is married and living in Seward, so she has been able to see quite a bit of him and his little children while she's been here. But let me tell you something interesting. It was she who had my washing machine when it was new. She left it in Moose Pass when she moved. That's how it came to Rev. Elliott who sold it to us. And now she again had her clothes washed in it. Small world! Eh? She had her clothes washed in it because the campers asked us if they could do laundry at our place. I couldn't help thinking how I had progressed from last fall when I used a scrub board to now when people are asking to use my laundry facilities. Well, the laundry system worked just fine. The machine is gas powered and has been sitting outdoors on a platform floor, which is the earliest stage of a washhouse that we will be building.

That first time they came up to do their wash, I had a chance to get acquainted. They had said that they would haul the water, buy the gas for the engine, and chop the wood to heat the water. I did let them haul water and heated it for them. Two of the girls then came back in the afternoon to do the washing.

A couple of incidents punctuated that afternoon. In the first place, in filling the machine, one of the girls, Katy, poured scalding water on her hand. She seemed to be much more devastated by the incident than was merited. In the course of caring for her I learned that because she was just recovering from a bout of bronchial pneumonia, she had been allowed to join the camp crew only at the very last minute. The first week of being here she had not been allowed to go to the campsite to work with the others. She had stayed at home base and helped Mrs. Knight cook, etc. She had felt very keenly about this lack of participation. And now when she had finally been allowed to join the workers, she had brought this catastrophe upon herself. I think the fact that she'd been delayed in joining in the work and the fear that she would, again, be incapacitated affected her more than the burn; she went to pieces. The pain was considerable, I'm sure, but I was more worried about her strange despair. In time, after she lay on our bed for a long period, she got control, and all was well. She has a slight blister on one finger, but we managed to treat the other parts of her hand and arm soon enough to prevent serious injury. At any rate, she's very happy because she's been able to go back to work. She is a lovely girl, and Harold says that she has turned out to be a dandy worker, both consistent and fast.

The second incident was when a girl named Cathy caught a pair of pants in the wringer and tore them unmercifully. She was horrified. She was chagrined. She was crushed. I couldn't see any cause for all the upset, because I knew that no one in this group would get all that upset about torn pants. They were just a pair of guy's jeans, after all.

Nevertheless, I promised her to do the best I could in the way of mending. Thank goodness for Augustine Boe's treadle sewing machine. I am so glad that she has been willing to trade her treadle for my electric. I have had fun sewing for Tommy. Anyway, in mending those jeans, I did a beautiful job. I spent hours on that silly pair of pants, but it had become a challenge to me. After checking on the owner's size, I just made them slightly smaller. I added a few seams here; put in some reinforcement there; moved a few loops. When I was finished, they looked very presentable. Harold was amazed at the results and, let's face it, so was I. When I returned them to her, I began to realize why the incident had assumed such proportions in her mind. It seems that she and the owner of the jeans had begun to have a shared interest beyond building a Bible camp. Aside from these incidents getting the camper's clothes washed was pretty routine.

We also had another incident with the folks at the Methodist work camp where we benefited greatly from their help. One of the young women, Kay, is not a college student but a fully trained nurse. She is Canadian and has been active in the Methodist church in Seattle where she is employed in the infant's department of a large hospital. And oh my, I had reason to be so grateful to her for her calm expertise! You see, one afternoon when I was changing wiggly Tommy, I gave him the Vaseline jar to hold and to play with. He was chewing on it with his new teeth. Suddenly I heard a sort of scraping sound and then saw him swallow hard. I grabbed the jar from him and noticed to my dismay that a chip had been bitten off the bottom. I was frantic and sick at the same instant. Fortunately, Harold was outside working and was able to respond to my distress. Harold rushed to the campsite to contact Kay. She was calm and suggested we try to get him to eat bread. She didn't seem to think that it was really urgent that we get him to the doctor in Seward, but she didn't try to talk us out of it.

We rushed off. I was in tears much of the way because of how careless I had been with this precious baby we had been given. Tommy was fussy and unhappy. I suspect now that he was reacting to my reaction.

This distance from Hope to Seward varies with one's emotions. Sometimes it is a nice leisurely trip when one can view lovely scenery, occasionally stop to stretch, and think of the trip as a time for sharing thoughts. Sometimes it is interminable, bumpy, and fraught with distress as it was that day. At the doctor's office, the nurse heard our story. She talked briefly with the doctor, and we were told to watch his stool for bleeding and for his excreting the glass. The doctor never even saw him. We went our sad way back over those seventy-five miles to home. Kay was a pillar of strength in the next hours while we waited for Tommy's system to reject safely the chunk of glass that had turned my world upside down.

Since then we have been much more careful about the kinds of things we allow within Tommy's reach. Who would have thought he could bite off a chunk of a Vaseline jar? From some of your letters, I can see that all of you are also learning the difficulties of being parents. Well, I suppose if we keep writing to each other and sharing our experiences we can learn from each other. So, listen to the voice of experience. Don't let your infant children play with Vaseline jars!

In addition to this important lesson about child care, the most important thing that our contact with these wonderful young people taught was that we need to firm our resolve to get on to another stage of our life even earlier than we had planned. We don't know exactly what kind of career is in our future, while Harold is working his way through law school. But right now, working with young people in the church or in the public-school system certainly seem like appealing options to us.

Say, what is the idea of all of you ganging up on me asking for more Alaskan stories in this last set of letters? If I keep using up all these stories in my letters how will I ever get a book about Alaska written? As you know, Granny Clark, with whom Harold and I have become very close, is the queen of Alaskan stories. I really do intend to get some of her stories into a book someday. But if Granny is the queen, I think Harold might be on the way to some kind of royalty in the Alaskan story department. It has been amazing to me to listen to him tell his stories to visitors and friends. Each retelling demonstrates refinement and improvement in timing and finesse. Since you have asked, I will share some of those he used to enthrall the work campers.

One old sourdough once stated that Alaska was bigger than Texas in every way, not just in landmass. As evidence, he named a few local characters who exhibited the ability to run wild with the truth. Harold recognized one of those named because he had met him in 1947. At that time Harold and two buddies were traveling down the Sterling Highway on their way to Homer. They stopped at the little store at Coopers Landing. They were the only customers, and no traffic was on the road going by. The owner and keeper of the store had recently acquired a wine license and had instantly changed from a life of sobriety to one who consistently sampled his for-sale spirits.

In his happy state of mind, he regaled the three boys with

stories of his life. Among those stories was how he had swum the river every day of his life for some years. In another, he told of how he'd used the river as a highway to deliver the mail when the river was frozen over. One of the boys asked if it wasn't a bit difficult to swim across the river when it was frozen. "Oh hell, boy, "he exclaimed, "You can't believe me. I'm the damndest liar in the world." Then without missing a beat, he launched into a tale about the giant ice worms that lived in the glaciers.

Another story Harold likes to tell is about how he was completely taken in by the tall tales of a woman who styled herself as" Alaska Nellie." She is the proprietor of a roadhouse out on the highway from Hope to Seward. The main room of the roadhouse is decorated with the mounted trophy heads of Alaskan animals. Each work of taxidermy is the take-off point for an amazing story about the life and times of Alaska Nelly. Her account of how she had stood up to the murderous charge of the huge Alaskan brown bear was riveting. She gave interesting accounts of how she had bagged the large Billy goat, and then the hazardous struggle of getting the head, cape, and meat back to camp. A mountain snow squall, a fall off a cliff and being caught in a rockslide did not stop her.

Although these stories did strain credulity, Harold was caught completely by surprise when he met the man one day who said he had shot the big ram in Alaska Nelly's display. This man went on to explain that he knew who had actually contributed every one of the other trophies that Nellie claimed as her own. If that man was honest, champion Alaskan liars are no respecter of gender.

Harold also likes to tell stories about Alaskan fliers. I suppose this is only natural for a former Air Corps pilot like Harold. One of Harold's favorite stories is about Tiny Sabaughsky. Tiny was a bush pilot who was the opposite of his nickname. Because he weighed in the neighborhood of three hundred pounds, there was not enough room for him and a parachute to be seated at the controls of his little aircraft. His acquaintances joked that there were no nerves in his entire body mass. The chronicling of some of his exploits may substantiate that claim.

His home base was Seward. On a return trip, he ran out of gas before reaching the landing strip. The only straight tree-less piece of land within gliding distance was the railroad. A perfect dead-stick landing wiped out his landing gear, but he walked away. The plane was removed from the tracks before the next train came through, and then it was repaired to fly again.

In another incident, Tiny misread the tide charts and came to Hope expecting to land on the beach at low tide. The tide was in, and fuel and weather concerns dictated that he had to land somewhere. He made a perfect short-field landing up the two-block main street of Hope. This emergency landing strip was so narrow that one wing tip knocked down the sign from Doc's store and the other wing tip took out a post holding up the porch roof on the house across the street. Nevertheless, a couple days later Tiny flew the repaired plane off the beach at low tide.

Perhaps the most unusual of Tiny's exploits was his landing on the bridge across the upper end of Kenai Lake. The weather had trapped him over the lake that was surrounded by moun-tains. The bridge was a long narrow one with low guardrails on either side. The forced landing was successful except the plane veered too near the guardrails and damaged the struts on one side. Tiny managed to taxi the damaged plane on across the bridge to a wide place in the road. The plane sat there for a few days while repairs were made, then he took off back across the bridge and flew home.

I wonder what it says about Harold that his favorite stories are about liars and flyers. Hmmm, that sounds like the title to a book, which is just what this letter is becoming! If I don't stop now, I'll never get all of it stuffed into an envelope with the rest of your letters and on its way to the next person in the round-robin. So, give my regards to your husbands and little ones.

Your Ex-Roomie,
Harriet

Hope, Alaska
July 30, 1954

Dear Mother

I missed church last week because of a cold. I missed it to-night because Harold didn't get back from Seward in time. We need to drive now that we live up on the bench. I'm getting to feel like a heathen. The worst of it is that I've really enjoyed going since the work campers have been here because they join their voices with ours to help override the monotone of our pastor.

There I go again after I had resolved to not be so critical of our pastor. Let me at least balance the slate a little. Harold is very impressed with his ability in working with young people. They are moving right along on the project and working with precision. Rev. Eliot has helped foster a sense of camaraderie among these kids and is skillfully leading them in their spiritual aspects of this camping experience. We have been critical of him so often that it is refreshing to see this side of him. Perhaps his true calling will be working with church young people.

In spite of Harold's intentions to have the car worked on at this time, He went to Wasilla last weekend and brought it back rather than leave it in the mechanic's shop. He needed some parts for the cat and didn't want to be without the car right now. I was glad he went because he could get a little visit in with Elsie, and goodness knows, we don't get together very often. Erma Ann came over here and stayed with me while he was gone. She and Colleen Stainbrook got ready for the dance here. I really enjoyed the primping and fussing that went on to transform two jean-dad teenagers into two lovely belles.

Harold brought a ten-gallon can of milk back from Elsie's. So, Monday evening the entire local youth fellowship was at our house rushing around gaily and having a big lark making ice cream. After the first few minutes when I was trying to get them all organized, I enjoyed the proceedings very much too. The idea was that they would make the milk Elsie and Dave donated up into ice cream, pack it down in ice and salt brine and sell it this weekend. Harold brought back paper quart containers, and so the process began. They wanted to experiment. I was all for sticking to plain vanilla, but all kinds turned out. No two batches were the same, and fortunately, it was all very good. Well, they made about twenty quarts or so which were packed down in ice, and then about five or six quarts which were packed down the kids ... not counting all the tasting, comparing, paddle licking, etc., that went on before.

Wednesday evening at their regular meeting, however, they decided to go ahead and canvas the neighborhood to see if the ice cream would sell. They sold it all...at a dollar a quart. After all, ice cream made with fresh milk rather than canned milk is a real delicacy. The revenue from this project will just about take care of the expenses they have in the new athletic equipment that the youth group bought.

The other evening the college work campers borrowed our freezer, and so it has really had a workout since we got it. Guess those state-reared kids are eager enough for ice cream to use canned milk. The freezer came back from its last excursion slightly bent. Harold thinks he can straighten it out. I surely hope so. We'd have loaned it anyway; even if we had known this would happen.

All this news about making ice cream reminds me of my fiasco with ice cream last fall. At the time I was too embarrassed to write about it. But since then Harold and others have told about it enough times that I have decided I need to own the story and tell it myself in self-defense. I don't remember what the occasion was, but we had some young people at the little white cottage in the town making ice cream. I do remember that we had to go way up Palmer Creek to find ice. I was mixing up the ice cream, sugar, vanilla and so on and listening to the animated conversation going on around me. I handed the bowl with the mix in it to Harold who poured it into the ice cream container and had one of the kids start the process of turning the crank. A few minutes afterward as I was clearing the counter, I noticed the eggs and the eggbeater lying on the counter -unopened eggs - unused eggbeater. I broke open the eggs into a small bowl and explaining why I asked Harold to stop the ice cream process and open the container. When this was accomplished, I poured the eggs down into the liquid mix feeling pretty smug that I had short-circuited the process of beating the eggs. The ice cream dashers could do that for me, and I wouldn't have to wash up the eggbeater.

With the usual joking about whose turn it was to turn the handle as the ice cream got firmer and firmer the anticipation of the dessert grew. When it was mutually decided by all present that the mix was firm and it was time to take out the dasher, we gathered around, bowls in hand. Out came the dasher and the kid who had spoken for that accepted it on a plate and began the process of consuming the ice cream. Then Harold began to dish up for the rest of us. He hadn't gone beyond the second bowl, I suspect when he brought up a large spoonful of ice cream with a frozen egg yolk lying on top like an undersized dull gold golf ball. Another spoonful brought up another egg yolk. There was much mirth and mortification. Mirth on the part of the ice cream consumers who happily discarded the egg yolks and ate the ice cream anyway, claiming that it tasted just fine. You already know who bore up under the mortification part of the equation. Since then, any ice cream mixes I've had anything to do with contained well-beaten eggs.

It's only about three weeks until Harold's hunting trip, and he is getting pretty excited. He's going into the interior with Jim Carter to hunt sheep. I guess sheep are supposed to be the choice wild meat. If they don't have any luck, they'll still have a wonderful time. I'm glad that he's getting the trip in, because, with our plans to come Outside for school, it may be a long time before he gets another chance.

Harold's hunting trip is having an impact on the interior decor of our home. Right now, our house is in a terrible mess. Harold is happily fixed up with all his shell loading equipment around in a disorganized

organization. He stayed up late last night and got up early this morning to load shells in preparation for the hunting trip. He and Jim Carter are like a couple of little boys in their excitement. It's good to see people like that; it's refreshing. To discuss plans, Harold goes up there, and Jim comes down here on the slightest provocation. Fortunately, those plans don't include any concerns over their absence around here. One of the Stainbrook girls will be staying with me while the men are gone.

Tommy is still a head shaker. The minute Harold steps in the door Tommy goes into his routine. Almost makes me dizzy to watch him. He's been laughed at so much that he thinks it's a sure approach. He grins happily as he shows off. Old patty-cake is too small time for him now; he's a big boy. He can shake his head. When Willard was here, I said something about Tommy's head coming unscrewed and falling off. Being the mechanic that he is, Willard just assured me that Tommy was screwing it on tighter.

Tommy's cold didn't amount to much. He was pretty sick last Saturday, but by Sunday morning he was back to normal. He still has a bit of a runny nose, however. Next time I count my blessings, I must remember to list being able to blow my nose. Poor little guy. How much happier would be his lot if he could blow his nose!

I have just decided that one of my problems in rearing my son is going to be his father. The other night I came back from working in the garden to find that Tommy had been having a glorious time roaming all over the floor. When I tell you that I usually keep Tommy in the playpen, I don't want you to have the concept of limitation. The playpen is really just a little corral made of four one inch thick boards fourteen inches wide. One advantage of owning a mill is that such an odd-dimension board is available. The boards are fastened together at the corners to form a pen six feet square and fourteen inches high with no top or bottom. The floor serves as a bottom wherever we locate the pen. Most of the time Tommy is happy there with the variety of toys and interesting objects that I place in there with him. But his daddy has other ideas. He enjoys letting Tommy be "free." Exploring the big world of our little cabin, examining the alarm dock, destroying old magazines, and that sort of thing. Of course, Harold watches him closely. However, because I can't watch him that closely every minute of the day, I am hoping that he won't out-grow the playpen too rapidly. But if Harold is soft with Tommy, I'm soft with Harold, so all has been harmony in this house.

Hardly seems possible that August is pressing so near. That means that the summer is slipping away. Soon it will be school time again. Harold has received his acceptance into law school at the University of Nebraska so this year the season will hold special meaning for us again as you know. We had thought we would have to wait to the second semester for him to start, but we were worried about being accepted as a beginner in law school the second semester. The problem was that according to Home Site regulations we couldn't retain ownership of our house if we didn't live in it long enough. We were really kicking ourselves that we hadn't bent every effort to getting moved up here sooner. Then just a couple of weeks ago Harold talked to the new Forest Service man, and it seems very likely that we can get our home site on an extension basis. I mean, we lease the land long term until we get a chance to start living on it again. This development has cleared the way for us to change our plans and Harold will be starting the first semester this fall. You see, it's just like you said in your last letter, things do have a way of just working out.

Guess, that's all for this time.

Love,
Your Alaskan daughter, Harriet

Hope, Alaska
August 13, 1954

Dear Mother,
Life certainly has its changing challenges. Here's the latest.
As you know, Alma has been very concerned about the high
school experiences of Erma Ann and Lewie. She has been considering many possibilities. Mom Walker has been aware of
this, of course, and has been doing some planning on their behalf.

Here's what came up. Last week Alma got a letter from
Mom telling her that the position of principal for a two-
teacher mission school at Velarde, New Mexico was available,
and Alma could have it. She would be furnished a place to live
and transportation each weekend to McCurdy and back. During the week she and Linda would stay in Velarde, and the two
older kids would live with Mom in her house and attend the
McCurdy Mission High School. Erma and Lewie would profit
immensely from the chance to be with other up-and-coming
young people. They wouldn't have any trouble scholastically
because they are both top students and the adjustments that
they'd have to make socially will surely be less than if they
waited another year and tried to make them on the college
level. Alma would be doing the administrative work at the
school and teaching the upper-level students. Linda would
be going to school under the second mission teacher. Alma
would have to be away from Ross, of course, and hates that.
But since she couldn't be separated from her children, she
would be willing to make that sacrifice for their eventual
good. Well, Alma accepted the offer.

I believe that they have chosen wisely. However, as you have probably already figured out, this situation causes us all to step back and rearrange financial plans. The original intention was for us to take most of the capital that the mill had on hand for our own travel expenses and early support. There are about a thousand dollars that can be scraped up. The Millers would then collect the outstanding money, and the profits from the lumber already sawed for their winter expenses. Of course, that can't be done now. Most of that available capital will be needed to get the Millers to New Mexico.

However, this doesn't change our own intentions to come out. The two of us have become ever more firmly convinced that Harold's future should be working with people. And even more convinced that his future is now -- not down the road a few years. So, we are coming Outside.

We're scurrying around in the attempt to dig enough capital up to foot both major moves. Harold is very determined. He's been peddling everything that's loose. We aren't selling eggs anymore because we've sold seventeen of our layers. I think we'll have enough eggs for ourselves for a while, but that's all. We're trying to sell the car. We are hoping to get enough for it to pay our way Outside and some living expenses. If we can't sell it, we'll have to put some money into it and get it repaired for a drive out. We won't know until the very last minute, I suppose, which we are going to do. We would like very much not to have to borrow any more money from you since our prospects of making a lot this winter are slim. But we'd appreciate your keeping the money available for just a little while.

Which brings me to another topic. Harold feels that the time has come to move on and release the mill to Ross. Harold has offered the whole mill setup to Ross for just our initial cash investment plus a small interest on the years involved. It is a terrific bargain for Ross, and I confess that I feel it is not quite enough to ask. But on the other hand, Harold will have accomplished his purpose in establishing a mill for Ross, and we'll still have some money. Very likely, the deal will go through. The money won't be forthcoming for some time. But it is gratifying to think that to some degree, Harold has been able to show his appreciation for all that Ross and Alma meant to him when he shared their home in Idaho.

I am helping Harold get ready for the hunting trip. He has a list a mile long with all the things he wants to accomplish before he leaves. Given recent events, he felt that he should give up the hunting trip. I encouraged him to go on with it because he may never again have such a chance so inexpensively. Fellows from the States pay small fortunes to make such a trip, and he'll be doing it for less than $40.00. Any meat they bring home will more than offset that cost. Since we plan to establish residence in Nebraska, which will save half the tuition cost, we won't be eligible next summer for hunting. So next week Harold and Jim Carter will be off to the Interior after mountain sheep and if they have time, caribou. If Harold doesn't get any meat at all, the experience should give him more than his money's worth in yarns to spin the next few years.

I plan to make good use of Harold's absence to get a lot done. I'll be sorting pictures, completing scrap-books and the like. Then when he comes back, I shall have a long string of accomplishments and the only conclusion he can possibly draw is that when he is around, I am too busy to accomplish things like that. He's sure to be impressed. Reckon?

The surveyors have been swarming around here lately. They are opening up a new section of land for home sites. These will be located between our place and the end of the road where the Methodist Camp is. Wouldn't you know after all the trouble we had getting a home site that all of a sudden, a whole group of new home sites would come available? While some may have richer soil, none of them will have the view that we have.

Oh! I wanted to put into this letter something that occurred to me the other day when I was thinking about all the work you do for the college. We're so proud of you, Mother. You are efficient, systematic and have that extra something that comes from dedication and love of people. After Daddy died, I was leery when you took the college bookstore job, for I felt it wasn't along your line. You've pleasantly surprised me, and now I have nothing but confidence in your handling any challenge that comes your way.

You remember having given me one of those new Scripto ballpoint pens. It has been just wonderful. You said that I would like it. I do. Thank you for that and for so much that I can't enumerate.

Love,
Your Alaskan daughter, Harriet

Hope, Alaska
August 20, 1954

Dear Clarke and Jean

Things have really, really been popping around here. We are really coming out, and we wanted you to know the particulars. We've only had one little fiasco when the cash from the mill needed to be used to get Alma and the children to New Mexico rather than fund our move. Maybe Mother told you about that. Alma has a chance at a teaching job in one of the little out-stations in the mission in New Mexico and thus a chance to put Erma Ann and Lewie in a bona fide high school for their senior year. So, Harold has been scurrying around like mad digging up a little cash. He is very amusing to watch. Suddenly nothing is safe from his eagle eye and his salesman's voice. He even has sold the engine off my washing machine, effective after we leave. The chickens have gone to various places at three dollars a head. Who knows what will go next!

We are leaving Anchorage the evening of Monday, the 13th of September, and will fly all the way to Denver where we'll catch a train, which will get us into Lincoln early, and I do mean early, the morning of the 15th. I wish I could give you the exact hour of that train's arriving, but it is somewhere around 3:30 a.m. or so. I understand that it is originating from the City of Los Angeles or possibly the City of San Francisco - one of "them cities," anyway. And of course, it'll be going through Denver. Them's the facts, Mac!

We're returning to you the semi-filled-out application you sent for the potential job at the Y.M.C.A. As you see, some of the questions are still blank. For example, salary expected will depend so much on the job. We're not clear if it would be a full-time job or just an "extra." If they want a Lincoln address on the address lines maybe that had better be left blank. Otherwise, you could fill in the Hope, Alaska address for us. This application isn't binding, is it? Naturally, we are interested in securing the best job all around that we can.

We were really impressed with the number of contacts you made on our behalf in the brief time that you must have had. We do appreciate it and hope that you never have cause to regret any efforts along the line.

A thought has just come up in the way of job possibilities. Perhaps there would be a rural church that needs a supply pastor. I know that some congregations are assigned young student pastors who supply while they start their way through college. Harold and I believe we could do justice to the parsonage duties as well as they or perhaps better, in fact.

Harold is now gone on his hunting trip. Harold and Jim Carter, a very close neighbor and pal of Harold's, have, for a long time, been planning an extensive hunting trip. When our immediate plans began to shape up toward a trip outside, Harold more or less thought he should give up the trip. I've encouraged him to go on it anyway. This is the kind of trip that young men dream about, and old men reminisce about. He and Jim are going into the interior to hunt mountain sheep. They will set up a base camp when they have driven as far as they can, and they will pack in their supplies to their hunting camp. The trip will last no longer than ten days and likely no fewer than seven. And the cost will be around forty dollars or less. Which, if you have ever priced Alaskan hunting trips, is an incredible bargain.

Colleen Stainbrook is staying with me during the nights now. She's a nice kid, but I didn't feel it necessary to have someone here. However, Harold insisted that this had to be. I am not finding her presence as much of an intrusion as I had feared, but I will be really glad when Harold gets back, and we can get on with the next stage of our lives. We are eager to see you all. It surely won't be long now.

Love,
Harriet

~~⊃ ⊂~~

Hope, Alaska
August 28

Dear Mom Walker,

Tommy is helping me write this letter. What set up this situation is that he has begun to declare loudly and firmly that he has outgrown his playpen whenever we put him in there. I wish he could have waited another two weeks. Now he is only happy when he is crawling around outside that confinement exploring things. He has the most inquisitive brain and about the quickest fingers in town. Of course, our house with its orange crate dressers and open shelves is ideal for a little demon bent on disorganizing things. Even though our rough lumber floor scratches up his legs right through his pants, he persists. I'll have to figure some way of keeping those busy legs covered with sturdier cloth.

As I mentioned, he is helping me with my writing, because right now he is standing here shaking the typewriter table. Since it is a rather unstable card table, he is very successful. However, I find that it doesn't bother me as much as it did this morning after I had the table all set for breakfast and he pulled the same little stunt, spilling hot chocolate all over. My, how he can reach and stretch. I used to have to move things about an inch from the edge of the table to elude him. But it keeps getting farther and farther that they have to be moved. And I know he's not growing quite that fast.

I'm expecting Harold to return from his hunting trip any time now. Maybe he'll arrive before I finish this letter so that I can include his news. I did hear last Monday night over the Mukluk Telegraph that he and Jim had returned to Anchorage from a successful sheep-hunting trip and that they were going out after caribou. I don't know just what constitutes a successful trip, but I suspect we'll have some fresh meat.

While Harold has been gone, Colleen Stainbrook has stayed nights with me part of the time and her sister Laura has come the rest of the nights. After all my protesting, I really did appreciate having them here. With the time of Harold's absence almost over, I realize it hasn't dragged nearly as much as I thought it might. I've had lots of people dropping by and have kept busy.

While she's been up here, Laura has been knitting a pair of socks for George Windle. None of this old heavy yarn and big needles stuff that works up fast. No, she's using fine gray yarn and fine needles. Ah! Love! The other afternoon she asked me to help her turn a heel. I pored over the instruction book. Wow! It looked so complicated that I was really impressed that I had ever managed to turn one heel, let alone as many as I have. After studying that information for a minute, I gave up and showed her how to do it as one Alma Miller taught me. "You do it this way. Watch!" The heel came out nicely, and we are both satisfied.

Well, by now you will have gotten over the initial excitement of the arrival of Alma and the children in New Mexico. I hope you are settling down to enjoying it all. I know you'll have a wonderful winter and by "you," I mean all five of you. It will do Alma worlds of good to get into a new environment for a while. As you may know, Lewie had finished up his correspondence work just before he left. "Only seven days of vacation!", He announced, thinking of the imminent start of school at McCurdy. But actually, he did take quite a bit of time off this summer. Correspondence work puts so much strain on a kid's willpower that before long it begins to wear thin. I'll say this for Lewie, he's been at it night and day since they heard about going outside. I'm glad especially for him because he must carry five hours to graduate next year, and it'll come easier this way, I'm sure.

Sure enough, as I predicted, Harold drove in just a little while ago. You'll not be surprised that this husband of mine had a wonderful time on his hunting trip and I'm very happy for him. He and Jim had each bagged a caribou, and each had gotten a sheep. The heads Jim is going to mount for trophies. I guess an Alaskan Dall Sheep makes a wonderful trophy and the meat is excellent.

Then too, Harold sold the car. He sold it to Elsie and Dave who had been planning to buy a car anyway. We had been planning to use the cash from the sale of the car to provide for our trip out. But Elsie and Dave can't give us all the money right away. Nevertheless, not having to drive out gives a week's extra time. Also, Harold scraped, around and got some more lumber orders. We're going to make it nice. It does seem that things are shaping up for us. Of course, we won't have a car when we get outside, and that might cramp our style, but if we need to economize anywhere, a car is surely a good place.

I can't believe it. It's just two weeks until we leave. We have reservations for flying out the 13th of September. We'll fly all the way to Denver and take the train to Lincoln. We'll get to Lincoln early, early in the morning of September fifteenth. I don't like to think of getting the Clarke Thomas family up at this terribly early hour, but someone has to meet us.

Gotta hurry to get this letter to the P.O. GIVE THE MILLER FAMILY A BIG HELLO!

Love,
Harriet

Lincoln, Nebraska
September 16, 1954

Dear Mother,

Let's see, I don't know just where to start. Perhaps it would be best to begin at the beginning. We left Hope around 2:00 Sunday afternoon and drove to Wasilla. We spent the night with Elsie's and then left on the bus in the morning for Anchorage. We got there around noon. Harold got us a hotel room for the day so that we would have a place to rest until the plane left that evening at 8:30. I felt that it was a bit of extravagance, but it proved to be so delightful and convenient with the baby and all, that many times I was glad for the expenditure. After we got on the plane, Tommy slept until sometime after we landed in Seattle. Small world, when you can sleep all the way from Anchorage to Seattle. We had about three hours in Seattle, but the time was lessened considerably since the airport where we were to land was fogged in, and we had to go to another one and then ride over to the first airport by bus to make our next connections. Still, I had plenty of time to give Tommy his breakfast and clean him up a little. So far, he had been no trouble.

The flight from Seattle to Denver, however, proved to be a problem. Tommy was sleepy but couldn't go to sleep. He fought it long and hard. We were all worn out. Just as the plane was coasting in for a landing, he fell asleep. Naturally, he woke up as we left the plane.

We had about five hours in Denver then, so we went downtown for supper and Harold got a haircut. Still, the little guy could not get to sleep. Worse yet, now he was thoroughly used to being held every minute. He finally fell asleep on the train.

Clarke met us, and we came right out here to his place and went to bed. I didn't see Jean because she was sleeping.

Tommy was a bit of a problem yesterday because there seemed to be no place here in Clarke and Jean's house where he could be left. We have that worked out better now. We have the bed where he can sometimes be, and we have the porch blocked off so he can play out there. So now we must settle down to getting him back on schedule. Last night he didn't want to go to sleep and cried for quite a while. Even though I knew I should just let him get to sleep by crying, I felt that I couldn't risk the disturbance because of Clarke and Jean. So, I held him and struggled with him. This went on until around 11:30 when Harold finally decided to take him down to the basement and just let him howl. That did the trick, I guess. He went right to sleep. A few minutes later here came Harold trudging up the steps with a very sound asleep baby.

He played by himself awhile this morning and is taking his nap now, so I'm hopeful that we'll have our little old Tommy back before long. I don't know how some parents manage with fussy children - walking the floor and all. Mercifully we've been spared all that. And we're not going to start it now just because Tommy's bright enough to be very, very naughty.

At this very minute, Harold is talking to the District Superintendent of the Methodist church here about the possibilities of doing supply work in a nearby parish. I don't know what will turn up. The Y.M.C.A. possibility is still strong, but they can't afford to pay over a hundred and fifty dollars a month and possibly not that much, and it would be very slim pickings. Harold's tuition will be a hundred and sixty dollars, and there will be the cost of books. Rent and the like have to be factored in. There might be someplace around where we could live inexpensively. Perhaps I could do babysitting during the day or something. We are really optimistic that all will work out. And with that attitude, we are exploring several possibilities.

Harold did go ahead and sell out our interest in the sawmill to Ross. He sold it for five thousand dollars to be paid some-time in the future. This price is very, very low. Actually, it is just about what we have in it, plus a small interest rate for the last years. But I think it's all for the best. Harold is now free to pursue other ideas. The only drawback is that we don't have any expectation of receiving anything monetary before the first of the year. But even so, I'm glad.

I must stop. Don't know now just when we'll get up to see you, but we plan to get there sometime soon. Harold has classes on Saturday, so our weekends are going to be brief. Thanks again for all your help and thanks for sending us the money. It was very good to get your letter wishing me a happy birthday. I surely have enjoyed my life so far and know to whom goes

much of the credit. Thank you for the life you gave me twenty-seven years ago today.

Love,
Your Nebraskan daughter, Harriet

Lincoln, Nebraska
October 1, 1954

Dear Grannie Clark,
I have a few minutes, which I will happily use to get this let-ter off to you. After I catch you up on the news from this part of the world I will be expecting - very soon- a nice letter from you bringing us up to date on how you have been feeling and your wonderful relating of life in that unique little Alaskan village named Hope, Alaska

I am grateful that we were able to fly out. We had a nice, un-eventful trip except that Tommy about wiggled us to death. There was so much for him to see and to try to touch that he wasn't still one minute.

Harold is almost through with his second week of law

school. He finds the work exacting but very interesting. I suspect that I may have to do some reading in his textbooks so that I'll know what he's talking about when he tries to discuss his assignments with me. It seems to me that even the language they use differs from our everyday language.

Tonight, the law wives are having a picnic for their husbands. Of course, I'm not yet acquainted with this group, but I did meet several of the members at a welcoming tea for new students' wives the first Sunday I was here. I believe the membership of this group consists of wives of both law students and professors.

We are still living here in Lincoln with my brother, Clarke, and his wife, Jean. For a while, we were not sure how we would settle and make our way in this new life, but now things are shaping up just fine. Harold has been offered the opportunity to be a lay pastor of a small Methodist church in Raymond, a little town near here. The church in Raymond is one of a two-church circuit so he'll be driving into the country for the second service each Sunday. The neighboring Presbyterian Church in Raymond has also asked him to supply. The churches schedule their times so that this three-service morning can be managed. In case it sounds like too much, and it is, I might mention that the last pastor who filled the three pulpits was also a professor at Wesleyan University. So, we believe that it can be done in addition to Harold's schooling. Now you get the picture. I'm going to be a preacher's wife for a while. Too bad you can't drop in at one of our services.

Raymond is just eleven miles from Lincoln. While the road isn't paved all the way, it is graveled where the pavement stops so shouldn't be too bad in winter driving. There is a lovely, big Methodist parsonage where we will live. We'll be moving into that by the middle of October. When I first saw it, I was astounded. There is a huge living room that extends the length of the house. Just behind it to the right is a dining room with a built-in buffet. And to the left is the pastor's study with one wall of built-in bookcases. Imagine a parsonage with a planned pastor's study. The kitchen is not as nice as the rest of the house, but it will be adequate. It has a basement where I can do the washing and hang the clothes on non-drying days. And the upstairs has a bathroom and three bedrooms with closets.

When I first saw the house, it was nicely furnished because the former pastor hadn't left yet. I've been trying to imagine all those rooms empty. When, in my mind, I start placing our few pieces of furniture I come up with about one piece of furniture in each room. Seriously, we have decided to live mostly in the back part of the main floor and leave the huge front room unfurnished. This will help with heating bills, and that room will make a nice gymnasium for Tommy to run in, well, crawl in. He has been walking some, but he still gets down on his hands and knees when he is in a hurry.

However as important as the house is, we are most excited about the opportunity for ministry. We have met some of the future parishioners and have been welcomed so warmly that we are eager to be part of this church community. There are young families with children as well as a fair representation of members in the generations above them.

I just got a letter from Mom Walker. She is really enjoying the Miller family living with her in New Mexico. I'm glad that it's working out for them. She says that Linda loves it in the Velarde School and is enjoying her new little girl companions. Alma who seems to be fitting easily into her teacher and principal roles feels that this year will be a good one for Linda. Erma Ann is adjusting smoothly to her challenges and new routine. Lewie is really in the thick of the football season. His coach says that he is the fastest man on the team. When he gets better at handling the ball, he should be a real asset to the team. I guess he got a little homesick for Alaska last Sunday, but on the whole, the entire family seems to be adjusting beautifully. They are as happy there as four transplanted Alaskans can be even though they miss Ross.

So, you can see, Grannie, how things have fallen into place

nicely for all of us former Hopeites. Harold and I will be purchasing a modest car next week, moving to Raymond in a couple of weeks, and begin experiencing the adventure that the months ahead may have in store for your Walker friends. I doubt very much that these months will offer anything like the richness of the frontier life that we experienced last year. And as I write this, I can see you smile at my use of the word "frontier." Yes, I know. It was nothing like your experiences of frontier life in the EARLY days of Alaska that your wonderful stories so colorfully relate. But it was a season in our life that I will always, always treasure.

Best wishes to you and everyone in Hope,
Your Alaskan Friend, Harriet

ABOUT THE AUTHOR

Harriet Leone Walker was born in Freetown, Sierra Leone, West Africa, of missionary parents in 1927. She was home-schooled with her brother and sister until she reached the age of ten when her parents returned to the United States and her father accepted the pastorate of the United Brethren Church in Coffeyville, Kansas.

In 1945 after completing high school in Coffeyville, she entered the denominational college in York, Nebraska. During her junior and senior years at York College, she was editor of the college newspaper. She graduated with honors in the class of 1949. Some years later further education at the University of Idaho earned her M.A. and Ph.D. degrees in Foundations of Education.

In June of 1949, she married Harold Walker, a York College classmate who had returned to college after serving as a B-29 pilot in World War II. With a few exceptions, she and her husband dedicated their professional years to public education. An example of an exception would be the year in Alaska described in this book. At that time their first son was born. He was joined later by two brothers and a sister.

During the early years of her marriage, Harriet Walker wrote articles for church and children's publications and for some time wrote the Sunday night programs used across the denomination for intermediate Youth Fellowship meetings. But her delight was in letter writing. Even in college, she had followed the practice of keeping carbons of letters that she typed. Through the years the material in her files changed from carbon copies of typed letters to computer copies and finally to e-mail printouts. Now in her retirement years, she used these files as resource material even as she added to them through letters she continued to write to family and friends.

71748989R00191

Made in the
USA
Middletown, DE